Walking in Cities

In the series *Urban Life, Landscape, and Policy,*
edited by Zane L. Miller, David Stradling, and Larry Bennett

Also in this series:

Edited by
Evrick Brown and Timothy Shortell

Walking in Cities

Quotidian Mobility as Urban Theory,
Method, and Practice

TEMPLE UNIVERSITY PRESS
Philadelphia • Rome • Tokyo

TEMPLE UNIVERSITY PRESS
Philadelphia, Pennsylvania 19122
www.temple.edu/tempress

Library of Congress Cataloging-in-Publication Data

Walking in cities : quotidian mobility as urban theory, method, and
practice / edited by Evrick Brown, Timothy Shortell.
        pages cm. — (Urban life, landscape and policy)
    Includes bibliographical references and index.
    ISBN 978-1-4399-1220-1 (hardback : alk. paper) — ISBN 978-
1-4399-1221-8 (paper : alk. paper) — ISBN 978-1-4399-1222-5
(e-book)   1. Sociology, Urban.   2. Cities and towns.   3. City and
town life.   4. Walking.   I. Brown, Evrick, editor.   II. Shortell,
Timothy, editor.
    HT151.W298 2015
    307.76—dc23
                                                                          2015013668

072216P

Contents

Figures and Tables

Walking in Cities

1

Introduction

Walking as Urban Practice and Research Method

TIMOTHY SHORTELL

alking in cities has a history as old as cities themselves. Walking predates urban settlement, of course, but it has always been a significant form of mobility in urban space. More than just a way of getting around, walking as a social activity was transformed by urbanization. Walking was fundamental to the new liberty of labor in cities. According to Tim Cresswell:

> The idea of mobility as liberty and freedom would have made little sense in feudal society. In the early modern period, as cities grew and people were displaced from the land, the practice and ideology of mobility was transformed. New mobile figures began to inhabit the landscapes of Europe. Mobility as a right accompanied the rise of the figure of the modern *citizen* who was granted the right to move at will with the bounds of the nation-state. (2006:15, emphasis in original)

The freedom to move from place to place—migration—was an important part of the politics of modernism in Europe, and the meaning attached to mobility changed the way ordinary people regarded the use of urban space. The ability to move around the city was understood as an important aspect of being a free man or woman.[1]

Walking remained a practical activity, by and large, but it was also increasingly associated with a way of living in the city, a way of extending the so-

[1] Men and women experienced this freedom differently, to be sure. In fact, one of the most visible manifestations of patriarchy is the control by men over the mobility of women.

cial realm beyond, and between, home and work. Walking connected the new rhythms of urban life to the reconfiguration of urban spaces. The birth of the "nocturnal city," for example, is the story of walking as quotidian mobility and the desire of authorities to control it (Schlör 1998). Discussing walking in nineteenth-century Europe, Joachim Schlör (1998:240) notes, "Nocturnal life in London and Paris, and in its beginnings in Berlin as well, begins to push 'outwards' into the streets. And it is precisely the public presentation of vice that becomes the dominant theme of debate about the city." This discourse produces the idea of the "dangerous classes," who circulate at night. The police and other moral enforcers struggled against the new kind of urban walking. According to one police chief: "There are three terrible enemies with which our age has to struggle almost everywhere . . . namely, *the proletariat, crime and prostitution*" (quoted in Schlör 1998:184, emphasis in original). The "danger" comes from the unauthorized uses of everyday mobility. Walking was a part of urban crime, to be sure, but also of collective political action. Walking was a form of agency.

The everyday mobility of the "dangerous classes" is an important part of the history of walking in cities. The places where poverty and street labor intersected with vice and crime were well-known neighborhoods, both for the people who lived in them and those who did not. In London, for example, the parish of St. Giles, site of the hospital for lepers, later a plague zone, and still later an infamous London slum, has long had the reputation of transience and mobs (Ackroyd 2009). The parish church was along the route where the condemned were taken from London—on foot, it should be noted—to be hanged.

Not all walking is as notorious as this. But everyday mobility is part of the vernacular urban landscape, where ordinary urban dwellers live. It is part of the repertoire used by the relatively powerless against the designs of the relatively powerful. But because this everyday mobility lies far beneath the circuits of capital and its control network, and the powerful social forces created by the flows of capital and information, it has been largely unnoticed in sociology. As the editors noted elsewhere, "Local politicians, workers, shoppers, protesters, busy commuters, tourists, *flâneurs*, panhandlers, urban ethnographers—these social actors and many more occupy the city streets as an essential part of their quotidian routines. Everyday mobility on the streets and public spaces of neighborhoods is such an ubiquitous part of urban life and culture that it is often overlooked" (Shortell and Brown 2014:1). As a social activity, walking is very much hiding in plain sight. While much has been written of "car culture" with regard to U.S. cities, there is relatively little on pedestrian culture. While sociology has investigated desegregation busing as part of the history of race relations in the United States, there is much less scholarship on walking as a context for intergroup interaction. But walking, in everyday and spectacular forms, is a significant part of urban rhythms and practices.

Modern cities offer more ways to engage in everyday mobility than earlier urban forms did. The presence of systems of public transportation, and the proliferation of private options beyond personally owned automobiles—what we might call semiprivate transportation—have made walking less singular;[2] it is now part of a tool kit of everyday mobilities in the cities discussed in the research contained in this volume. Though contemporary urban dwellers may walk less—less often and fewer miles—this does not mean that walking is less important as a social activity. Technological advancements have made walking more of a choice. For example, Sonia Lavadinho (2014) demonstrates how walking is part of the mobility repertoire of hypermobile people in order to balance range and speed in a multimodal urban context. Both Hilary Ramsden (2014) and Federica Gatta and Maria Anita Palumbo (2014) identified new practices of walking in cities that reflect intentional efforts to "get to know" the city (for fun or for profit), to take it less for granted.

As was the case in earlier periods, walking reflects the systematic inequalities that order contemporary urban life. Walking has different meanings for different groups of people, in part because it reflects different motives and different mobility resources. For elites, mobility reflects a lifestyle choice: "Those 'high up' are satisfied that they travel through life by their heart's desire and pick and choose their destinations according to the joys they offer" (Bauman 1998:86). For the powerless, mobility is often forced; the poor and vulnerable are sometimes running away from something or toward something better. Of course, there are some for whom mobility is denied entirely—by imprisonment or by segregation (Ohnmacht, Maksim, and Bergman 2009). Our contemporary moment of globalization has made travel across borders easier than ever before, but not equally easily for everyone. "Some of us enjoy the new freedom of movement *sans papiers*. Some others are not allowed to stay put for the same reason" (Bauman 1998:87).

The inequality manifest in the "big mobility" Zygmunt Bauman discusses is recapitulated in "small mobility" of the everyday variety. Walking can be a way of temporarily "taking possession" of urban space, and therefore, an assertion of agency by the relatively powerless against official forms of authority.[3] At the same time, walking can make the relatively powerless more vulnerable, as well. It increases exposure to street crime for those residents of poorer, high-crime neighborhoods, who learn strategies for walking as a result. As important, it

---

[2] Consider the controversies surrounding new mobile apps linked to new forms of car service (Chen 2012; Irwin 2014; Scott 2014).

[3] The protests that occurred in Ferguson, Missouri, in August 2014 are a compelling example of this. The mass collective action by residents of the majority black town protesting the homicide of an unarmed black youth by a white police officer often provoked additional violence by police (including the state highway patrol and later the National Guard), who were aggressively focused on maintaining control. The protests were often described in the media as "riots"—as urban protests often are—but when one considers the context, they were clearly the result of long-standing issues of racial inequality. The repeated attempts by protesters to occupy the streets in defiance of municipal authorities constituted an important form of social agency. The protesters were saying, in a manner, that we'll be in the streets until the injustice is addressed.

increases exposure to aggressive urban policing, which poses a different kind of danger (Vitale 2014a, 2014b).[4]

Motility and Mobility

Walking is usually associated with everyday life. As such, we tend to view it as an activity that is instrumental and habitual (or as phenomenological sociologists would say, pretheoretical), as so many everyday routines are. Indeed, it is fair to say that most walking is done with purpose (even if the purpose is recreation) and without much reflection on walking as such. In this regard, it is tempting to view walking as only minimally social or cultural. But that would be a mistake.

Walking invokes a number of important social processes, and I want to note some of its important qualities here. The chapters that follow consider in more detail how walking intersects with sociological dimensions such as gender, race and ethnicity, social class, and power.

It is important to start with the distinction between motility and mobility. According to Vincent Kaufmann, motility "can be defined as the capacity of a person to be mobile, or more precisely, as the *way in which an individual appropriates what is possible in the domain of mobility and puts this potential to use for his or her activities*" (2002:37, emphasis in original). That capacity is a combination of access, skills, and appropriation. *Access* refers to the choices available. We can characterize this aspect of motility as a relative quantity of resources, so that it is meaningful to speak of more than or less than when comparing individuals. Some urban dwellers have more options for getting from one place to another. Kaufmann (2002:38) notes that *skills* "refer to the *savoir-faire* of those involved." This includes physical capacity, of course, but also knowledge of the operations necessary for a mode of mobility. Even walking on the sidewalk in a large city requires a practical knowledge of traffic and pedestrian norms. Urban dwellers have different expectations with regard to different kinds of social actors (tourists, the elderly, parents with strollers, and so forth); this represents a sophisticated knowledge of the use of public space. Finally, appropriation concerns an individual's sense of his or her access and skills in a particular situation. "Appropriation is constructed through the interiorisation of standards and values, and as such has to do with gender and the point reached in a person's life course" (Kaufmann 2002:39). We would add social class position to the list of factors, as well.

"Spatial mobility," Kaufmann (2002:40) continues, is "a phenomenon that revolves around four main forms: migration, residential mobility, travel, and daily mobility." These four forms represent a typology along two dimensions, duration and relation to the "living area." Short duration activities within the living area are daily mobility, and those outside the living area are travel. Long

---

[4] Indeed, the initial confrontation between the police officer and Michael Brown in Ferguson was prompted by pedestrian activity—walking in the road instead of on the sidewalk.

duration activities within the living area are residential mobility, and those out-side it are migration.

Since our topic is walking in cities, we will focus on the daily mobility type. Urban walking could be part of the other types, as well—tourists certainly walk in cities and some mobility resources are surely related to migration—but the relation of motility to mobility will be adequately illustrated with a discussion of daily mobility. Kaufmann points out that specific instances of mobile activity can represent more than one type. But the kinds of activities that the contributors analyze in this volume mainly concern mobility of short duration in a fairly restricted geographic area. Daily mobility is embedded in specific parts of cities—neighborhoods and other places.[5]

The ability and willingness to use one's motility (to appropriate a specific daily mobile activity) puts walking squarely in the realm of urban culture. Kaufmann notes, "Motility thus defines not only a propensity for mobility in terms of intensity, but also a propensity to realize certain forms of mobility in-stead of others, and to maintain a pace of life more or less oriented toward short temporal durations" (2002:44). Allowing for constraints resulting from social inequalities, this view preserves the agency of the urban dweller, in recognizing that he or she makes choices based on available resources and preferences. In this regard, we can consider the transition from motility to mobility to be a mat-ter of specific lifestyles. Kaufmann (2002:45, emphasis in original) concludes, "In this context, *the acquisition of motility and its transformation into mobility is built through the compromises made between aspirations, projects and lifestyle and is linked to multiple logics of action.*"

Bringing Pierre Bourdieu into the discussion enables us to understand how motility/mobility is structural as well as phenomenological. Individuals make decisions about how to acquire and appropriate motility, but these decisions are not merely instrumental choices. One of the logics of action, then, derives from the norms of social groups. In any social location, some kinds of mobile activi-ties are more valued and others are less valued. Patterns of daily mobility reflect social preferences and tastes as well as the desire to exchange one's "mobility capital" for specific forms of everyday activity. The decision to walk to work or to walk for leisure, for example, may reflect the availability of another resource: time—a form of conspicuous consumption, of a sort. One sees this in spaces where social classes combine but do not integrate; distinctions of daily mobility manifest in "parallel play" as Judith DeSena (2009, 2012, and Chapter 8 in this volume) has shown in her research on Greenpoint in Brooklyn.

The ability to appropriate possible mobilities for speed also reflects class and status differences. Faster and more direct forms are generally more valuable, and therefore not equally available to all urban dwellers. In global cities, where the

---

[5] I am using *place* here in the urban culturalist sense, of urban spaces that are invested with particu-lar emotions, such as love or fear, and therefore meaningful as specific parts of the city. Places are the parts of an individual's mental map of the city.

cost of living continues to rise faster than most incomes, daily mobility certainly manifests structural inequality and, increasingly, class segregation.

The Use of Urban Space

Cities are places of strangers. Urban dwellers must spend significant amounts of time (and a significant variety of forms of interaction) in the presence of others personally unknown to them. As a result, urban life is structured by difference. Urban dwellers learn to interpret the signs of difference—and as these differences are usually hierarchical, the status order—as a part of their everyday activities. Urban dwellers are well socialized into this kind of visual literacy. Timothy Shortell and Konrad Aderer (2014:113) explain:

> As groups practice their culture in local social spaces, through their quotidian mobility and performances of identity, they embed signs of their collective identity in those places. This is sometimes done intentionally, but most often is simply the by-product of people using and inhabiting urban space. These signs become meaningful to members of both the in- and out-groups—though not necessarily communicating the same thing to members of the majority and minorities.

We acquire this information through primary and secondary socialization and through the media. It is an important part of everyday life in the city; we are generally unaware of the process by which we read urban space even as it guides our behavior.

The differences that urban dwellers read are rarely parallel instances, where the value attached to one identity is equal to the value attached to another. As Bourdieu (1990) noted, because our social space is hierarchical, our public space is also. Jerome Krase and Timothy Shortell (2013:193) elaborate: "Because urban spaces are also subject to the effects of social inequality as class, racial, and ethnic hierarchies, societies often mark their urban territories with differential meanings, from slums and ghettos to 'silk stocking districts.'"

Krase and Shortell (2011) apply Roman Jakobson's structural semiotics to extend a distinction made by Erving Goffman (1959) between intentional and unintentional signs of identity. They explain the difference between *expressive* signs of collective identity and *phatic* signs. The former reveal the affective state of the producer of the sign; these are the signs we produce when we want to proclaim our identity, our pride of place (in the sense of geographical place or of status). The latter are signs produced as a by-product of ordinary activities. They are oriented to confirming in-group memberships and facilitating contact. Krase and Shortell note:

> In addition to ethnic differences, class antagonisms also generate competition for the use and control of social space. In some instances, phatic

signs of working-class life become transformed into expressive signs of middle-class "hipster" authenticity. Globalization encourages the appropriation of phatic signs for expressive consumption; the distance introduced by commodification tends to make the products empty of local, distinctive content—turning "something" into "nothing," as Ritzer (2003) might say. Sometimes neighborhood residents push back against such encroachment and, in doing so, produce more phatic and expressive signs of their class identity. (2011:372)

As symbolic interactionists argue, we are interpretable objects for each other. The use of public space is very much a practice of "folk hermeneutics." Walking is especially important for reading urban space because the pace is sufficiently slow to allow sensory intake. We can pay attention to the signs of collective identity while walking more effectively than other forms of quotidian mobility, such as biking or car riding.

Henri Lefebvre (1991, 1992, 1996) is one of the most important theorists of everyday life and of urban space. He saw the city as related to a particular organization of everyday life. Like other urban theorists, he uses the metaphor of language or text to describe the city. "The city *writes* and *assigns*, that is, it signifies, orders, stipulates," he observes (1996:102, emphasis in original). As a site, the city mediates the "near order" of everyday life and its institutions (family, local groups) and the "far order" of the state and ideology. To decipher the city as text, one needs to know both the level of the everyday as well as the level of ideology and the organization of production. He notes that global processes have influenced the space and time of the city: "By enabling groups to insert themselves, to take charge of them [global processes], to *appropriate* them; and this by inventing, by sculpting space (to use a metaphor), by giving themselves rhythms. Such groups have also been innovative in how to live, to have a family, to raise and educate children, to leave a greater or lesser place to women, to use and transmit wealth" (1996:105, emphasis in original). Indeed, Lefebvre even offers a definition of the city as "plurality, coexistence and simultaneity in the urban of *patterns*, ways of living urban life" (1996:109, emphasis in original).

Lyn Lofland (1998) and Elijah Anderson (1990) have described social behaviors and strategies that effect a claim to public space. It is useful to think of these behaviors as strategic rather than habitual, even though that implies a motive in particular instances, because these patterns of behavior require social skill to enact. They are learned and reflect agency. Patterns such as incivility, uncooperative motility, exaggerated displays of confidence (swagger), and even grouping generate claims of possession. When behaviors appropriate to the private spaces (or less public) are introduced into public spaces, others generally interpret this to be a claim to that space (Anderson 1990; Lofland 1998).

Anderson (2011) examined public spaces where diversity is tolerated, generally for the sake of commerce; he calls such spaces "cosmopolitan canopies." In his analysis of Philadelphia, Anderson notes the fragility of these canopies.

Ethnic and class differences reflect power hierarchies, and there are instances in which members of the more powerful group try to exercise their privilege to control public space. Just as inequality gives some urban dwellers more mobility choices, it also gives them more strategies for the use of public space. Advantages in the one are related to advantages in the other.

Despite this, Anderson explains, when cosmopolitan canopies function, they are often regarded as essential to the public life of the city; they are certainly significant to the economic life of central districts in contemporary cities. One of the most interesting aspects of cosmopolitan canopies is that they tend to flatten motility/mobility differences. Public parks and shopping malls allow members of different social groups (across racial and class hierarchies, according to Anderson) to engage in similar patterns of everyday mobility.[6]

Urban culturalist theory is a relatively new way to reflect on and to investigate urban space in which the focus is on "the *lived* culture of cities and not merely their economic or political 'structures' and demographic profiles" (Borer 2006:174). Studies have examined public, parochial, and private spaces. Michael Ian Borer summarizes: "Many of these studies have shown how place matters for individuals' experiences of social life more than simply providing the background or setting for actions and interactions. In fact, we have seen how places can structure interactions between people and can act as identity markers for the people who inhabit, revere, and travel through them" (2010:96). Particular parts of cities are meaningful places—they have what we sometimes call "personalities"—and urban dwellers relate to them on this basis. The variety of places in a city is part of what makes it distinctive. As Borer (2010) reminds us, modern global cities are too big and too complex to be experienced in totality.

The meaning making of urban places is dynamic. This is partly the result of the flows of people and cultural practices that occur in the course of daily mobility. But it is also related to the connection between memories of a place and imaginings of its future—movement in space is always related to the passage of time. The meanings we attach to a place are always embedded in time, both specific time (now) and abstract or ideal time.[7] This is especially important for how urban dwellers understand the vernacular landscape.

Toward a Sociology of Walking

Much of the social scientific work on urban walking begins with Walter Benjamin's (1983) theorizing of the *flâneur*. John Rennie Short (2012:121) calls the

---

[6] Not all parks or malls are cosmopolitan canopies, of course. Anderson compares some instances of both in Philadelphia to reveal how those that are not work to limit mobility for the less powerful (less affluent).

[7] Nostalgia is an important part of urban life. Our feelings about a specific place are often colored by a sense of some idealized past, and this often orients us to some idealized future. Conflict between groups in particular neighborhoods often take particular forms as a result of differences in the ways groups relate temporally (real and symbolic) to the space.

concept "a lens for understanding and representing cities undergoing globalization." For Benjamin, Charles Baudelaire was the original *flâneur* and his walking was a way of experiencing, and celebrating, the dynamic and sensual vitality of the modern city, represented by nineteenth-century Paris (Tester 1994). In contemporary cities, the dandy urban walker is joined by walkers of other types, some of whom have come from far away.

Short (2012) observes the arrival of an important new kind of urban walker: the global nomad. He explains, "Globalization's inherent interurban quality facilitates a new kind of *flânerie*, that of the global nomad, as another process to serve the experiencing, charting, and the conferring of 'globalizing' to a city" (133). The kind of everyday mobility the global nomad engages in is situated in a different class location than the *flânerie* of the nineteenth-century aesthete. It comes from an altered cosmopolitanism, where the meaning of national identity is disconnected from particular nation-states. The global nomad is transnational and transurban.

Inspired by the *flâneur*, the contemporary researcher of urban life and culture can use walking as a method. Walking around urban spaces is a way of seeing them from the perspective of ordinary urban dwellers. Walking in urban neighborhoods can also be a form of "working the street," that is, forming social connections with residents as a means for gathering ethnographic data (Brown 2012).

Giampaolo Nuvolati (2014) compares the ethnographer and the *flâneur*, recognizing both similarities and differences. Most significant of these differences concerns the kind of knowledge of the city produced by their instrumental walking: "Normally in the *flâneur*'s activities poetic suggestions are permissible, while for the ethnographer the scientific description is required" (25).

Guy Debord (1957, 1958, 1961) and his Situationist colleagues tried to bring some revolutionary poetry into the scientific study of cities. They developed a walking method to explore possibilities for a new urbanism, centered around the *dérive*. Similar to the wanderings of the *flâneur*, the *dérive* is a different kind of mobility. *Flânerie* is an aesthetic practice; it is about producing a narrative of the city. In contrast, the *dérive* is an attempt to identify the characteristics of urban space that create the fields and vortexes that determine the rhythm and tempo of urban life.

The *flâneur* wanted to know the city, but the Situationists wanted to change it. The *dérive* was one practice in an effort to study the city using psychogeography. If the modernist city, dominated by the logic of mass consumer capitalism, could domesticate urban dwellers, they reasoned, then psychogeography might reveal ways to restore the untamed and unexpected qualities of urban life.

Iain Sinclair (1997, 2002, 2011, 2013) is the most prominent of the contemporary psychogeographers. Merlin Coverley (2010:122) describes his style as one in which "urban wanderer, local historian, avant-garde activist and political polemicist meet and coalesce." As is fitting for the psychogeographer working in London fifty years after the Situationists predicted imminent doom for urban culture—based on their readings of the changes to Paris—Sinclair has a keen eye for the dystopias of neoliberal capitalist society. The practitioners of psychogeography are more likely to be writers than urban researchers, but the concerns of both substantially overlap. I believe that this approach needs to be recovered as a part of urban ethnography (as a set of related techniques). The emphasis on everyday life and daily mobility is in keeping with the phenomenological and interactionist traditions I have described here.

In a similar way, Jean-François Augoyard (2007) recognized that quotidian mobility is like a text and applies a rhetorical analysis to reveal much about the meaning of vernacular urban space. He studied the walking patterns of a group of residents of public housing in Grenoble. He introduces the study by saying, "This work takes the *step* as its point of departure under a variety of headings" (2007:3, emphasis in original). He is, in a sense, asking his respondents to perform a kind of psychogeography on their neighborhood.

Augoyard (2007:7) begins with the observation that the urban space that people typically know through usage is small and fragmented: "broken sections of neighborhoods scattered at the will of the fragmented activities that are our lot (work, domicile, leisure, consumption)." Our experience in these places is at odds with planners' designs, even of more integrated areas such as a public housing complex, because usages are determined by forces broader than sanctioned activities and official uses.

Augoyard asked his respondents to take notes about their routine walks, and he then interviewed them about what they had recorded. His rhetorical analysis is partly about how the residents of the complex talked about their quotidian mobility. But its greater significance is the application of some categories of rhetoric to the quotidian mobility itself. "Through the practice of one's walks, everyday life seems to take on the look of a language. The steps taken would expound spatiotemporal actions whose overall configuration would have a *style*. . . . Let us speak, rather, of a *walking rhetoric*" (2007:26, emphasis in original).

His main focus is on how different walking strategies enact ways of appropriating public space. In his view, "In fact, the qualification of appropriation depends neither on the quantity of the space traveled through nor on the constancy of territorial limits but, rather, on the degree of possibilities it includes. The 'trace' of a route signals an action and the way in which it unfolds in everyday time" (2007:16–17).

In individuals' routine walks, Augoyard suggests, one's sense of the meaning of space contains gaps. With regard to daily mobility—walking to and from work or school, walking to and from shopping, walking for leisure—not all parts of a walk are equally meaningful; some parts of the route are left out of the narratives the walkers construct. Augoyard terms this "ellipsis." When our walks are structured by avoidance of specific areas, we substitute alternates for the avoided territory. This is "paratopism."

In contrast to these forms of exclusion, combinatory figures involve redundancy. Augoyard notes, "Now, in examining people's walks, one can see that *the essential features of walking activity unfold in the mode of redundancy"* (2007:51, emphasis in original). Redundancy is an essential feature of everyday life: "This is probably the case for all forms of everydayness" (51). He notes a playfulness in walking, "metabole." "Metabole is always carried out in one's walks with a poetic, ironic, or playful tone to it. The space walked is valued for itself. The exhaustiveness toward which this form of redundancy tends expresses precisely the gratuitous character of the act" (52). The motive would seem to be to experience variety, "to diversify a site that can be walked in a multitude of directions" (54).

As an approach to psychogeography, or a phenomenology of urban walking, this rhetorical analysis could be quite useful. Urban dwellers may not realize how the decisions they make when appropriating their motility constitute a kind of text that structures the meanings that they attach to the activity. But seeing walks as "figures of speech" that use exclusions and redundancy can contribute to an ethnographic approach to quotidian mobility that places the urban dwellers' sense of place at the center of analysis.

William Helmreich (2013) notes that though New York has been the object of a great deal of sociological research, rarely does the research attempt to know the city as a totality. Toward that end, he devised a method to walk every street in every neighborhood in the city. He claims to have walked about six thousand miles. "I covered almost every block in Queens, Manhattan, Staten Island, Brooklyn, and the Bronx, including seldom-traversed industrial sections of the city" (2013:3). His method is auto-ethnographic combined with improvised unstructured interviews with some of the people he encounters.[8]

Helmreich makes a strong case for walking as a tool of urban ethnography. "Walking is critical to the task because it gets you out there and lets you know the city up close. However, you cannot merely walk *through* a city to know it. You have to stop long enough to absorb what's going on around you" (2013:3, emphasis in original). Walking is also a way to study walkers in the city, though that is not one of Helmreich's main concerns.

Like Lefebvre, Helmreich argues that to know a city you need to know its rhythms and cycles. He walked during the day and in the evening, during the week and on the weekends and holidays, when there is more activity on the streets. Of course, there is seasonal variation also. This approach is effective at focusing on everyday life. It is a part of the culture of New York that everyone lives, in varying degrees, but because it is everyday life, we often do not reflect on it as cultural practice. This is what he means by "the city that no one knows."

---

[8] All ethnography faces the same dilemma: to balance breadth and depth. One reason that so few have tried to study a city like New York as a totality is because the choice of that kind of breadth comes at a sacrifice of depth. Helmreich spent four years on this project and collected a lot of interesting narrative bits, but the sociological analysis is thin and it is hard to get a sense of which details are part of patterns and which are unique. The research in this volume, like most of the literature, offers greater depth with less breadth.

The strongest part of the study is the description of the patterns of intergroup interaction, the kind of everyday cooperation that characterizes all global cities. New York is a collection of many ethnic groups, the full range of races, of natives and immigrants, of different religious communities, and, of course, of different social classes. The city is not without conflict, but much of everyday life is a matter of implicit cooperation. New York is not a "melting pot" as much as a mosaic.

Using a much more modest auto-ethnographic approach—riding the B68 bus in Brooklyn—Krase (2012) arrives at the same conclusion. Krase investigated how people across social groups—ethnic, linguistic, religious, and racial—interact in the quotidian setting of public transportation. He suggests, "There is perhaps no better way to appreciate the embodied or inhabited nature of living with cultural difference . . . than by using public transportation in global cities such as Brooklyn" (2012:239). He continues, "We might argue that, in essence, multiculturalism is an unintended consequence of globalization" (239).

Along with greater attention to everyday mobility, urban researchers are focusing more on the embodied and emplaced nature of urban life. The urban culturalist perspective has called attention to the ways in which urban dwellers form affective attachments to particular places in the city, and that this is a key aspect of urban experience. We develop feelings about urban places in large measure as a result of the ways that our bodily senses mediate our routine activities in urban spaces. Sociologists, anthropologists, and geographers are elaborating on the complexity of these processes (see, for example, Adams and Guy 2007; Crossley 2006; Hsu 2008).

Walking is a significant urban activity, in part, because its pace is slow enough to draw in a multisensory experience. Much has been written about the importance of seeing the city and vision in urban interactions (Simmel 1924). Other bodily senses are being added to the picture in more recent scholarship. The city is experienced by its odors (Low 2006; Porteous 2006) and sounds (Bull 2000; Wissmann 2014), as well as its appearance. In general, we can think about this as "somatic work" of urban dwellers, or "the range of linguistic and alinguistic reflexive experiences and activities by which individuals interpret, create, extinguish, maintain, interrupt, and/or communicate somatic sensations that are congruent with personal, interpersonal, and/or cultural notions of moral, aesthetic, and/or logical desirability" (Vannini, Waskul, and Gottschalk 2012:18). This somatic work is guided by social norms, which urban dwellers learn through experience and socialization.

One of the most important contemporary researchers of urban walking as an embodied phenomenon is Jennie Middleton (2009, 2010, 2011). She has used walking diaries and in-depth interviewing to explore how walking is connected to the affective experience of time, space, and place (2009) as well as the material and technological aspects of everyday vernacular urban life (2010) in London. One of the most important insights of this research is the claim that "the intensification of certain senses at certain times that makes us aware of corporeal planes of experience" (2010:577). This is particularly significant for understanding of the sociability of urban mobility, and especially how it can be deployed strategically. One of the most profound feelings of power comes from acting in mass actions in public space. However much one might be inclined to favor collective action as a political tactic, it is primarily in the movement of a large group of people in public space that one experiences social movement power as a material fact.

Theorizing on everyday life has established the importance of habitual, or pretheoretical, processes (Jacobsen 2009). Indeed, one could argue that this quality is the defining feature of "the everyday." In quotidian mobility, the materiality of urban life is experienced through the interaction of bodies (the individual and others, usually strangers) with things and places, unfolding over time. Urban dwellers may not always be aware of why they make the mobility choices that they do, but these patterns are essential to the formation of affective bonds—positive and negative—to urban places. Middleton's research shows "how decisions to walk are not only made up of factors relating to the built environment or people's health, as frequently considered in the policy arena, but need to also be understood as intimately bound up with people's day-to-day routines" (2011:2858). She continues, "Understanding habit as situated and part and parcel of the unfolding action of urban pedestrian movement enables the transformative potential of habitual walking behaviour to be realized" (2859).[9] This becomes especially clear in Part IV of this volume. This transformative potential is vital to the public realm, as Lefebvre (1991, 1992) also noted.

As urban experience is multisensory and embodied, many urban researchers incorporate sensory research strategies into their tool kits. Sarah Pink (2009) has written more lucidly than anyone else on sensory ethnography. She notes, "One might argue that sensory experience and perception has 'always' been central to the ethnographic encounter, and thus also to ethnographers' engagements with the sociality and materiality of their research" (10). As the researchers in this volume demonstrate, auto-ethnography is one way for urban researchers to more fully engage sensory research, because it puts researchers in the streets, as it were, with the people in the communities they study. It also puts the researcher in the everyday rhythms of the people being studied. Embodiment is about understanding both space and time as phenomenological and material. As Pink (2009:17) points out, connecting the sensing body with the landscape is a way to gain insight into "the constitution of the self and the articulation of power relations." This is a necessary task to understand how the dimensions of race and ethnicity, gender, social class, and politics structure urban social life.

This volume is divided into four parts: race and ethnicity, gender, social class, and power and politics. A brief introduction to each part describes the chapters in the part and highlights their points of correspondence. Most of the

---

[9] Middleton is interested in sustainable mobility. This is not a major theme in the present volume, though Kristen Williams and Amber Wiley provide some discussion of the topic in Chapters 9 and 10, respectively.

research presented here is focused on cities in the United States, but there are important points of comparison. A broader view, such as this, is necessary to develop a meaningful sociological understanding of walking as a form of quotidian mobility in urban spaces.

REFERENCES

Ackroyd, Peter. 2009. *London: A Biography*. New York: Anchor Books.
Adams, Mags and Simon Guy. 2007. "Editorial: Senses and the City." *Senses and Society* 2(2):133–136.
Anderson, Elijah. 1990. *Streetwise: Race, Class and Change in an Urban Community*. Chicago: University of Chicago Press.
———. 2011. *The Cosmopolitan Canopy: Race and Civility in Everyday Life*. New York: Norton.
Augoyard, Jean-François. 2007. *Step by Step: Everyday Walks in a French Urban Housing Project*. Minneapolis: University of Minnesota Press.
Bauman, Zygmunt. 1998. *Globalization: The Human Consequences*. New York: Columbia University Press.
Benjamin, Walter. 1983. *Charles Baudelaire: A Lyric Poet in the Era of High Capitalism*. Translated by H. Zohn. London: Verso.
Borer, Michael Ian. 2006. "The Location of Culture: The Urban Culturalist Perspective." *City and Community* 5(2):173–197.
———. 2010. "From Collective Memory to Collective Imagination: Time, Place, and Urban Redevelopment." *Symbolic Interaction* 33(1):96–114.
Bourdieu, Pierre. 1990. *In Other Words: Essays towards a Reflexive Sociology*. Stanford, CA: Stanford University Press.
Brown, Evrick. 2012. "An Ethnography of Local Politics in a Brooklyn Caribbean Community." Pp. 313–336 in *The World in Brooklyn: Gentrification, Immigration, and Ethnic Politics in a Global City*, edited by Judith N. DeSena and Timothy Shortell. Lanham, MD: Lexington Books.
Bull, Michael. 2000. *Sounding Out the City: Personal Stereos and the Management of Everyday Life*. Oxford: Berg.
Chen, Brian X. 2012. "A Feisty Start-Up Is Met with Regulatory Snarl." *New York Times*, 2 December. Retrieved August 24, 2014. http://www.nytimes.com/2012/12/03/tech nology/app-maker-uber-hits-regulatory-snarl.html.
Coverley, Merlin. 2010. *Psychogeography*. Harpenden, UK: Pocket Essentials.
Cresswell, Tim. 2006. *On the Move: Mobility in the Modern West*. New York: Routledge.
Crossley, Nick. 2006. *Reflexive Embodiment in Contemporary Society*. London: Open University Press.
Debord, Guy. 1957. *Report on the Construction of Situations*. Translated by Ken Knabb. Retrieved August 5, 2014. http://www.bopsecrets.org/SI/report.htm.
———. 1958. *Theses on Cultural Revolution*. Translated by Ken Knabb. *Internationale Situationniste #1*. Retrieved August 5, 2014. http://www.bopsecrets.org/SI/1.cultural -revolution.htm.
———. 1961. *Perspectives for Conscious Change in Everyday Life*. Translated by Ken Knabb. *Internationale Situationniste #6*. Retrieved August 5, 2014. http://www .bopsecrets.org/SI/6.everyday.htm.

DeSena, Judith N. 2009. *Gentrification and Inequality in Brooklyn: New Kids on the Block*. Lanham, MD: Lexington Books.

———. 2012. "Gentrification in Everyday Life in Brooklyn." Pp. 65–88 in *The World in Brooklyn: Gentrification, Immigration, and Ethnic Politics in a Global City*, edited by Judith N. DeSena and Timothy Shortell. Lanham, MD: Lexington Books.

Gatta, Federica and Maria Anita Palumbo. 2014. "Walking through Urban Transformation: Fieldwork in the Northeast of Paris." Pp. 245–262 in *Walking in the European City: Quotidian Mobility and Urban Ethnography*, edited by Timothy Shortell and Evrick Brown. Farnham, UK: Ashgate.

Goffman, Erving. 1959. *The Presentation of Self in Everyday Life*. New York: Anchor Books.

Helmreich, William B. 2013. *The New York Nobody Knows: Walking 6,000 Miles in the City*. Princeton, NJ: Princeton University Press.

Hsu, Elisabeth. 2008. "The Senses and the Social: An Introduction." *Ethnos* 73(4): 433–443.

Irwin, Neil. 2014. "Uber, Lyft and a Road Map for Reinventing the Ride." *New York Times*, 11 July. Retrieved August 24, 2014. http://www.nytimes.com/2014/07/12/upshot/uber-lyft-and-a-road-map-for-reinventing-the-ride.html.

Jacobsen, Michael Hviid. 2009. "The Everyday: An Introduction to an Introduction." Pp. 1–41 in *Encountering the Everyday: An Introduction to the Sociologies of the Unnoticed*, edited by Michael Hviid Jacobsen. Basingstoke, UK: Palgrave Macmillan.

Kaufmann, Vincent. 2002. *Re-Thinking Mobility: Contemporary Sociology*. Aldershot, UK: Ashgate.

Krase, Jerome. 2012. "Riding the Bus in Brooklyn: Seeing the Spectacle of Everyday Multicultural Life." Pp. 237–258 in *The World in Brooklyn: Gentrification, Immigration, and Ethnic Politics in a Global City*, edited by Judith N. DeSena and Timothy Shortell. Lanham, MD: Lexington Books.

Krase, Jerome and Timothy Shortell. 2011. "On the Spatial Semiotics of Vernacular Landscapes in Global Cities." *Visual Communication* 10(3):367–400.

———. 2013. "Seeing New York City's Financial Crisis in the Vernacular Landscape." Pp. 188–217 in *Cities and Crisis: New Critical Urban Theory*, edited by Kuniko Fujita. London: Sage.

Lavadinho, Sonia. 2014. "Walking between Planes: Why Hypermobile People Take to Walking in the City." Pp. 75–90 in *Walking in the European City: Quotidian Mobility and Urban Ethnography*, edited by Timothy Shortell and Evrick Brown. Farnham, UK: Ashgate.

Lefebvre, Henri. 1991. *The Production of Space*. Translated by Donald Nicholson-Smith. Malden, MA: Blackwell.

———. 1992. *Eléments de rythmanalyse*. Paris: Éditions Syllepse.

———. 1996. *Writings on Cities*. Translated and edited by Eleonore Kofman and Elizabeth Lebas. Malden, MA: Blackwell.

Lofland, Lyn H. 1998. *The Public Realm*. New York: Aldine.

Low, Kelvin E. Y. 2006. "Presenting the Self, the Social Body, and the Olfactory: Managing Smells in Everyday Life Experiences." *Sociological Perspectives* 49(4):607–631.

Middleton, Jennie. 2009. "'Stepping in Time': Walking, Time and Space in the City." *Environment and Planning A* 41:1943–1961.

———. 2010. "Sense and the City: Exploring the Embodied Geographies of Urban Walking." *Social and Cultural Geography* 11(6):575–596.

———. 2011. "'I'm on Autopilot, I Just Follow the Route': Exploring the Habits, Routines, and Decision-Making Practices of Everyday Urban Mobilities." *Environment and Planning A* 43:2857–2877.

Nuvolati, Giampaolo. 2014. "The *Flâneur*: A Way of Walking, Exploring and Interpreting the City." Pp. 21–40 in *Walking in the European City: Quotidian Mobility and Urban Ethnography*, edited by Timothy Shortell and Evrick Brown. Farnham, UK: Ashgate.

Ohnmacht, Timo, Hanja Maksim, and Manfred Max Bergman. 2009. *Mobilities and Inequality.* Burlington, VT: Ashgate.

Pink, Sarah. 2009. *Doing Sensory Ethnography.* London: Sage.

Porteous, Douglas. 2006. "Smellscape." Pp. 89–106 in *The Smell Culture Reader*, edited by Jim Drobnick. Oxford: Berg.

Ramsden, Hilary. 2014. "A Walk around the Block: Creating Spaces for Everyday Encounters." Pp. 225–244 in *Walking in the European City: Quotidian Mobility and Urban Ethnography*, edited by Timothy Shortell and Evrick Brown. Farnham, UK: Ashgate.

Ritzer, George. 2003. "Rethinking Globalization: Glocalization/Grobalization and Something/Nothing." *Sociological Theory* 21(3):193–209.

Schlör, Joachim. 1998. *Nights in the Big City.* London: Reaktion Books.

Scott, Mark. 2014. "Uber Wins a Reprieve in Berlin." *New York Times*, 18 August. Retrieved August 24, 2014. http://bits.blogs.nytimes.com/2014/08/18/uber-wins-a -reprieve-in-berlin.

Short, John Rennie. 2012. *Globalization, Modernity, and the City.* London: Routledge.

Shortell, Timothy and Konrad Aderer. 2014. "Drifting in Chinatowns: Toward a Situationist Analysis of Polyglot Urban Spaces in New York, Paris, and London." Pp. 109–128 in *Walking in the European City: Quotidian Mobility and Urban Ethnography*, edited by Timothy Shortell and Evrick Brown. Farnham, UK: Ashgate.

Shortell, Timothy and Evrick Brown. 2014. "Introduction: Walking in the European City." Pp. 1–20 in *Walking in the European City: Quotidian Mobility and Urban Ethnography*, edited by Timothy Shortell and Evrick Brown. Farnham, UK: Ashgate.

Simmel, Georg. 1924. "Sociology of the Senses: Visual Interaction." Pp. 356–361 in *Introduction to the Science of Sociology*, edited by R. E. Park and E. W. Burgess. Chicago: University of Chicago Press.

Sinclair, Iain. 1997. *Lights Out for the Territory.* London: Granta.

———. 2002. *London Orbital.* London: Penguin.

———. 2011. *Ghost Milk: Recent Adventures among the Future Ruins of London on the Eve of the Olympics.* New York: Faber and Faber.

———. 2013. "Diary." *London Review of Books* 35(9):38–39. Retrieved August 2, 2013. http://www.lrb.co.uk/v35/n09/iain-sinclair/diary.

Tester, Keith. 1994. "Introduction." Pp. 1–21 in *The Flâneur*, edited by Keith Tester. London: Routledge.

Vannini, Phillip, Dennis Waskul, and Simon Gottschalk. 2012. *The Senses in Self, Society, and Culture: A Sociology of the Senses.* New York: Routledge.

Vitale, Alex S. 2014a. "How to End Militarized Policing: We Can Undo the Policies Facilitating Police Violence in Ferguson." *The Nation*, 18 August. Retrieved August 23, 2014. http://www.thenation.com/article/181307/how-end-militarized-policing.

———. 2014b. "Paying in Blood for Over-Policing: Broken Windows Is the New Stop and Frisk." *New York Daily News*, 19 July. Retrieved August 23, 2014. http://www.nydaily news.com/opinion/paying-blood-over-policing-article-1.1872536.

Wissmann, Torsten. 2014. *Geographies of Urban Sound.* Farnham, UK: Ashgate.

I

Race and Ethnicity

ategorical knowing of neighborhoods and ethnic groups became the apparent mainstay for outsiders of places of stigma in urban environments. The so-called ghetto communities and barrios not only promote physical, social, and economic isolation for those within their boundaries but extend that isolation to those guilty by phenotypical association. As Elijah Anderson (2011) explained, the iconic ghetto represents a hovering image that associates all African American males with the menacing and fearful lower-class residents most middle-class white people wish to avoid. Nikki Jones and Christina Jackson (2012) discussed how this process of avoidance works through discursive redlining through informal conversational declarations that discourages interaction with African Americans. They discuss how discursive redlining developed as a common practice by those in San Francisco to warn the newcomers to avoid the perceptively troubled areas and people surrounding San Francisco's Fillmore District.

As with the iconic ghetto, it is not a location that is ultimately relevant and should be avoided, but "the people, their bodies, and their behaviors that are the problem" (Jones and Jackson 2012:106). It is the pervasive creation of the hazardous ghetto, the barrio, and other places of stigma fused to a category of people with its stubborn dismissiveness of alternative narratives based on limited contact with the "other" that persists and carries a reality that can be challenged by the *flâneur* and others who choose to investigate the authentic identity of a place.

The chapters in this part discuss and emphasize the social reality of the city from the "ground up" through the purview of race. There is a diversity of methods with a core experiential theme of quotidian mobility ranging from solo walks to "go-alongs" employing public transportation. The common theme of exploring the city through a communal copresence, with the shared aim of investigating the racial and ethnic production of space and city life, is explored in each of these chapters. They present a layered production of urban life that, as argued elsewhere, may challenge a hegemonic gaze and conventional view of a city (Holgersson 2014).

In Chapter 2, Rebecca Williamson deploys Henri Lefebvre's (2004) *Rhythmanalysis* as an ethnomethodological tool to understand the indigenous production of space in a suburb of Sydney, Australia, that has undergone multicultural change through an influx of immigrants. Meanwhile, local authorities attempt to control the usage of space by altering the immigrants' sense of "situated belonging." Williamson provides a theoretical discussion distinguishing the *flâneur*, psychogeography, and rhythmanalysis to note the importance of the latter as a means for grasping local semiotics. This understanding is made possible through the researcher surrendering or "letting go" to acquire and absorb the rhythms of community.

In Chapter 3, Shanshan Lan investigates how Chinese immigrant workers develop their knowledge about race through street-level interaction when mainstream discourse apparently emphasizes an increasingly color-blind culture. Race-based knowledge is gained through the street-level daily life experiences of residents as they navigate the streets of Chicago. She looks at walking as a daily routine for Chinese immigrants and African Americans, noting how the two attempt to negotiate a form of civil inattention while taking class differences of the latter into account. She also highlights how local city boosters work to prescribe what Jerome Krase (2012) refers to as tourist-friendly "ethnic theme parks" catering to the perception of tourist assumptions of a fictive and pedestrian-friendly Chinatown while noting the disjuncture with the reality of Chinese-immigrant neighborhoods. She concludes with a brief discussion on the sensorial facets of walking as a research method while sharing the experience of navigating the streets as a researcher.

In Chapter 4, Ernesto Castañeda, Kevin Beck, and Josué Lachica take the reader through the everyday experience of three neighborhoods—Manhattan, New York; San Diego, California; and El Paso, Texas—through various mobility means, including walking, driving, and public transportation, to dispel the prevailing conception of "El Barrio." For example, Castañeda, Beck, and Lachica discovered diversity in the East "Spanish" Harlem neighborhood of Manhattan after taking a stroll in the area. What is apparently prominent in a Latino neighborhood is not only the presence of a Spanish-speaking population but the businesses catering to a Mexican clientele who may not be neighborhood residents and are more likely commuters from elsewhere. Similarly, San Diego's Barrio Logan is experiencing racial and ethnic change as proximity to trendy areas like the Gaslamp Quarter has a ripple effect on rising rents, making it an unlikely settlement for first-generation immigrants in recent years. The artistic evidence of its Mexican heritage is shown on the murals of Chicano Park under the Coronado Bridge, laying claim to the neighborhood's ethnic past with an uncertain future. Meanwhile, the transnationalist character of El Segundo Barrio and Chihuahuita with its proximity to Ciudad Juárez in Mexico contributes to what they argue is "a continuous presence of Mexican culture and Mexican residents throughout" the two neighborhoods.

The thematic presence of an experiential discussion to place reveals the common thread of a social reality of the city and spatial cultural production. Overviews by Williamson, Lan, and Castañeda, Beck, and Lachica contain similarities of the impact of the built environment with a call for understanding the authentic construction of neighborhoods from the "ground up." In light of the overwhelming push for the creation of pedestrian- and tourist-friendly areas, there is a definitive tension between differential presentations of a city. On the one hand, there is the prevailing commercialized image of the city, heavily marketed through the inclusion of safe, sterile fabricated places while carving out and marginalizing the "other" from the mainstream discourse contributing to the generic classification of "dangerous" ghetto communities. On the other hand, there are presentations of urban life highlighted by these three chapters that call for an understanding of the city by those removed from the vernacular.

REFERENCES

Anderson, Elijah. 2011. *The Cosmopolitan Canopy: Race and Civility in Everyday Life.* New York: Norton.

Holgersson, Helena. 2014. "Challenging the Hegemonic Gaze on Foot: Walk-Alongs as a Useful Method in Gentrification Research." Pp. 207–224 in *Walking in the European City: Quotidian Mobility and Urban Ethnography*, edited by Timothy Shortell and Evrick Brown. Burlington, VT: Ashgate.

Jones, Nikki and Christina Jackson. 2012. "'You Just Don't Go Down There': Learning to Avoid the Ghetto in San Francisco." Pp. 83–109 in *The Ghetto: Contemporary Global Issues and Controversies*, edited by Ray Hutchison and Bruce Haynes. Philadelphia: Westview.

Krase, Jerome. 2012. *Seeing Cities Change: Local Culture and Class.* Burlington, VT: Ashgate.

Lefebvre, Henri. 2004. *Rhythmanalysis: Space, Time and Everyday Life.* New York: Continuum.

2

Walking in the Multicultural City

The Production of Suburban Street Life in Sydney

REBECCA WILLIAMSON

This chapter brings together a discussion of walking as a research method and as a ubiquitous facet of urban life. It situates this routine activity within the context of migration-led diversity in cities. In doing so, it follows a call to integrate migration studies with research on the production of urban life, in order to reterritorialize processes of transnationalism and international migration (Hall and Datta 2010; Massey 1994; Smith 2005). In the context of Australia and other immigration countries, discussions of migrants' experiences of urban settlement or incorporation have tended to focus on generalist concerns about social cohesion and migrants' willingness to integrate around specific policy-relevant issues (for example, labor market integration) (Amin 2002; Vasta 2013). Questions of migrant belonging largely remain scaled in relation to the geographical boundaries of the nation-state (Bauder 2012; Çağlar and Glick Schiller 2011), despite the emerging forms of transnational mobility, connectivity, and reconfiguration of citizenship associated with globalization and international migration (Sassen 2002). Such framings privilege static and singular notions of belonging, where movement and multiple identities are inherently problematic (Castles, Hugo, and Vasta 2013; Papastergiadis 2005). This work is interested in how these dynamics play out in global cities, where ethnocultural diversity is likely to increase. More specifically, it seeks to outline how diverse, quotidian modes of inhabiting and being mobile in city spaces mediate migrant identities and their sense of situated belonging.

In this chapter I argue that using a fine-grained, ethnographic approach to examine embodied migrant place-making practices or "local cultural becomings" (Carruthers 2013) is an important dimension of understanding forms of lived multiculturalism. In particular, I explore how multicultural belonging is constituted through local rhythms of place making and everyday mobilities. Walking is taken as both a methodological frame and object of study to illuminate everyday patterns and forms of dwelling in a multicultural locality—in this case, a highly ethno-culturally diverse main street in suburban Sydney, Australia. Walking as an embodied practice—and the structural conditions that shape it—is a particular focus in this chapter. Henri Lefebvre's (1996, 2004) rhythmanalysis is used to explore the temporal and spatial dimensions of walking as a form of everyday mobility, as a way of better understanding the nuances underlying the daily production of space. In doing so, it examines how this methodological tool can inform critical conceptions of the diverse city and the place of new residents within it.

The chapter first offers a brief review of the theoretical strands that inform ethnographic approaches to everyday mobility and their contribution to imagining cosmopolitan urban space. It then paints a picture of the everyday rhythms of street life in the main street of Campsie, a multiethnic suburb in Sydney. I provide several snapshots of the mundane patterns of quotidian mobility and migrant place making in Campsie before considering the variance of normative rhythms that might also shape pedestrian activity on the street. I then critically examine the relational interplays between and among these rhythms, and I argue that they are part and parcel of the everyday production—and contested politics—of lived multiculturalism.

Theorizing the Mobile City from the Ground Up

One way of researching how multiculturalism is experienced, negotiated, and mobilized in (sub)urban space is to engage more fully with ethnographic, phenomenological, and mobility-centric approaches to the study of urban life. This is by no means a novel approach. Imagining the city by framing its inhabitants as sensorial and receptive mobile beings draws on a legacy of influential scholars of space such as Georg Simmel, Walter Benjamin, Lefebvre, and Michel de Certeau. The embodied perspective of the *flâneur* or psychogeographer counters the technocratic perspectives of the bureaucrat and planner, re-envisaging urban life from the ground up. Ethnographic approaches to studying differentiated modes of dwelling in urban spaces, forms of (im)mobility, and the structural conditions that create them were also legitimized by some proponents of the Chicago School of urban sociology. Observing and partaking in the life of the city through walking became an important ontological and methodological approach, the social importance of which was further developed through the work of theorists such as Jane Jacobs (1961) and William H. Whyte ([1988] 2009).

Contemporary scholarship has focused on the extent to which urban life is transformed through processes of globalization and neoliberalization. The city is an emergent, networked, complex, and contingent space, produced both by global and by local flows, and constituted through an assemblage of human and nonhuman objects that reconfigure forms of dwelling and belonging in the city

(Amin and Thrift 2002). Studies that highlight the centrality of differing forms of mobility have complicated how we think about the spatial politics of the city. Conceptions of space and proximity have been reconfigured through the critical attention given to physical, virtual, imaginative, and corporeal mobilities as part of processes of globalization and time-space compression (Urry 2007). Places are produced through a multitude of "moorings" and mobilities (Cresswell 2006), where *mobility* refers to a social practice with social meaning and involves "an appropriation and transformation of the space encountered during this practice" (Jiron 2010:129). As Doreen Massey (1994) has argued through the notion of a "global sense of place," localities are more than bounded, physical territories; they are also defined through movement, linkages to other places, and multiple conceptions of place, and they are continually reproduced. From this perspective, place is "a porous and emergent expression of multiple intersecting mobilities, rather than an ordinary, essential and bounded unit that mobilities work to threaten or disrupt" (Bissell 2013:2). The types of mobility that shape cities of diversity are multiple and include international migratory trajectories and transnational flows of people, goods, and capital to the minutiae of mundane mobilities in everyday life (walking, cycling, taking public transport). The capacity to move—across countries or just around your local suburb—and the various structural and socio-material conditions that shape mobility impact on the subjectivity, sociality, and sense of belonging of urban inhabitants (Bissell 2007; Middleton 2009; Sheller and Urry 2000). Thus, systems of mobility like transnational migration can intersect with and unsettle notions of immutable community, territory, and place-based identity, and are profoundly political and unevenly distributed (Sassen 2002).

In this context, research into urban cosmopolitanism in diverse cities requires a consideration of how residents negotiate the city through different types of mobility. Migrants engage in home-building practices in urban settings that draw on the spatial knowledge that they carry with them, their diasporic practices, and the dominant socio-spatial logics of the places they come to inhabit. The production of multiculture involves not only the everyday negotiation of exchanges across difference but also the socio-spatial and sensory dimensions of these encounters (Amin 2002; Fincher and Iveson 2008; Noble 2009; Wise and Velayutham 2009). Urban space is organized around hegemonic notions of landscape, place, and order that make particular modes of dwelling in, moving through, and belonging in space normal and commonsense. These spatial logics in turn impact the way in which strangers in the city are defined and encountered, and—by extension—how lived multiculturalism is experienced in the everyday life of the city (Bugg 2013; Fincher and Iveson 2008; Trudeau 2006; Wise 2010). Much of the literature of multiculturalism in the city focuses on social interactions between strangers, forms of recognition (Taylor 1992), and nonrecognition of difference (or "indifference to difference") (Tonkiss 2003). It is worth noting that the way people maneuver, mingle and "dwell in motion" in local spaces also shapes intercultural encounter and the production of a multicultural urban ethos (Fincher and Iveson 2008). Moreover, it raises important questions about the everyday dynamics or urban ethos of the city and what this communicates about the right of others to inhabit urban space. It is these questions that form the basis of the following discussion.

Methodologies of the City and Everyday Mobility

How might the connections between migration-led diversity, urban cosmopolitanism, and micro-mobilities—and the "messiness" of everyday life—be approached from a methodological perspective? Ethnography allows a multilayered understanding of urban space and places the researcher amid the intricacies and idiosyncrasies of the lives and spaces he or she is researching; ethnographers are participants as well as observers in the multisensory world of the city. They participate in and observe its complexities to create an interpretation of city life that operates as one urban discourse. The present research draws on ethnographic research of a multiethnic neighborhood in Sydney that included residence in the neighborhood, interviews with local migrant residents and local key informants,[1] participant observation, and photography of the varied use of local public spaces. This approach was supplemented by participants' self-drawn mental maps—tapping into residents' localized spatial knowledge— and the researcher's own mapping exercises tracing the micro-mobilities and activities in local public spaces (Low 2000), including the main street, a local urban park, the public library, and a pedestrianized mall.[2] While a mixed methods approach attempted to capture how diversity is negotiated in suburban public spaces—and how such negotiations shaped migrants' sense of belonging—it was while walking along the main street and its surrounds that my most vivid impressions of the lived multiculturalism of the place were formulated. Sometimes this was in my capacity as researcher and "participant observer," and at other times as a resident, a walker, a runner, and a consumer. Walking enabled critical observation and it propelled me into the very relationality and spatiality of the street I was examining. Moreover, in a couple of instances, some of the most interesting exchanges with participants occurred while walking to or from the location of the interview. Despite this, it was not one of the methods I privileged in my initial reflections on my research data. And indeed there has been a lack of recognition of walking as an ethnographic or social scientific method in its own right (but see, for example, Cheng 2014; Elsheshtawy 2013; Pink 2008).

Several theorists have argued that as an ethnographic approach, walking is an embodied "tactile gaze" (Saeter 2011) that allows for both objective and sub-

---

[1] This group of informants included council staff, migrant support and housing support workers, local ethnic community leaders, and real estate agents.

[2] These localities were chosen because they were key sites of local migrant place-making practices. This selection also draws on literature that highlights the role of such urban spaces in contestations over public space (see, for example, Fincher and Iveson 2008; Hall 2012; Low 2000; Mitchell 1995).

jective engagement in the flows and rhythms of the street. Just as the *flâneur*'s experiences represent "a kind of palimpsest of multiple perspectives: visual and corporeal, social and historic" (Saeter 2011:186), the ethnographer-as-walker is situated within the multiplicity of life worlds on the street, and must continuously negotiate the subjective experience of walking with and the "objective" stance of the observer. Lefebvre encouraged urban researchers to allow themselves to be captured by city rhythms in order to study them; "to let go, give in and abandon oneself to its duration," to be part of the production of urban dynamics (1996:219). He used the idea of 'rhythmanalysis' to explain such an embodied approach to understanding the different geographies and temporalities of the city. Rhythms, he explained, are how the "everyday" appropriates a particular place and time; they are a way of "localizing time" and "temporalizing place."

In his analyses of Paris and other cities, he follows the cacophony of rhythms in the street, observing the traffic lights, the flow of cars, the pace and milling of pedestrians, the voices, noises, and smells of the street, which overlay and interact with a variety of the cyclical rhythms: of nature, of day and night, the seasons, the climate, the growth of trees. Places are made up of multiple, repetitive, overlapping, conflicting, and synchronized rhythms that create the "symphony" or "polyrhythmicity" of the urban (Lefebvre 1996:223). In this way, rhythmanalysis enables an analysis of local place as dynamic, multidimensional, and porous, always in a process of becoming (Edensor 2010). But understanding how to apply rhythmanalysis as a methodological tool is—like other aspects of Lefebvre's work—"frustratingly elusive" (Amin and Thrift 2002:19). Rhythmanalysis does provide a tool for attending to more detailed, multisensory descriptions of how places are produced. Rather than speaking abstractly about "atmosphere" and "vibrancy," a focus on rhythms highlights the unique temporalities and spatialities that mediate and constitute urban social life. Here, *walking*—as methodological tool and object of research—both produces and is produced by urban rhythms. The imprints on material space and embodied experiences of walking can be used to trace wider systems of mobility, modes of belonging, and the discourses and social structures that shape street life. As de Certeau (1984:71) posits, walking can "give shape to how places are and should be dwelt in and used." The following discussion analyzes several snapshots of walking in the street, the social structures that shape pedestrian activities, and how they might contribute to the multiculture of Campsie, drawn in part from my experiences and observations of walking in the suburb and from interviews with residents. It provides one means to theorize how everyday rhythms of place facilitate or hinder certain kinds of sociality, difference, and a particular multicultural imaginary.

Situating Multiculture: An Ethnography of Beamish Street

Sydney is one of the most ethnically diverse cities in the world as a result of high levels of migration, which has transformed the city's social geography.

Ethno-cultural diversity is managed through an official policy of multiculturalism that institutes the right to the expression of cultural identity and the right
to equal opportunity and participation in society. One major criticism leveled
at national discourses of multiculturalism is that they often fail to take into account the forms of lived or "grassroots" multiculturalism and situated politics
of identity that occur on a daily basis (Wise and Velayutham 2009).

My research focuses on a particular suburb in southwestern Sydney, an
area on the edge of a belt of middle-ring suburbs with a largely working-class
and ethnically diverse population. Decline in manufacturing employment
has combined with spatial histories of social deprivation that continue to in-
tertwine with migrant settlement patterns. The suburb of Campsie is the commercial and administrative center for the City of Canterbury, located thirteen
kilometers from Sydney's central business district, and it is one of many suburbs situated along the southern and western railway lines with concentrations
of immigrants. Its population is highly diverse: 63 percent of the residents were
born overseas, 60 percent of the total population are from non-English-speaking
backgrounds, predominantly from China, South Korea, Lebanon, India, Vietnam, and Nepal. It has been a gateway suburb for new migrants since the
postwar era and remains popular with new arrivals: In 2012, 30 percent of the
overseas born population arrived in the last five years. The suburb is characterized by relatively high deprivation and precariousness, measured by household
variables such as low income and educational attainment, high unemployment,
poor English-language skills, and unskilled jobs.

The town center hosts a number of community and ethnic welfare organizations, particularly those working with migrants and refugees. It is a popular
shopping center, known for its inexpensive "Asian" goods, green grocers, discount chemists, and specialist ethnic food. In recent years, local authorities and
businesses have marketed Campsie as the "Seoul of Korea" to reflect the strong
Korean presence in the locality, although recent demographic shifts have seen
Koreans move to more affluent parts of the city, which has undermined the
relevance of this marketing label. Campsie borders the gentrified Inner West
suburbs and has been earmarked for strategic redevelopment like many of the
town centers with transport hubs connecting into the central city. Increasingly,
it is being marketed as an up-and-coming "cultural quarter" to middle-class
professionals and young families seeking property within a short commute of
the city. While affordable housing has been a key draw to the area, gentrification has begun to raise property prices and displace sectors of the population—
particularly recent migrants with lower incomes—into the surrounding less expensive residential areas.

Upon starting fieldwork, I was immediately struck by the visible diversity
and the hustle and bustle of the main street. Shoppers jostle, dawdle with trolleys, and pause to chat while shopkeepers haul crates and rearrange vegetables,
commuters stream to and from the station, mothers push prams, and elderly
residents ponder life on sidewalk benches. During the day, it is a perpetually
busy space: a constant flux of bodies, goods, shopping trolleys, and cars. Much

of this activity is concentrated along Beamish Street's pedestrian footpaths. The main street seems to embody a sense of social density and "amiable disorder" (Whyte 2000:228, quoted in Blomley 2011:22) combined with ethnocultural diversity that differs from many of the other more ordered, affluent, automobile-dominated, hyperregulated, or commercialized urban spaces in Sydney. Beamish Street is a 1.6-kilometer stretch of road that bisects the town center, and it forms the social and commercial heart of the suburb.

The central section of the street is composed of mixed low-rise retail space with a train station positioned midway along the street. It is characterized by a variety of long-established businesses reflecting the migration histories of the area—Greek, Italian, Anglo-Australian, and Lebanese businesses—interposed with more recently established Indian, Bangladeshi, Indonesian, Vietnamese, Korean, and Chinese shops. Businesses range from hair and beauty salons, butchers, bakeries, fabric shops, medical and holistic health centers, discount pharmacies, Asian DVD shops, shoe and clothing shops, and several older-style pubs, traditionally associated with the Anglo-Australian working-class community. As such, a range of migrant cultures are visible—some more prominent than others—and they coalesce in a multilayered and mildly disordered streetscape of shop signs, ethnic products, multilingual street and print media, diverse spoken languages, modes of interaction, exotic smells, and migrant bodies. The street is a microcosm of the processes of migrant-led urban transformation that have shaped Sydney as a global city. It is a kind of informal public space that "situates and connects," gathering bodies together in proximity while "focusing and expanding the possibilities for contact between different individuals and groups" (Hall 2012:6).

Traversing the street almost daily over a period of six months, I became familiar with its ordered chaos and ebbs and flows, which began to raise questions about the forms of social organization that produced such rhythms, and how this contributes to the area's unique forms of everyday multiculturalism. In the following discussion, several sets of rhythms are outlined that produce the diverse temporalities and spatialities that coalesce on Beamish Street. It begins with a general overview of the everyday rhythms of the street, particularly as they relate to migrant place-making practices, drawing on Lefebvre's (1996:222) distinction between cyclical and alternating rhythms. Other emergent and dominant spatiotemporal logics are then explored by examining different modes of walking in the street, including those associated with place making and different ways of governing and appropriating diversity. Finally, I discuss how Beamish Street operates as a space of ordinary cosmopolitanism or "multiculture" that is partially forged through the production of everyday rhythms and walking.

The Everyday Rhythms of Beamish Street

The way people move through urban spaces is strongly marked by multiple forms of temporality and spatiality (Edensor 2010; Middleton 2009). In other words, pedestrian movements involve different localized experiences of time and space. The spatiality and temporality experienced by people with a disability, in a hurry, or new to a place may diverge from linear clock time and from the spatial logics underlying policy and planning perspectives. Lefebvre's (1996:222) distinction between cyclical rhythms "with big and simple intervals" that are manifestations of social organization and the more intense "alternating rhythms" that occur at short intervals is drawn on to tease out some of the complex, everyday rhythms that constitute the multicultural dynamics of Beamish Street.

Cyclical Rhythms

Diurnal rhythms begin from the relative stillness of the early morning, which is disrupted around 7:00 A.M. by the arrival of delivery vans unloading vegetables to the green grocers—the cooler morning air is punctuated by the rattling of metal hand trolleys, the clattering of plastic crates, and by the scent of fresh coriander. The shops begin to roll up their wall-to-wall doors and stack tables, boxes, and shopping trolleys full of fruit and vegetables for the trickle of early morning customers. They are joined by commuters hurriedly walking toward the train station or converging in quiet swells around several bus stops along the street. These pedestrian numbers are augmented by the school run—strollers, children's voices, and coaxing parents—which is soon displaced by a steady flow of pedestrians and shoppers. This culminates in the lunchtime surge of residents and local workers around the restaurants, dumpling and bread shops, where one traverses pungent pockets of fish sauce or the soft warm smell of hot bread, before a postlunch lull of activity.

Rhythms intensify in the afternoon and early evening with the surges of after-school and after-work crowds. The train station is a central node in these flows of pedestrians, connecting the localized rhythms of the street to the wider rhythms of work and the city's public transport systems. The station channels commuters, workers, and students in the morning (a steady flow) and more sporadic movements of elderly shoppers, mothers, and students during the day. In the evening, returning commuters are expelled into the main street and surrounding residential areas. The crowd exiting the station is so dense that one local resident described it as people "walking like ants." The "vibrancy" of the street is enhanced by the fact that the shops are open late—the density of bodies lugging bags of shopping, milling around the vegetable stalls, and ducking in and out of pharmacies only abates around 7:00 or 8:00 P.M. By late evening shoppers are minimal, and any buzz along the street is oriented around the restaurants and the local pubs. By 10:00 P.M. this subdued nighttime economy lapses into the restorative rhythms of the night, a stillness broken only by occasional traffic and shift workers returning home.

Over the week these various cyclical rhythms are repeated with slight variances until the weekend, when the intensity of shoppers and pedestrians ratchets up, particularly on Saturday morning. Sunday sees a more languid pace, shoppers still stream along the main street, but the routes are more varied with more people milling around, going to church, or meandering through the Sunday rotary market in the pedestrian mall with its tables of secondhand goods. While the rhythms generated through capitalist imperatives do indeed shape the street to a large extent, it has not—at least, not yet—led to a total appropriation or homogenization of everyday rhythms. Instead, they are overlaid and intersected by a range of other rhythms: the opening times of local schools and English-language training centers, the weekly programming of language-specific activities at the local library and ethnic community centers, paydays for pensions and welfare benefits, the work rhythms of shift workers, the annual rhythms of cultural and religious festivities, the rhythms of home life, and countless others.

Cyclical rhythms produce a sense of familiarity and routine that structures social life on the street. For recent migrants to the area, gradually falling into the pattern of these rhythms marks a transition toward feeling more "at home" and "local." Many of the recently arrived residents I spoke to valued Beamish Street as a social space that punctuated and oriented their daily geographies and mental maps. For newer migrants (especially those not connected into the temporalities of regular waged employment), the rhythms of sociability of the street were a central feature of their everyday mobilities around the neighborhood. This may involve more direct and organized forms of social interaction (for example, joining a book club at the local library, classes at local English-language institutes, and the site-specific sociality of ethnic shops along Beamish Street) or more indirect interactions associated with forms of copresence and sharing public spaces with others (fleeting exchanges with shopkeepers, being "out and about" amid crowds of shoppers, taking children to the playground in the park).

In the apparent chaos of Beamish Street, such rhythms of social interaction and everyday mobilities along the street are "coordinates through which inhabitants and visitors frame and order the urban experience" and circumvent disorder (Amin and Thrift 2002:17). For local residents and shopkeepers, the predictability of everyday rhythms of mobility along the street—demonstrated through a largely unconscious, normative knowledge of the activities along the street—constituted their localness. A local shopkeeper noted the familiarity of the ebbs and flows of populations who are seen to be definitively "in place" on the street: groups of elderly Chinese and Korean residents resting on the benches in the pedestrian mall connecting to the main street, a group of elderly Greek men who clustered outside the Greek green grocer, the young mothers shopping and pushing prams along the street, the passing rumble of time-tabled public buses. But he also spoke of observing a regular group of unemployed Anglo-Australian men and women—labeled by local residents and shopkeepers as "drug dealers"—who regularly hung out on the benches on the corner of the main street during working hours and sporadically headed along the main street individually or in groups of two. The shopkeeper referred to their irregular and erratic patterns of dwelling in the space by stating that they "gallivant in that area," a whimsical term that associates them with cyclical and familiar yet sometimes unpredictable rhythms that were "out of place" in the street. However, their familiar presence was also part of the everyday production of the streetscape; indeed, one local businessman commented that the same people had been sitting there since his business began twenty years ago. Local knowledge of rhythms and micro-mobilities thus works to identify appropriate and deviant behaviors and bodies, particularly those associated with unproductive rhythms in a space otherwise associated with "productive" rhythms of consumption and legitimized sociality.

Alternating Rhythms

The alternating rhythms of the street highlight the "daily grind" of everyday life, made up of more fleeting but equally obdurate encounters punctuating linear time (Lefebvre 2004:30). The flow of people in and out of shops and the pace of pedestrians along the street have their own temporalities, intricacies, encounters, and micro-rhythms. Shoppers hover, push, or barter with the shopkeeper as they check the price of tomatoes or Vietnamese mint. People weave through the crowds pushing appropriated supermarket shopping carts from the local chain supermarket store or prams loaded with children, shopping, hovering, and merging at points, calling to and chatting with shopkeepers or neighbors, pausing at traffic lights, or slowing outside the butcher or the hot bread shop, to peer into the windows with Chinese/English or Korean/English signs. People stop and rest on benches located along the main street, or cross into the quieter space of the pedestrian mall positioned halfway along the road, to loiter, chat, or sit under shade umbrellas and rest weary feet. The rhythms of car traffic punctuate street life: short bursts of acceleration, the rumble of buses, and car horns amid crawling, exhaust-emitting traffic.

The idea of alternating rhythms helps highlight the range of spontaneous everyday interactions and activities that are contingent on the "in-between" spaces and times that intersect with cyclical rhythms. There are many moments of encounter that occur along the street and *between* specific sites of more organized sociability: greeting a neighbor at the green grocer, sharing a joke or sense of impatience with fellow shoppers in a shop queue, requesting a translation of a Korean-language sign in the butcher's window, an impromptu conversation with a fellow inhabitant of a sidewalk bench, tossing a coin to one of the rare buskers (street performers) playing on the street, an exchange with one of those pesky prophesizing church collectors. The socio-materiality of the street—with a limited amount of seating—facilitates this type of proximity, as well as pedestrian density. Social interactions of this kind are akin to what Bissell (2013:9) refers to as neighborhood "loops," where movement itself constitutes relations of proximity with "near-dwellers" and the potential for encounter lies in the "in transit" moments of everyday mobilities.

For some, these unordered and spontaneous rhythms were a source of anxiety that disrupted a normative socio-spatial ordering of the street. One local Australian-born resident with a migrant background noted that in the past:

> You wouldn't hear people talking at the top of their voices . . . everyone was very quiet, respectful—it was the English way. Everyone kept to the left! There was an order about everything. When new migrants came, like my parents, you just fit in, you learnt to queue up, walk to the left. But when other migrants came in, all that changed . . . I mean, some of these migrants have come from places like China, where there are a million people in one little city—there is no order to anything and it's just the survival of the fittest . . . People are walking and you have to get out of the way otherwise they'll knock you out! (Tania, interview transcript, November 2012)

For this resident, ethno-cultural diversity connotes a disordered streetscape and disrupted pedestrian etiquette that belies wider fears about the impact of migration on the transformation of familiar neighborhood spaces. For others, irregular, spontaneous rhythms were integral to the vitality of the street and to a sense of local belonging. A newly arrived Korean resident told me:

> When I go to Big W [a chain department store], I don't need to speak to other people too much. But when I am strolling around Beamish Street, there are lots of Chinese and other stores, I can speak with other people, and I can hear other people. So many times I am strolling around Beamish Street . . . You can get a lot of useful information from them [the shops] . . . What to do, and [what you] should not do in Australia, and how to raise our kids, and how to communicate with Australian people. It's very informative. (Michael, interview transcript, June 2012)

Encounters like these that occur "en route" highlight not only how pedestrian-consumer mobilities blur the line between public and private space but also how interactions while walking along the street can constitute a form of homeliness and emplaced sociality. They perhaps also evoke aspects of what Lefebvre referred to as the urban in its pure form: "a place of encounter, assembly, simultaneity" ([1970] 2003:118).

Rhythms of Homemaking and Translocality

The more generalized cyclical and alternating rhythms of Beamish Street intersect with a range of other spatial and temporal patterns that are particularly relevant to the production of everyday multiculturalism and migrant place making. Beamish Street is replete with a variety of ethnic specialty food and "one-stop" shops that cater to migrants from various backgrounds. For some visitors and local migrant residents, especially those who are recently arrived, they are key translocal nodes around which their everyday mobilities are oriented, linking customers with other familiar—if distant—localities. They are part of a habitus composed of familiar signage, imagery, smells, sounds, languages, and faces (Wise 2010) and operate as community hubs, sources of social interaction and gossip, where intimate social exchanges as well as everyday transactions can occur. As Hall and Datta (2010) have argued in relation to visual signscapes in London, these material dimensions of urban space evoke material and embodied links between the street and its neighborhood, while also drawing the locality into wider spatial networks of (global) "routes/roots" connected with migrant entrepreneurs and their customers.

Sometimes this meant replicating a sense of the everyday rhythms of a homeland. As one Chinese migrant explained: "In Beamish Street there are more than ten Chinese shops. So we live here as we live in Shanghai. Each morning, the same . . . and we can talk in Chinese, so we are feeling convenient [sic]." For this elderly couple, the regular pattern of social interaction in local shops and in the nearby pedestrian mall, where they sometimes met friends, was integral to their sense of feeling at home in Campsie and in Australia. However, at the same time such cyclical rhythms could also enhance a feeling of otherness or diasporic distance when compared with the everyday rhythms of sites of previous residence. Several recent migrants commented on the lack of nighttime rhythms along the street, which created a very different experience of local place and time compared with life in Seoul or Hong Kong, for example. Some migrants found that this curtailed their rhythms of sociality and impacted on their engagement in local life, as one middle-aged female resident, originally from Hong Kong, noted: "Sometimes during the first few years I felt horrible [coming home after work]—too early to go to sleep. [At] seven o'clock you can't see even one person in the street."

Diurnal street rhythms follow the tune of shop opening times, which, as Edensor (2010:13) has argued, runs the risk of turning "polyrhythmic landscapes into isorhythmic ones," where alternative rhythms are made indistinguishable from shopping rhythms. In Beamish Street these commercial temporalities have been appropriated by migrant entrepreneurs: The daily rhythms of the street have been transformed by the institution of a particular pattern of opening hours associated with businesses owned by local, "hardworking," "Asian" proprietors—that is, entrepreneurs and business owners from Korean, Chinese, and Vietnamese backgrounds. The move by the local council to extend shop opening times until 10:00 P.M. creates rhythms of consumption based on a kind of ethnicized temporality, which one local official referred to as fundamentally different from "Caucasian [business] hours." Multiculture is here associated with transformation of consumption rhythms, where translocal senses of place are interposed with "local cultural becomings" (Carruthers 2013:214). This local cultural economy extends pedestrian activity and thus the sociality of the street, yet it is also inevitably situated within the political economy of the city, generative of forms of socioeconomic inequality where extended opening hours are a necessity to business survival.

Consuming Multicultural Diversity: The Rhythms of Appropriation

The rhythms of multiculture on the street are intertwined with organic, ground-up rhythms of homemaking, as well as economic imperatives and rhythms of consumption. One particular example highlights the extent to which these rhythms of multiculture have become increasingly appropriated into local economic development and the symbolic economy of the city, focused on the promotion of ethnic precincts (Collins 2006) and consuming ethno-cultural difference (Hage 1997; Jordan and Collins 2012). Recently a Campsie Food Tour has been initiated by a charitable organization that incorporates several of ethnic food businesses in Campsie. The tours, like the annual Campsie Food Festival organized by the council, is marketed to the general (often white, middle-class) public and aims to promote intercultural understanding in marginal, multiethnic suburbs through food, transforming these spaces into sites of encounter as well as sites of consumption. Visitors (and indeed some residents) feel they have "stepped into China or Korea," as one food tour participant informed me as we trailed a tour guide with a microphone and tour guide flag past bemused local residents. A walk along Beamish Street is transformed into a site of intrepid exploration where "outsiders" can be subjected to "ethnic rhythms" through encounters with local food and chefs. "Food multiculturalism" (Flowers and Swan 2012) facilitates transversal interactions and laudable goals such as transforming negative perceptions of low socioeconomic areas. However, it may also transform such spaces into sites of "cosmo-multiculturalism" (Hage 1997) in which the middle class are able to encounter and consume "the global" (articulated as cultural distance) or "authentic culture" in local spaces without having to encounter the social disadvantage, overcrowding, precarious employment, and poverty that are also part of the neighborhood's social fabric. This spectacle runs the risk of further essentializing, depoliticizing, or disembedding cultural practices and identities. Multicultural rhythms are thus appropriated and presented through engineered and selective and sanitized representations of diversity mediated by food consumption and made even more authentic by the multisensory experience of walking or traversing localities of multiculture.

But what happens to the everyday mobilities that constitute this space if the balance between these various rhythms shift, for example, through gentrification and the privatization of public space? Recent local government plans to create a one-way street through the local pedestrianized mall off Beamish Street is one such example. Ostensibly, the plan aims to create a "cosmopolitan eat street" to reenergize the local economy, but this plan could otherwise be interpreted as evidence of the neoliberal urge to restructure what, according to urban authorities, is often considered "ailing public space." But these visions either ignore the organic rhythms of street life already existing in and coproducing the space or deem them unproductive and deficient. The top-down project—which is partially funded by local developers who are building residential complexes above the mall—prioritizes the commercialization of pavement space for restaurant and cafés over current public uses. In an interesting twist of rhetoric, the planning proposal prioritizes vehicular access through the mall as a way of ensuring pedestrian safety, drawing on the concept of having additional "eyes on the street." This redefinition of pedestrian space where everyday rhythms are oriented solely around consumption or stage-managed civic events disregards existing organic rhythms of the street.

The Rhythms of Government: Regulating Pedestrian Diversity

The rhythms of the street cannot be grasped without taking into account another set of socio-spatial logics. The rationalities that produce the materiality of the built environment inevitably shape the way people move through and use local public spaces. These include governance techniques instituted by the local council such as local development controls, zoning laws, and public space regulations, variously shaped by state and federal legislation, as well as town-planning discourses, practices, and histories. While the "smokescreen" neutrality of technocratic and bureaucratic forms of knowledge that shape urban spaces has been highlighted in critical urban studies, it is worth noting that these governance logics are also highly historically contingent (Blomley 2011; Valverde 2011). How do these socio-spatial logics regulate street life, and how might this work to differentiate everyday mobilities and rhythms over others?

Because of high pedestrian traffic, the local government has invested significant funds in the design and upkeep of the pavement to ensure the unimpeded access of pedestrians, particularly in the areas of high retail turnover density. According to the local council, footpaths are solely for the provision of "a safe and accessible path of travel for pedestrians along shopfronts" (Canterbury City Council 2012), and ensure a "viable and vital" local economy. As well as dominant rationalities of economic development, this framing of pedestrian access and footpath use accords with the discourse of pedestrianism that Blomley (2011) argues underlies much municipal governance of urban spaces. *Pedestrianism* refers to the highly normalized legislative and bureaucratic logics that prioritize the unimpeded movement of cars, objects, and people on sidewalk spaces over other social and civic functions. The publicness of the sidewalk is emptied of any humanist interpretations of public space as a site of assembling or exercising citizenship rights, and instead merely signifies the absence of private encroachment and obstruction on sidewalks.

The diversity of rhythms that constitute the everyday multiculture of Beamish Street are shaped by urban planning logics, which are based on sometimes conflicting discourses of public safety, the regulation of pedestrian space, and the promotion of a vibrant cultural quarter. Pedestrian flows are physically routed in certain ways by a number of pedestrian safety measures, for example, installing raised pedestrian crossings, bollards, and median fencing. Some material interventions discourage gathering in groups or responsibilize citizens into proper, risk-averse behaviors and modes of walking, such as the No Loitering signs, lack of seating, or the large signs pictorially warning walkers to beware of "bag thieves." But like most public spaces, there are continuous contestations and subversions. Despite the signs, people do still assemble in small groups at "bottleneck" points along the road: a glut of bodies, trolleys, shopping bags, and prams around which people push and eddy.

Local businesses also challenge bureaucratic ways of organizing street rhythms. The council has the continuous task of dealing with local businesses that circumvent the footway merchandising display regulations. The regulations entail paying fees for displaying retail products on public pavement space (which were until recently among the highest in Sydney). From a governance perspective, this is a form of private encroachment on public space, and it highlights the council's priorities of avoiding impediments to the flow of pedestrian-consumers. Yet, as a local administrator admitted, these displays contributed to the multicultural aesthetics of the street that actually attracted consumers to the area, and thus accorded with the council's place-marketing visions of colorful cosmopolitanism. Combined with a lack of resources to continually police these practices, and what one local businessman complained was a "fear of getting rapped over the knuckles for discrimination," there was a degree of flexibility to the implementation of street regulations. Residents I spoke to also appreciated the enhanced porousness between life on the street and individual retailers that blurred the lines between public and private space and contributed to the multisensory cacophony that was familiar to local residents.

These seemingly minor contestations over the use of the sidewalk highlight how an aesthetics of order is being negotiated in relation to the rhythms of everyday multiculture in Beamish Street. A range of normative, governmental, and capitalist rhythms shape the everyday mobilities that produce the rhythms of the street, but, as Valverde (2011) points out, such regimes are partial, contingent, and open to negotiation and contestation, and they never entirely dominate the everyday rhythms shaped by and shaping pedestrian activities and social life along the street.

Producing Spaces of Cosmopolitan Encounter?

Walking the street—as practice and as a method—brings to the fore the different multifarious rhythms that orchestrate daily street life, as well as the extent to which these rhythms produce spaces of multiculture. The various rhythms of the high street both facilitate and hinder spontaneous and sustained intercultural encounters. This kind of interaction—variously captured through concepts such as cosmopolitan conviviality (Gilroy 2004), everyday multiculturalism (Wise and Velayutham 2009), cosmopolitan urbanism (Binnie 2006), and "situated multiplicity" (Amin 2006)—work to make difference ordinary (Wessendorf 2010).

Diversity and difference were absorbed into the often almost-unconscious forms of habituated walking and rhythms of sociability enacted along the main street and around the suburb, creating an affective landscape oriented around familiarity and belonging. Indeed, for many of my participants, this "ordinariness of difference" was an integral component of the spatialities of homeliness in the suburb. But this was not always the case: tracing cyclical, alternating, and normative rhythms of street life also highlights instances where disruption, discontinuity, and feelings of disjuncture occur. Moreover, it is important to keep in mind that these processes of familiarization and place making do not apply only to residents who are recent arrivals: the increase in diversity in cities has meant that it is not only the migrant who requires the social and cultural skills to be able to live with multiple spatial and temporal senses of a local place (Hall 2012:6; Wise 2011).

Yet, as we have seen in the discussion above, the rhythms of place and the modes of walking that constitute it are also partly produced through official modes of managing diversity, which shape planning priorities and are instantiated in the built environment of the street. These are, in turn, intertwined with capitalist rhythms that localize discourses of productive and marketable diversity, gentrification, and middle-class consumer quests for authenticity (Zukin 2010). Some scholars (Amin 2002; Binnie 2006; Fincher and Iveson 2008) have argued that while quotidian intercultural exchanges in public spaces can be facilitated, they cannot be engineered or coerced; to do so runs the risk of a "colonization of the encounter" by either governmental or market forces. Urban regeneration plans and food tours may seek to appropriate or design out certain rhythms of sociality, but they can also provide spaces of emergent sociality and resistant or subversive rhythms: residents who contest the plans or local ethnic businesses that refuse to participate in the food tours. And perhaps the slow-moving place-marketing and regeneration strategies can never keep up with the forms of cultural resistance and adaptation that make place-based rhythms so dynamic (Edensor 2010). As Degen (2010:23) asserts, "A locality adapts, refractures, reworks and at times even discards these regeneration processes." Tracing the rhythms of walking and sociality provide one way to tease out the different agencies and agendas producing local urban configurations without necessarily dividing them into "folk rhythms" and "governmental rhythms." Instead the questions become, whose rhythms "intensify, alter, or disappear" as different groups make their claim to space? (Degen 2010:25). What forms of power and inclusion are being instantiated through such rhythms, and who benefits?

Conclusion

By studying everyday rhythms that constitute pedestrian life in the street, we can begin to get a sense of how nonexceptional, everyday spaces—like a multiethnic retail strip—demonstrate micro-level processes of spatial legitimation in a plural society. Walking is an everyday mobility that has transformative potential and structural resonance. Residents and visitors to Beamish Street, whether migrants or not, create routes, pathways, connections, and patterns through the space that shape the lived experience of the street. In other words, these habitual individual and collective routing practices along the street "produce situated rhythms through which time and space are stitched together" (Edensor 2010:8). As such, walking in its manifold forms is an integral part of suburban rhythms that work to produce phenomenologies of "local" familiarity. As I have argued, this emerges from a unique assemblage of spatial logics and a multiplicity of rhythms that produce the everyday mobilities and sociability that characterize the street.

However, rhythms are not necessarily democratic; certain spatial and temporal patterns dominate others, rendering some more visible, acceptable, or "authentic." As Lefebvre (1996:226) argues, rhythms highlight both presence and absence; they both hide and reveal the forms of social organization and normative structures shaping everyday life. Applying this approach to diverse urban spaces is one way of tracing how city spaces facilitate or obstruct inhabitants' "right to their own spatiality and a right to encounter" (Fincher and Iveson 2008:13). In doing so, it contributes to questions such as the following: At which scales are human-level rhythms being shaped? Whose mobilities are being enabled and whose are being hindered, designed out, or synchronized with more "appropriate" rhythms?

The multiculture of Beamish Street is generated through different sociospatial logics that variously converge, synchronize, or clash, spawning either smooth modes of sociality or arrhythmic frictions. Although policies of gentrification, and the appropriation of ethnic difference by market structures, have a homogenous starting point, namely, the pursuit of capital accumulation, it is evident that such processes unfold in complex ways and engage with different articulations of multiculture. Tracing the different rhythms of Beamish Street, it becomes clear that there is no easy divide between quotidian, "organic" rhythms, those that are the outcome of consumerist and governmental appropriations of ethnic diversity, and indeed those that are the product of the researcher's participation and gaze. Nor can it be argued that the mere presence of multiethnicity creates an urban space that is somehow more sociable, egalitarian, or authentic. Indeed, as Lefebvre states, "rhythms of the self and rhythms of the other, those of presence and those of representation, cannot be separated" (1996:236). Studying everyday rhythms as produced through micro-mobilities on the street is a starting point—and a methodological tool in its own right— for elucidating the relationalities between the diverging, yet interdependent, rhythms of urban multiculture.

REFERENCES

Amin, Ash. 2002. "Ethnicity and the Multicultural City: Living with Diversity." *Environment and Planning A* 34(6):959–980.
———. 2006. "Collective Culture and Urban Public Space." Woodrow Wilson International the Centre for Scholars; Development Bank of South Africa; Centre de Cultura

Contemporània de Barcelona, Barcelona. Retrieved March 28, 2014. http://www
.publicspace.org/en/text-library/eng/b003-collective-culture-and-urban-public-space.

Amin, Ash and Nigel Thrift. 2002. *Cities: Reimagining the Urban*. Cambridge: Polity.

Bauder, Harald. 2012. "Nation, 'Migration' and Critical Practice." *Area* 45(1):56–62.

Binnie, Jon. 2006. *Cosmopolitan Urbanism*. New York: Routledge.

Bissell, David. 2007. "Animating Suspension: Waiting for Mobilities." *Mobilities* 2(2):
277–298.

———. 2013. "Pointless Mobilities: Rethinking Proximity through the Loops of
Neighbourhood." *Mobilities* 8(3):1–19.

Blomley, Nicholas. 2011. *Rights of Passage: Sidewalks and the Regulation of Public Flow*.
New York: Routledge.

Bugg, Laura Beth. 2013. "Citizenship and Belonging in the Rural Fringe: A Case Study of
a Hindu Temple in Sydney, Australia." *Antipode* 45(5):1148–1166.

Çağlar, Ayşe and Nina Glick Schiller, eds. 2011. *Locating Migration: Rescaling Cities and
Migrants*. Ithaca, NY: Cornell University Press.

Canterbury City Council. 2012. *Canterbury Development Control Plan 2012*. Sydney:
Canterbury City Council. Retrieved January 2, 2013. http://www.canterbury.nsw
.gov.au/resources/documents/CDCP_P3A_footpath_use_V7F.pdf.

Carruthers, Ashley. 2013. "National Multiculturalism, Transnational Identities." *Journal
of Intercultural Studies* 34(2–3):214–228.

Castles, Stephen, Graeme Hugo, and Ellie Vasta. 2013. "Rethinking Migration and
Diversity in Australia: Introduction." *Journal of Intercultural Studies* 34:115–121.

Cheng, Yi'en. 2014. "Telling Stories of the City: Walking Ethnography, Affective
Materialities and Mobile Encounters." *Space and Culture* 17:211–223.

Collins, Jock. 2006. "Ethnic Diversity and the Ethnic Economy in Cosmopolitan Sydney."
Pp. 135–148 in *Landscapes of the Ethnic Economy*, edited by David H. Kaplan and
Wei Li. Lanham, MD: Rowman and Littlefield.

Cresswell, Tim. 2006. *On the Move: Mobility in the Modern Western World*. New York:
Routledge.

de Certeau, Michel. 1984. *The Practice of Everyday Life*. Berkeley: University of California
Press.

Degen, Monica. 2010. "Consuming Urban Rhythms: Let's Ravalejar." Pp. 21–31 in
Geographies of Rhythm: Nature, Place, Mobilities and Bodies, edited by Tim Edensor.
Farnham, UK: Ashgate.

Edensor, Tim. 2010. "Introduction: Thinking about Rhythm and Space." Pp. 1–18 in
Geographies of Rhythm: Nature, Place, Mobilities and Bodies, edited by Tim Edensor.
Farnham, UK: Ashgate.

Elsheshtawy, Yasser. 2013. "Where the Sidewalk Ends: Informal Street Corner Encounters
in Dubai." *Cities* 31:382–393.

Fincher, Ruth and Kurt Iveson. 2008. *Planning and Diversity in the City: Redistribution,
Recognition and Encounter*. New York: Palgrave Macmillan.

Flowers, Rick and Elaine Swan. 2012. "Eating the Asian Other? Pedagogies of Food
Multiculturalism in Australia." *Portal Journal of Multidisciplinary International
Studies* 9(2):1–30.

Gilroy, Paul. 2004. *Postcolonial Melancholia*. New York: Columbia University Press.

Hage, Ghassan. 1997. "At Home in the Entrails of the West: Multiculturalism, Ethnic
Food and Migrant Home-Building." Pp. 99–153 in *Home/World: Space, Community
and Marginality in Sydney's West*, edited by Helen Grace, Ghassan Hage, Lesley
Johnson, Julie Langsworth, and Michael Symonds. Sydney: Pluto.

Hall, Suzanne. 2012. *City, Street and Citizen: The Measure of the Ordinary*. London: Routledge.

Hall, Suzanne and Ayona Datta. 2010. "The Translocal Street: Shop Signs and Local Multi-culture along the Walworth Road, South London." *City, Culture and Society* 1:69–77.

Jacobs, Jane. 1961. *The Death and Life of Great American Cities: The Failure of Town Planning*. Ringwood, Victoria: Penguin.

Jiron, Paola. 2010. "Repetition and Difference: Rhythms and Mobile Place-Making in Santiago de Chile." Pp. 129–143 in *Geographies of Rhythm: Nature, Place, Mobilities and Bodies*, edited by Tim Edensor. Farnham, UK: Ashgate.

Jordan, Kirrily and Jock H. Collins. 2012. "Symbols of Ethnicity in a Multi-Ethnic Precinct: Marketing Perth's Northbridge for Cultural Consumption." Pp. 120–137 in *Selling Ethnic Neighborhoods: The Rise of Neighborhoods as Places of Leisure and Consumption*, edited by Volkan Aytar and Jan Rath. New York: Routledge.

Lefebvre, Henri. 1996. *Writings on Cities*. Oxford: Blackwell.

———. [1970] 2003. *The Urban Revolution*. Minneapolis: University of Minnesota Press.

———. 2004. *Rhythmanalysis: Space, Time and Everyday Life*. New York: Continuum.

Low, Setha M. 2000. *On the Plaza: The Politics of Public Space and Culture*. Austin: University of Texas Press.

Massey, Doreen. 1994. *Space, Place and Gender*. Minneapolis: University of Minnesota Press.

Middleton, Jennie. 2009. "'Stepping in Time': Walking, Time, and Space in the City." *Environment and Planning A* 41(8):1943–1961.

Mitchell, Don. 1995. "The End of Public Space? People's Park, Definitions of the Public, and Democracy." *Annals of the Association of American Geographers* 85:108–133.

Noble, Greg. 2009. "'Countless Acts of Recognition': Young Men, Ethnicity and the Messiness of Identities in Everyday Life." *Social and Cultural Geography* 10(8):875–891.

Papastergiadis, Nikos. 2005. "Mobility and the Nation: Skins, Machines and Complex Systems." *Willy Brandt Series of Working Papers in International Migration and Ethnic Relations* 3(5):1–29. Retrieved June 19, 2013. http://dspace.mah.se/dspace/handle/2043/1862.

Pink, Sarah. 2008. "Mobilising Visual Ethnography: Making Routes, Making Place and Making Images." *Forum: Qualitative Social Research* 9(3). Retrieved March 3, 2014. http://www.qualitative-esearch.net/index.php/fqs/article/view/1166/2575.

Saeter, Oddrun. 2011. "The Body and the Eye: Perspectives, Technologies and Practices of Urbanism." *Space and Culture* 14:183–196.

Sassen, Saskia. 2002. "Towards Post-National and Denationalized Citizenship." Pp. 277–292 in *Handbook of Citizenship Studies*, edited by Engin F. Isin and Bryan S. Turner. London: Sage.

Sheller, Mimi and John Urry. 2000. "The City and the Car." *International Journal of Urban and Regional Research* 24(4):737–757.

Smith, Michael Peter. 2005. "Transnational Urbanism Revisited." *Journal of Ethnic and Migration Studies* 31(2):235–244.

Taylor, Charles. 1992. "The Politics of Recognition." Pp. 76–93 in *Multiculturalism: Examining the Politics of Recognition*, edited by Amy Gutmann. Princeton, NJ: Princeton University Press.

Tonkiss, Fran. 2003. "The Ethics of Indifference: Community and Solitude in the City." *International Journal of Cultural Studies* 6(3):297–311.

Trudeau, Daniel. 2006. "Politics of Belonging in the Construction of Landscapes: Place-Making, Boundary-Drawing, and Exclusion." *Cultural Geographies* 13:421–443.

Urry, John. 2007. *Mobilities*. Cambridge: Polity.

Valverde, Mariana. 2011. "Seeing like a City: The Dialectic of Modern and Premodern Ways of Seeing in Urban Governance." *Law and Society Review* 45(2):277–312.

Wessendorf, Susanne. 2010. "Commonplace Diversity: Social Interactions in a Super-Diverse Context." *Working Papers, Max Planck Institute for the Study of Religious and Ethnic Diversity*. Retrieved June 11, 2013. www.mmg.mpg.de/workingpapers.

Whyte, William H. 2000. *The Essential William H. Whyte*. New York: Fordham University Press.

———. [1988] 2009. *City: Rediscovering the Center*. Philadelphia: University of Pennsylvania Press.

Wise, Amanda. 2010. "Sensuous Multiculturalism: Emotional Landscapes of Interethnic Living in Australian Suburbia." *Journal of Ethnic and Migration Studies* 36(6): 917–937.

———. 2011. "'You Wouldn't Know What's in There Would You?' Homeliness and 'Foreign' Signs in Ashfield, Sydney." Pp. 93–108 in *Translocal Geographies: Spaces, Places, Connections*, edited by Katherine Brickell and Ayona Datta. Farnham, UK: Ashgate.

Wise, Amanda and Selvaraj Velayutham. 2009. *Everyday Multiculturalism*. New York: Palgrave Macmillan.

Vasta, Ellie. 2013. "Do We Need Social Cohesion in the 21st Century? Multiple Languages of Belonging in the Metropolis." *Journal of Intercultural Studies* 34(2):196–213.

Zukin, Sharon. 2010. *Naked City: The Death and Life of Authentic Urban Places*. Oxford: Oxford University Press.

3

Race and the Politics of Space

Doing Walking Ethnography in Urban Chicago

SHANSHAN LAN

I t is well known among anthropologists that "race" is no longer a scientifically valid concept in denoting human biological variation, but as a social con- struct it still plays an important role in structuring the daily life experiences of different populations in contemporary U.S. society (Harrison 1995; Omi and Winant 1993). Unfortunately, the general American public's understanding of race is still fraught with confusion. More often than not, race is considered to be "a fuzzy jumble of behavior, culture and biology: a deep and primordial mix of a bit of culture and a lot of nature" (Goodman 2005:18). Post-racial thinking in the United States today exemplifies this confusion. Celebrating Barack Obama's election as the end of racism in the United States not only upholds a biological interpretation of race based on skin color but reinforces the black-white binary in defining U.S. race relations. Scholars have noted that the post–civil rights reconfiguration of whiteness is often marked by the replacement of race with code words like *culture* or *ethnicity,* and the posing of one minority against another (Gotanda 1995; Matsuda 1993; Prashad 2000; Visweswaran 1997). This changing racial rhetoric of multiculturalism and colorblindness enables the U.S. nation-state "to perpetuate racial domination without making any explicit ref- erence to race at all" (Omi and Winant 1993:7). Meanwhile, it also poses enor- mous constraints to minority groups' struggle for racial equality and justice. My ethnographic research in Chicago asked the following question: How do Chinese immigrant workers develop their knowledge about race when main- stream discourses about race and racism are increasingly challenged and erased in a so-called color-blind or post-racial society?

When I started my preliminary dissertation research in Chicago's Chi- natown in summer 2003, I was a naive graduate student who believed that talking to people from different racial and ethnic backgrounds was the best way to gather research data. However, during my first month in the field I was constantly frustrated by people's lack of interest in my questions; they either walked away quickly or preferred to talk about something else. Then something happened that profoundly changed my relationship with my informants. One afternoon I was walking back to Chinatown after finishing an interview with two Chinese artists in Bridgeport. Being a poor graduate student, I had neither a car nor a cell phone at that time. While I was walking in the neighborhood, several white teenagers came from behind. They yelled racial slurs and imitation Chinese at me and threatened to beat me up. I was scared and started running as fast as I could. When I reached the tunnel that connects Bridgeport to Chinatown, another white teenager riding a bicycle appeared. He made wicked faces at me and tried to hit me with his bike. For several days I could not recover from the shock of the incident. My heart was filled with anger, humiliation, and helplessness. Fortunately, people in the Chinese immigrant community comforted me. They shared with me their personal experiences of being harassed in Bridgeport and taught me about the various hidden racial boundaries in the city. As I got to know more and more people in the Chinese community, my own little "traumatic experience" faded in comparison to the interracial harassment and hate crimes that Chinese immigrants coped with daily. However, this incident marked my true initiation into the immigrants' world and their acceptance of me as a member of the community.

It is through walking that I discovered the Chinese presence in Bridgeport, a historically white working-class community adjacent to Chicago's Chinatown. It is also through sharing stories of walking with my research subjects that I discovered the paradoxical absence and presence of race in the daily lives of Chinese immigrant workers in Bridgeport (Prendergast 1998). Though they are frequently the targets of white interracial harassment, Chinese immigrants seldom articulate their plight in racial terms. This disjuncture between race as an American ideological construct and race as a lived experience both perplexed me and motivated me to explore an alternative knowledge system developed by Chinese immigrants in navigating multiracial Chicago. As a woman born and raised in China, I was often mistaken in the field by non-Chinese speakers as a new immigrant who did not speak English. The plus is I gained an understanding of the racialized experience of my working-class Chinese American research subjects.[1] The minus is I had to cope with the psychological trauma and emotional hurt of interracial harassment on a very personal level. Often I found myself a walking embodiment of the contradictions and complexities

---

[1] By *Chinese American*, I am referring to both Chinese immigrants and American-born Chinese. Since foreign-born Chinese represent 76 percent of the Chinese American population both in Chicago and the suburbs, it is important to write their stories as a major part of the Chinese American experience (Lau 2006:170). By treating Chinese immigrants as Chinese Americans, I am also challenging prevailing stereotypes of Asian immigrants as foreigners to the United States.

in the entanglement of race with other modes of social differentiation, such as class, gender, language, place of origin, and so forth.

As noted by Tim Ingold and Jo Lee Vergunst (2008:1), walking is a profoundly social activity just like talking, because "in their timings, rhythms and inflections, the feet respond as much as does the voice to the presence and activity of others." Walking proved to be a particularly useful ethnographic method for me because it provided me a unique perspective in comprehending the physical, emotional, socio-spatial, and epistemological dimensions of racial meanings and dynamics in a daily life urban setting. Reflections on my interactive learning experience in the field helped me develop the concept of racial learning, which became one of the key words in my monograph *Diaspora and Class Consciousness: Chinese Immigrant Workers in Multiracial Chicago* (Lan 2012). In the book, I define racial learning as the development and accumulation of knowledge about racial differences and racial hierarchies through daily life experiences in various transnational, local, institutional, and community settings. The book argues that the racial learning of Chinese immigrant workers is conditioned not only by their transnational migration experience but by their various and contradictory racializations in relation to poor African Americans and Latinos in a multiracial urban environment. What is missing, however, is a critical reconsideration of my own racial learning experience in the field. This chapter represents my attempt to explore the politics and poetics of doing walking ethnography in a racialized urban environment (Rieder 1985).[2] Specifically, I am interested in teasing out the relationship between walking, narratives about walking, and the accumulation of racial knowledge by the vulnerable ethnographer (Behar 1996)

Multiracial Politics in Chinatown and Bridgeport

Chicago's Chinatown differs from those of San Francisco, Los Angeles, and New York in many ways. While the latter attract scholarly attention for their sweatshop workers, illegal immigrants, and economic potential, there are no similar studies on Chicago's Chinatown, which depends solely on the restaurant industry (Bao 2001; Bonacich and Appelbaum 2000; Kwong 1997; Lin 1998; Zhou 1992). Moreover, while Chinatowns in the two coastal areas are undergoing economic depressions and population decline, Chicago's Chinatown is expanding southwest to its adjacent Bridgeport neighborhood. According to Yvonne Lau (2006:173), about 26 percent of Chicago's entire Chinese population lives in the city's Chinatown. In comparison, only 14 percent of the Chinese in New York, 8 percent of the Chinese in San Francisco, and less than 3 percent of the Chinese in Los Angeles still live in the cities' Chinatowns (Zhou 2009:48). Put together, the Chinese population in Armour Square (where the historical Chinatown is located) and Bridgeport account for 48 percent of all Chinese

---

[2] By *poetics* I mean the sensorial embodied and phenomenological experience of walking.

in Chicago (Lau 2006:170). This concentration of Chinese immigrants in Chicago forms a sharp contrast with the Chinese American population in the two coastal areas, who mainly reside in multiracial suburban communities dubbed by scholars as "ethnoburbs" or "suburban Chinatowns" (Chen 1992; Fong 1994; Horton 1995; Li 1998). Compared with other Asian immigrant groups in Chicago, Chinese Americans also display the most striking class polarity. While the median household income for Chinese families in Chicago averages $36,853, suburban Chinese households in DuPage and Lake Counties, where the majority of middle-class Chinese Americans are concentrated, average $91,393 and $94,506 (Kim 2006:161).

Scholars have noted that communities are not merely physically bounded entities but intersections of a multitude of social political relations and human imaginaries (Anderson 1991; De Genova 2005; Gregory 1998; Võ and Bonus 2002). Instead of being a self-isolated urban enclave, Chicago's Chinatown community has always been part of the multiracial city landscape. To its east and southeast, there is a concentration of African Americans in Near South Side, Douglas, and Grand Boulevard, which is historically known as the "Black Belt."[3] To its west, there are Pilsen and Little Village, the two largest Mexican American communities in Chicago. And the "core" of Chinatown, Armour Square, used to be an Italian neighborhood. The expansion of the Chinese population into Bridgeport began around the 1980s and 1990s, due to a new wave of immigration prompted by the 1989 Tiananmen Incident and the 1997 return of the British colony of Hong Kong to mainland China. Since affordable rentals in Chinatown are hard to find, most new immigrants ended up in Bridgeport, where real estate prices are 20 to 30 percent lower. By 2002, the estimated Chinese population in Bridgeport exceeded Chinatown's and reached ten thousand (Kennedy 2002).

Bridgeport was, until recently, a white working-class neighborhood known for its history of resistance against housing desegregation and for its substantial antiblack racial violence. The neighborhood has been home to different waves of European immigrants: Irish, Germans, Lithuanians, Czechoslovakians, Poles, Ukrainians, and Italians. Politically, it remains an Irish stronghold: five of Chicago's mayors have hailed from Bridgeport, including Mayor Richard M. Daley, whose term ended in 2011. During the 1919 race riot, athletic clubs in the stockyards district played a major role in hunting and killing blacks on the streets. The number of injuries in that district was the highest among all seven riot districts identified by the Chicago Commission on Race Relations (1922). In the following decades, chronic violence against blacks in Bridgeport kept the

[3] The Social Science Research Committee at the University of Chicago has unofficially divided the city of Chicago into seventy-seven community areas. Near South Side, Douglas, and Grand Boulevard are the three community areas east of Chinatown. Douglas and Grand Boulevard used to be the Bronzeville community that Drake and Cayton described in *Black Metropolis* in 1945.

Black Belt from expanding to the southwest side (Hirsch 1983).[4] In 1965, when a group of multiracial civil rights activists paraded in the neighborhood in protest of housing segregation in Chicago, hundreds of Bridgeporters threw eggs and tomatoes, showed Ku Klux Klan signs, and shouted, "Two-four-six-eight, we don't want to integrate" and "Oh, I wish I was an Alabama trooper. That is what I'd really like to be-ee-ee. Cuz if I was an Alabama trooper, I could kill the niggers legally" (Biles 1995:112).

The multiracial transformation of Bridgeport began in the 1980s and lasted throughout the 1990s, with an influx of immigrants from Asia and Latin America that reconstituted the neighborhood's demography to 26 percent Asian American, 30 percent Latino, and 41 percent white.[5] These changes, however, cannot obscure the glaring fact that African Americans continue to be virtually excluded from Bridgeport. Today African Americans constitute only 1.05 percent of Bridgeport's population. They nonetheless continue to play an important role in the neighborhood's racial imagination. For example, in 1997, a thirteen-year-old African American, Lenard Clark, was beaten into a coma by three white adolescents while biking in a park near Bridgeport. It was reported that the offenders later bragged how they had taken care of the "niggers" in their neighborhood.[6] In another example, on June 25, 2000, an African American man was parked at a gas station in Bridgeport, when four young people came over to his truck. The victim got out of the truck to see what was wrong. One of the youths said, "Hey nigger, you are in the wrong neighborhood. We'll kill you." The victim got back into his truck and started to drive away, while the perpetrators threw several bricks and bottles at him. A police sergeant happened to be driving by, and he arrested the offenders.[7]

In their study of residential patterns of immigrant minorities in the United States, Richard Alba and Nancy Denton (2004) note a discrepancy between the increasing heterogeneity of urban populations and the reification of racial differences: "At the broadest level, we argue that the trend for immigrants and for the racial hierarchy has been toward greater heterogeneity and toward a loosening of once more rigid structures, while for places of residence, despite greater diversity at the neighborhood level, there has been a hardening of the urban residential structure" (237). The same thing can be said of Bridgeport, where racial integration was achieved mainly in the physical and geographical sense. While the arrival of Chinese immigrants revitalized Bridgeport's real estate market, tensions between Chinese Americans and more established residents, mainly white people, also increased. On November 3, 1999, two male Asian American teens were walking along a Bridgeport street when they were assaulted by three white

[4] It must be noted that the gangs involved in these attacks were Irish Americans; most other ethnic groups did not take part in the violence.
[5] Data obtained from Northeastern Illinois Planning Commission Data Research and Forecasting Group; see http://www.nipc.org/forecasting/PL-Profile-ccas/pca60.xls (last visited April 12, 2006).
[6] "Chicago: The Streets Where Black Kids Ain't Allowed" (1997) and Fedarko and Grace (1997).
[7] Data obtained from the Chicago Commission on Human Relations (2003).

male teens, who shouted racial epithets and beat up the Asian boys.[8] In 2000, a Chinese restaurant on Halsted Street was set on fire. Believing the crime was racially motivated, the owner eventually moved out of Bridgeport to the suburbs (Olivo and Avila 2004). These are just two recorded hate crimes. According to many Chinese residents in Bridgeport, there are numerous unreported cases of interracial harassment happening on a daily basis. Steve, a twenty-year-old Chinese American college student who grew up in Bridgeport, told me, "Harassment? It happens so often that it has become normal. I've gotten used to it."[9] Tony, a Chinese American community organizer, expressed to me his feelings of alienation in Bridgeport, "I happen to live in a place called Bridgeport, but all my friends are in Chinatown."[10]

The multiracial politics in Bridgeport and Chinatown makes urban walking a crucial domain in examining the racialization of space, the making and unmaking of interracial boundaries, and the performance of gendered and racialized stereotypes in daily life settings. In the rest of this chapter, I examine three different types of walking practices in multiracial Chicago: walking as a daily routine for Chinese and African Americans; walking as cultural consumption for white tourists; and walking as a research method for the urban ethnographer. As noted by Martin Manalansan (2000:1), "Ethnography can be likened to a cartographic project, mapping out and opening up spaces, relationships, and meanings for possible interventions and resistance." Doing walking ethnography in urban Chicago not only prompted me to critically reflect on the relationship between different types of walking but enhanced my knowledge of deeper structural reasons behind urban walking.

Walking as a Racialized, Gendered, and Classed Experience

Various scholars have noted the relationship between walking, the built environment, and the social dimensions of urban walking. Compared with driving and cycling, walking is more difficult and time-consuming. Yet it offers more opportunities for social interactions and building rapport with locals (Conley 2012; Helmreich 2013; Middleton 2009). According to William Helmreich (2013:10), driving creates "a physical wall" between the driver and the neighborhood. Erving Goffman (1963:17) notes that automobile traffic lacks the "richness of information flow and facilitation of feedback" of face-to-face interaction. Jim Conley (2012:224) explores the differences between walking, driving, and cycling by paying special attention to "how the speed of vehicular units

---

[8] See Chicago Commission on Human Relations (1999:13). Racial classification in this hate crime report stops at the Asian American level and does not deal with any individual subgroups among Asian Americans. In reality, these two Asian American teenagers are Chinese immigrants from a local Chicago public school. I interviewed their teachers, local community leaders, and the social workers who helped the victims and their parents bring the offenders to court.

[9] Personal interview, November 1, 2003.

[10] Personal interview, July 14, 2004.

and the material qualities of their shells afford or constrain interactions with others." While noting the "vulnerability of the pedestrian 'shell' to its environment," Conley's (2012:226) emphasis is on pedestrian outfits such as boots, coat, scarf, hat, or hood, rather than on the racialized and gendered bodies encapsulated in them. This chapter questions the universality of walking as a type of socially interactive mobility by probing into the various structural constraints on urban walking, such as race, class, and gender. For working-class Chinese immigrants and poor African Americans, urban walking may not be out of choice but out of necessity. For the female graduate student ethnographer, urban walking can be a highly personal experience where special precautions need to be taken in order to avoid potentially dangerous situations. Yet it can also be a useful ethnographic method that promises fascinating encounters with research subjects from different racial and class backgrounds.

In the Bridgeport and Chinatown neighborhoods, urban walking as a routinized practice is largely restricted to working-class Chinese immigrants and poor African Americans owing to their limited access to public transportations and private vehicles. The two groups' structural marginalization in U.S. society is reinforced by historically racist state policies such as urban renewal and housing segregation, which caused the rapid deterioration of living environment in the city and increasing dangers for urban walking.[11] Today, if one goes to Chinatown, one can still see the legacies of the urban renewal in the 1960s: hemmed in by elevated expressways on the east, west, and south sides, Chinatown is connected to the outside world by a number of tunnels. Many of the tunnels are old, dirty, flooded on rainy days, and poorly lit, which make them easy hiding places for crime. For working-class Chinese immigrants who live in Bridgeport, walking to Chinatown became a daily routine since many of them depend on the ethnic economy for job opportunities and social support. However, in order to reach Chinatown, they have to walk across several tunnels under Highway 55. Since those tunnels are located at the borderland between two police districts—District Twenty-One and District Nine—they become ideal sites for petty crimes such as robbery, purse snatching, and physical assault. The offenders are usually white teenagers and the victims are usually elderly or middle-aged Chinese women who do not speak English and are not physically able to fight back.

When I moved in with a working-class Cantonese family in Bridgeport in the summer of 2004, I told my landlady, Aunt Lu, that I was scared walking across these tunnels because I had had some bad experiences during the previous summer. Aunt Lu soothed my fear with her knowledge from experience:

Don't be afraid. Every time you walk to Chinatown, always go through the tunnel leading to the Chinese American Senior Housing. That one is the shortest and the safest compared to all the other tunnels. I walked through it every day. See this bag I am carrying? It's so plain looking that it won't

---

[11] For more details, see chapter 1 of Lan (2012).

catch people's attention. I tie the string of the bag to my arm so that it cannot be snatched from me so easily. I never wear any rings or necklace otherwise I might get jumped.[12]

My conversation with Aunt Lu marked the start of a series of learning experiences about the various hidden racial landscapes in the city. In order to minimize their chances of being victimized while walking around the neighborhood, Chinese immigrants have developed intimate knowledge of physical boundaries in a multiracial urban environment.

Another racial learning moment occurred when I interviewed Victor, a twenty-one-year-old college student who grew up in Bridgeport. Knowing that I was new to the neighborhood, Victor carefully explained to me the streetwise knowledge he had accumulated over the years:

As long as you know some rules here, you will be fine. Rule one, never go out after dark; rule two, when someone says stupid things to you like "Ching Ching Chong Chong," ignore them and walk away; rule three, don't stare at people; rule four, always look back when you are walking alone and make sure no one is after you; rule five, don't appear threatening to them; rule six, always choose a busy street whether driving or walking. Never go into a dark street.[13]

In his study of a mixed-race neighborhood in Philadelphia, Elijah Anderson (1990) finds that both white and black residents' understandings of "street etiquette" and "street wisdom" are racially coded. In a similar vein, Victor's elaboration on the rules of the street is a manifestation of his intimate knowledge of the racialized inner-city landscape. As noted by Michael Omi and Howard Winant, "'Etiquette' is not a mere universal adherence to the dominant group's rules, but a more dynamic combination of these rules with the values and beliefs of subordinated groupings" (1986:62). Paul's streetwise knowledge is not merely a surviving strategy for working-class Chinese immigrant youth but a reflection of the hierarchical relations inscribed in a multiracial urban space.

The Making and Unmaking of Interracial Boundaries

I was sitting in a Chinatown bakery with Paul, a middle-aged Chinese American architect, when he gave me the following advice, "Don't go to the other side of the railway track unless you want to risk your life." Then he told me the story of the Canadian doctor: "Beyond that bridge, it is dangerous. There is lots of violence, gangs on the other side. Several years ago, a Chinese doctor from Canada came to visit. He and his family couldn't find a taxi on Cermak road.

[12] Conversation, July 17, 2004.
[13] Personal interview, August 3, 2004.

They decided to walk back to their hotel in downtown Chicago. They got robbed on Cermak and State Street and the doctor got killed. He was just a tourist. He didn't know the area."[14] The railway mentioned by Paul is the elevated rapid transit line that runs along the Dan Ryan Expressway, popularly known as EL by Chicago residents. The Canadian tourist incident happened in 1979, near the Hilliard Homes, a high-rise public housing project (Brodt 1980). Twenty-four years later, in 2003, when I started doing my fieldwork in Chicago, the tunnel on Cermak and Wentworth still remained a forbidden area for Chinese Americans. According to Paul, the Canadian doctor lost his life because he was an outsider to the community and thus had no knowledge where the racial boundary between Chinese and African Americans was and why the crossing of the boundary could be fatal. Paul was kind to tell me the story, obviously viewing me as an outsider to the community, as well.

Although the Dan Ryan Expressway serves as a physical boundary between Chinatown and its neighboring black community, this geographical/racial boundary is largely porous because several tunnels underneath the highway provided easy connections between the two communities. However, boundary-crossing activities near the tunnels are highly asymmetrical: while African Americans feel safe coming to Chinatown to eat or do grocery shopping, few Chinese would venture to the other side of Dan Ryan. Aside from the tunnel near which the Canadian doctor was killed, the one connecting Chinatown and Ickes Homes on Twenty-Fourth Street proved to be another sore spot. The tunnel became a contentious issue between Chinese and African Americans because it provided a shortcut for criminal activities. Some African Americans were reported to steal, rob, and shoplift in the Chinese businesses and run back to their housing project through the tunnel. Concerned with the safety of their community, the Chinese side wanted to close the tunnel. However, since African American children needed to walk through the tunnel daily to attend an elementary school in Chinatown, the black community complained about discrimination on the Chinese side. The issue dragged on for almost thirty years until 2001, when the Illinois Department of Transportation decided to seal the tunnel as part of the restructuring of the Dan Ryan Expressway.[15] Despite the fact that Chinatown was not the only community affected by petty crimes from Chicago Housing Authority housing projects—the black community east of Dan Ryan suffered from more severe crimes—these stories of the tunnels gave rise to discourses of fear and danger within the Chinese American community, which served to perpetuate racial stereotypes against African Americans.[16]

[14] Personal interview, June 29, 2003.
[15] This account is based on personal interviews with Chinatown residents, community leaders, and Commander Stanley from the Twenty-First Police District. Another source for the story of the tunnel can be found in Yao (1977:47–49). By the time the tunnel was sealed, African American children no longer needed to cross it to attend school in Chinatown because a brand-new elementary school had been built in their neighborhood.
[16] For the plight of high-rise public housing, see Venkatesh (2000) and Popkin et al. (2000).

For the Chinese immigrant community in the Chinatown area, the image of the beggar is always a racialized and gendered one. There are generally two types of beggars in Chinatown: poor African American mothers with children asking for money to feed the little ones, and disabled African American males who are on crutches or in wheelchairs. They usually place themselves in front of tourist sites or near the entrance to Chinese bakeries or grocery stores, where there is a constant flow of people. However, some Chinese business owners thought the beggars were hurting their businesses. Others believed they were bringing down the image of Chinatown. The Chinatown Chamber of Commerce once urged people not to give money to beggars. The Chinese business owners' negative attitudes toward African American beggars reflect the policing of interracial boundaries in the marketplace and the circumscribed physical mobility of poor African Americans in Chinatown. However, the Chinese boundary-making strategies are also mediated by class distinctions within the African American population. Middle-class African Americans who patronize restaurants and gift shops in Chinatown on weekends or holidays are usually treated much better than poor African Americans from the public housing east of Dan Ryan Expressway are. In fact, business owners in Chinatown are the most experienced in judging whether a black customer has money or not by their outward appearance. Ling, the daughter of my Cantonese landlord, who works part-time in a Chinatown teashop, mentioned to me that her boss laughs and jokes with African American customers when they are well-dressed. When they are poorly dressed, she whispers to Ling, "Watch out!"[17]

In summer 2004, as I came back to Chicago's Chinatown, I noticed that children, both African Americans and Chinese Americans, from a local elementary school were working on a mural in the tunnel near which the Canadian tourist was killed in 1979.[18] Lisa, one of the Chinese American teens working on the mural, explained to me: "Our mural project is to bridge the racial gap. I think people in Chinatown are too conservative; they don't want any changes."[19] The mural depicts Asia on side and the African continent on the other, with Chicago in the middle. A blue ocean wave carries people from one continent to another. Unfortunately, the human figures in the mural have no visible facial features. The only faces floating in the ocean are Peking opera masks. While the transformation of the tunnel from a dangerous place to a bridge connecting the two communities may echo the changing U.S. rhetoric of multiculturalism and diversity, the use of Peking opera masks to replace human faces with natural skin tones also speaks of the limitation of a color-blind racial ideology. A few steps away from the mural, I found a notable sign at the foot of a Chinese pavilion: NO LOITERING, NO SLEEPING, NO DRINKING. It is common knowledge to Chinatown

---

[17] Conversation with Ling, July 2, 2004.
[18] It is worth noting that community murals are extremely common in Chicago—especially in Mexican neighborhoods—and are often used for connections between communities.
[19] Personal interview, July 22, 2004.

residents that African Americans love to sit in the pavilion to rest after they are done with grocery shopping. The juxtaposition of these two contrasting symbols is ironic: the mural as the potential site for the creation of interracial space, and the prohibitory sign as the means of policing interracial boundaries. Together they speak of the contradictions and complexities in the making and unmaking of interracial boundaries between Chinese and African Americans. They also remind us that social space is lived and changing all the time.

Walking as Cultural Consumption for White Tourists

While walking is a daily routine for working-class Chinese immigrants and poor African Americans who live near Chinatown and Bridgeport, it turns out to be a well-planned leisure activity for suburban white tourists who travel to Chinatown on weekends and special Chinese holidays for a taste of ethnic adventure. One of my Korean American friends told me the following story: "Once I was walking in Chinatown with a friend, two white tourists came and they insisted taking a picture of us standing in front of the Chinatown Gate. They said a picture of Chinatown must include some Chinese people in it. I told them we were not Chinese, but they said it did not matter. I was so annoyed by the experience."[20] My Korean American friend's story shows the politics of representation and the objectification of Chinatown in the eyes of some white tourists. Under the powerful white gaze, Chinatown can only be a homogeneous ethnic enclave for Chinese, and the presence of Korean Americans is an anomaly and must be suppressed and erased. Despite the protest of my friend, the two white tourists chose to represent Chinatown the way they wanted. In other words, Chinatown exists more vividly in their imagination than in real-life experiences. As temporary visitors in the neighborhood, suburban white people know little about the hidden racial landscape in the community, and they also show little interest in the daily survival experiences of working-class Chinese immigrants.

Chinatown residents and white tourists remain largely invisible to each other because of their distinct knowledge, expectation, and utilization of the urban built environment. Because of the increase of cars and tourists on weekends and special holidays, some Chinese immigrants deliberately avoid going to Chinatown on those occasions. I spent the Chinese New Year Day of 2005 with Aunt Lu's family in Bridgeport. We had vegetarian food, according to the Hakka tradition. While we were eating, we could hear the sound of fireworks and drums from Chinatown. "That must be the Chinese New Year Parade," I said excitedly. Aunt Lu did not seem to share my enthusiasm. "We never go to the parade. It is too crowded, with too many people from outside Chinatown," she said casually. For Aunt Lu's family, the presence of white tourists in Chinatown had little to do with their everyday life. By refusing to participate in the parade, the family

[20] Conversation, March 13, 2006.

refused to accommodate the white gaze, which often functions to turn their daily lives into a spectacle. By staying at home, the family also showed their determination to celebrate the Chinese New Year at their own pace.

Although white tourists only visit Chinatown on weekends and holidays and their walking activities are mainly restricted to the business area, they still played an important role in reshaping the physical and social landscape in the Chinese American community. Since the economy of Chicago's Chinatown depends mainly on the restaurant industry, the necessity to attract a large number of tourists became the primary concern for some Chinatown merchants and community leaders. In 1980, the *Chicago Tribune* announced civic leader G. H. Wang's ten-million-project for the commercial revitalization of Chinatown. At the heart of Wang's plan was the construction of an Oriental-looking parking garage at the northeast corner of Wentworth and Cermak, near the site where the Canadian tourist got killed. Wang was quite explicit about racial concerns in building the garage. He believed that besides relieving parking problems in an overcongested Chinatown, the building of a parking facility would ease visitors' anxieties about crime near the Chinatown area. "Chinatown itself, I would say is very safe and secure, but it is bordered by housing projects" (Brodt 1980). Apparently, the visitors envisioned by Wang who would bring economic revitalization to Chinatown were white suburbanites entertaining the idea of ethnic adventures in Chinatown yet deterred by its closeness to the "projects." Therefore, the building of a parking garage near the border between the Chinese American community and the African American community would help police the boundary between the two communities and thus minimize the possibility of white visitors' encounters with African Americans.

Besides the garage, Wang also proposed to build a Chinese pagoda and Oriental friendship gardens in the community. To culminate his plan to "make Chinatown more like Chinatown," Wang suggested putting ethnic decorations on everything from little news shacks and telephone booths to flower planters and restaurant directories. Charles Soo, the manager of the Wang project, told a *Tribune* reporter, "We want Chinatown to have the authentic Oriental atmosphere that tourists and other visitors can enjoy" (Brodt 1980). Wang's plan to "Orientalize" Chinatown represents some middle-class Chinese Americans' efforts to balance building a vibrant Chinese American community and meeting the Orientalist gaze of mainstream American society.[21] In order to counter stereotypes of the inner city as an urban wasteland haunted by poverty and crime, some Chinese American community leaders had to resurrect the Orientalist image of Chinatown as an exotic Eastern paradise for the purpose of attracting curious Euro-American visitors. In summer 2004, the Chinatown Chamber of Commerce launched a tourist program called "Summer Fun in Chinatown." They planned to introduce rickshaw rides in the neighborhood

---

[21] What Wang defines as an "authentic Oriental atmosphere" represented middle-class Chinese Americans' perceptions of what Euro-American tourists would expect.

in order to attract more visitors. Jimmy Lee, the chamber's spokesman, told a reporter, "Rickshaws and pedicabs are identified with the Chinese culture . . . Chinatown has always wanted to . . . get some pedicabs to the community because of its long tradition in the Asian American countries and culture." Lee also hoped that the pedicabs would bring about 15 to 25 percent growth in foot traffic in Chinatown.[22] Although the rickshaw project failed to materialize, it still illustrates how the image of the exotic ethnic enclave has been straitjacketing the development trajectory of the Chinatown neighborhood. The ideological presence of the white gaze proves to be more powerful than its physical presence in Chinatown.

Walking as a Research Method for the Anthropologist

In January 2005, I managed to get an internship position in a social service agency in Chinatown while still carrying on my dissertation research. Since the job required me to travel to the suburbs frequently, I had to purchase a used car in order to fulfill my work-related responsibilities. It was when walking ceased to be a daily routine that I began to realize the importance of walking as a research method. Even though I did not deliberately choose walking as a research method, the embodied and performative nature of urban walking, with its racialized, gendered, and classed implications, had transformed my personal walking experiences into highly politicized and emotionally charged field encounters (Cheng 2013; Wunderlich 2008). Unlike Charles Baudelaire's gentleman *flâneur*, who managed to participate in city life while simultaneously maintaining a critical distance, the female graduate student ethnographer could not remain a detached observer in the field. Sharing my experience of being personally harassed in Bridgeport with my working-class Chinese research subjects helped me temporarily cross the boundary between the insider and outsider (Võ 2000). It also facilitated several "go-along" trips with my informants (Kusenbach 2003), during which I simply allowed myself to perform the stereotype of a non-English-speaking new immigrant woman. In this way, I managed to blend in with my research subjects and learn to experience the multiracial cityscape from their perspectives. It was precisely through interactive learning experiences between the vulnerable anthropologist and my working-class immigrant informants that the dynamic, elusive meanings of race and class can be partially illuminated.

Cheng (2013:2) notes that walking ethnography is constituted not only through "walking" per se but through "the sensorial aspects of our bodies such as seeing, hearing, and feeling." Sharing my personal feelings of fear, anger, anxiety, and helplessness in the field with my research subjects strengthened the emotional bond between us, yet it also reminded me of the temporary nature of my ethnographic walking and pushed me to reflect on the relationship

[22] Chang (2004).

between urban walking, race, and the sensorial/affective domain. During my first few months in the field, I was easily upset or frustrated when I experienced negative encounters with white people in the street or when I heard stories of Chinese being victims of interracial harassment in the neighborhood. I kept telling my Cantonese landlord, Uncle Lu, "Why aren't you angry? This is racial discrimination!" However, the Lu family did not share my emotional distress. It was only after I left the field that I realized it was my privileged position as a researcher that had influenced my different reactions toward everyday racism in Bridgeport. I was angry at negative interracial encounters in Bridgeport because I had been used to living a sheltered life on an elite university campus and I was not prepared for the tough life in an urban neighborhood. I had no problem naming racial discrimination because I was armed with all the textbook knowledge about race and class. What I lacked was localized spatial knowledge (see Williamson, Chapter 2 in this volume), familiarity with the rhythms of urban walking, a constant awareness to stay alert while walking around (e.g., the street etiquette explained to me by Victor), and a strong will to survive in a racialized urban environment. Moving beyond my personal emotional responses to interracial harassment enabled me to reinterpret my research subjects' apparently indifferent attitude toward race as masking deeper levels of alternative racial knowledge formation process.

In addition to my personal walking experiences and sharing of these experiences with my informants, I also collected many stories about walking. By examining how walking was narrated and represented in individual personal stories, I was able to discover the hidden racial boundaries and hierarchical power relations inscribed in a multiracial cityscape. Gathering stories of walking also enabled me to reflect on the relationship between different types of walking and their different rhythms of sociability (Lefebvre 2004; see Williamson, Chapter 2 in this volume). Echoing Rebecca Williamson's observation that rhythms of sociability and familiarity are associated with particular sites and particular temporalities, I found that although poor African Americans are a common presence in Chinatown on weekdays, they did not enjoy the same level of sociality as Chinese immigrants both in public spaces and in ethnic shops. The different manners in which Chinese and African Americans walk in Chinatown reflect the complex process of the making and unmaking of interracial boundaries between the two groups. While white tourists frequent Chinatown mostly on weekends and special holidays, as a racially privileged group they have been unwittingly impacting the community infrastructure and future development trajectories of Chinatown. White tourists may be physically present in Chinatown, but their experience of the neighborhood is largely based on their Orientalist gaze: Chinatown as an exotic ethnic enclave. For this reason, these tourists remain largely oblivious to the daily plight of working-class Chinese immigrants struggling to survive in a racialized urban environment, and their version of the Chinatown experience remains distinct from the version of my Chinese informants. Walking as an ethnographic research method transgresses the boundaries between walking as a daily routine and walking as a carefully planned special event. It enables the ethnographer to both physically experience the material realities of race in daily life practices and analytically reflect on the hierarchical power relations inscribed in the relationship between different types of walking and the multiracial urban landscape.

REFERENCES

Alba, Richard and Nancy Denton. 2004. "Old and New Landscapes of Diversity: The Residential Patterns of Immigrant Minorities." Pp. 237–261 in *Not Just Black and White: Historical and Contemporary Perspectives on Immigration, Race, and Ethnicity in the United States*, edited by Nancy Foner and George M. Fredrickson. New York: Russell Sage Foundation.

Anderson, Benedict. 1991. *Imagined Communities: Reflections on the Origin and Spread of Nationalism*. New York: Verso.

Anderson, Elijah. 1990. *StreetWise: Race, Class, and Change in an Urban Community*. Chicago: University of Chicago Press.

Bao, Xiaolan. 2001. *Holding Up More Than Half the Sky: Chinese Women Garment Workers in New York City, 1948–92*. Urbana: University of Illinois Press.

Behar, Ruth. 1996. *The Vulnerable Observer: Anthropology that Breaks Your Heart*. Boston: Beacon.

Biles, Roger. 1995. *Richard J. Daley: Politics, Race, and the Governing of Chicago*. DeKalb: Northern Illinois University Press.

Bonacich, Edna and Richard P. Appelbaum. 2000. *Behind the Label: Inequality in the Los Angeles Apparel Industry*. Berkeley: University of California Press.

Brodt, Bonita. 1980. "Chicago's Chinatown Area Plans to Go More Oriental." *Chicago Tribune*, 6 March.

Chang, Rita. 2004. "Pedicabs Coming to Chicago." *Crain's Chicago Business*. 9 July. Retrieved May 25, 2013. http://www.chicagobusiness.com/apps/pbcs.dll/article?AID= 9999200013111.

Chen, Hsing-shui. 1992. *Chinatown No More: Taiwanese Immigrants in Contemporary New York*. Ithaca, NY: Cornell University Press.

Cheng, Yi'En. 2014. "Telling Stories of the City: Walking Ethnography, Affective Materialities, and Mobile Encounters." *Space and Culture* 17(3):211–223.

Chicago Commission on Human Relations. 1999. *Hate Crime Report*.

Chicago Commission on Race Relations. 1922. *The Negro in Chicago*. Chicago: University of Chicago Press.

"Chicago: The Streets Where Black Kids Ain't Allowed." 1997. *Revolutionary Worker Online*, 6 April. Retrieved May 22, 2015. http://revcom.us/a/firstvol/900-905/901/lenard.htm.

Conley, Jim. 2012. "A Sociology of Traffic: Driving, Cycling, Walking." Pp. 219–236 in *Technologies of Mobility in the Americas*, edited by Phillip Vannini, Lucy Budd, Christian Fisker, Paola Jirón, and Ole B. Jensen. New York: Peter Lang.

De Genova, Nicholas. 2005. *Working the Boundaries: Race, Space, and "Illegality" in Mexican Chicago*. Durham, NC: Duke University Press.

Drake, St. Clair, Horace R. Cayton. 1993 (1945). *Black Metropolis: A Study of Negro Life in a Northern City*. Chicago: University of Chicago Press.

Fedarko, Kevin and Julie Grace. 1997. "Chicago's Last Hope." *Time*, 7 April. Retrieved May 22, 2015. http://www.time.com/time/magazine/article/0,9171,986149-1,00.html.

Fong, Timothy. 1994. *The First Suburban Chinatown: The Remaking of Monterey Park, California*. Philadelphia: Temple University Press.

Goffman, Erving. 1963. *Behavior in Public Places: Notes on the Social Organization of Gatherings*. New York: Free Press.

Goodman, Alan. 2005. "Three Questions about Race, Human Biological Variation and Racism." *Anthropology News* 46(6):18–19.

Gotanda, Neil. 1995. "A Critique of 'Our Constitution Is Color-Blind.'" Pp. 257–275 in *Critical Race Theory: The Key Writings that Formed the Movement*, edited by Kimberle Crenshaw, Neil Gotanda, Gary Peller, and Kendall Thomas. New York: New Press.

Gregory, Steven. 1998. *Black Corona: Race and the Politics of Place in an Urban Community*. Princeton, NJ: Princeton University Press.

Harrison, Faye V. 1995. "The Persistent Power of 'Race' in the Cultural and Political Economy of Racism." *Annual Review of Anthropology* 24(1):47–74.

Helmreich, William B. 2013. *The New York Nobody Knows: Walking 6,000 Miles in the City*. Princeton, NJ: Princeton University Press.

Hirsch, Arnold R. 1983. *Making the Second Ghetto: Race and Housing in Chicago, 1940–1960*. Cambridge: Cambridge University Press.

Horton, John. 1995. *The Politics of Diversity: Immigration, Resistance, and Change in Monterey Park, California*. Philadelphia: Temple University Press.

Ingold, Tim and Jo Lee Vergunst, eds. 2008. *Ways of Walking: Ethnography and Practice on Foot*. Burlington, VT: Ashgate.

Kennedy, Kerrie. 2002. "Chinatown Returns to Center Stage: For Chinese-Americans and Immigrants, the Old Enclave Becomes the Hottest Place in Town." *Chicago Tribune*, 2 January.

Kim, Kiljoong. 2006. "The Korean Presence in Chicago." Pp. 154–167 in *The New Chicago: A Social and Cultural Analysis*, edited by John P. Koval, Larry Bennett, Michael I. J. Bennett, Fassil Demissie, Roberta Garner, and Kiljoong Kim. Philadelphia: Temple University Press.

Kusenbach, Margarethe. 2003. "Street Phenomenology: The Go-Along as Ethnographic Research Tool." *Ethnography* 4(3):455–485.

Kwong, Peter. 1997. *Forbidden Workers: Illegal Chinese Immigrants and American Labor*. New York: New Press.

Lan, Shanshan. 2012. *Diaspora and Class Consciousness: Chinese Immigrant Workers in Multiracial Chicago*. New York: Routledge.

Lau, Yvonne M. 2006. "Chicago's Chinese Americans: From Chinatown and Beyond." Pp. 168–181 in *The New Chicago: A Social and Cultural Analysis*, edited by John P. Koval, Larry Bennett, Michael I. J. Bennett, Fassil Demissie, Roberta Garner, and Kiljoong Kim. Philadelphia: Temple University Press.

Lefebvre, Henri. 2004. *Rhythmanalysis: Space, Time and Everyday Life*. New York: Continuum.

Li, Wei. 1998. "Anatomy of a New Ethnic Settlement: Chinese Ethnoburbs in Los Angeles." *Urban Studies* 35(3):479–501.

Lin, Jan. 1998. *Reconstructing Chinatown: Ethnic Enclave, Global Change*. Minneapolis: University of Minnesota Press.

Manalansan, Martin. 2000. *Cultural Compass: Ethnographic Explorations of Asian America*. Philadelphia: Temple University Press.

Matsuda, Mari. 1993. "We Will Not Be Used." *UCLA Asian American Pacific Islands Law Journal* 1(1):79–84.

Middleton, Jennie. 2009. "'Stepping in Time': Walking, Time, and Space in the City." *Environment and Planning* 41(8):1943–1961.

Olivo, Antonio and Oscar Avila. 2004. "Chinatown's New Reach Expands Its Old Borders." *Chicago Tribune*, 18 July.

Omi, Michael and Howard Winant. 1986. *Racial Formation in the United States from the 1960s to the 1990s.* New York: Routledge.

———. 1993. "On the Theoretical Status of the Concept of Race." Pp. 3–10 in *Race, Identity, and Representation in Education*, edited by Cameron McCarthy and Warren Crichlow. New York: Routledge.

Popkin, Susan J., Victoria E. Gwiasda, Lynn M. Olson, Dennis P. Rosenbaum, and Larry Buron. 2000. *The Hidden War: Crime and the Tragedy of Public Housing in Chicago.* New Brunswick, NJ: Rutgers University Press.

Prashad, Vijay. 2000. *The Karma of Brown Folk.* Minneapolis: University of Minnesota Press.

Prendergast, Catherine. 1998. "Race: The Absent Presence in Composition Studies." *College Composition and Communication* 50(1):36–53.

Rieder, Jonathan. 1985. *Canarsie: The Jews and Italians of Brooklyn against Liberalism.* Cambridge, MA: Harvard University Press.

Venkatesh, Sudhir Alladi. 2000. *American Project: The Rise and Fall of a Modern Ghetto.* Cambridge, MA: Harvard University Press.

Visweswaran, Kamala. 1997. "Diaspora by Design: Flexible Citizenship and South Asians in U.S. Racial Formation." *Diaspora* 6(1):5–29.

Võ, Linda Trinh. 2000. "Performing Ethnography in Asian American Communities: Beyond the Insider-versus-Outsider Perspective." Pp. 17–37 in *Cultural Compass: Ethnographic Explorations of Asian America*, edited by Martin F. Manalansan IV. Philadelphia: Temple University Press.

Võ, Linda Trinh and Rick Bonus, eds. 2002. *Contemporary Asian American Communities: Intersections and Divergences.* Philadelphia: Temple University Press.

Wunderlich, Filipa Matos. 2008. "Walking and Rhythmicity: Sensing Urban Space." *Journal of Urban Design* 13(1):125–139.

Yao, Tai-Ti Tsou. 1977. "Solving Communication Problems in Chicago's Chinatown." Master's thesis, University of Illinois at Chicago.

Zhou, Min. 1992. *Chinatown: The Socioeconomic Potential of an Urban Enclave.* Philadelphia: Temple University Press.

———. 2009. *Contemporary Chinese America: Immigration, Ethnicity, and Community Transformation.* Philadelphia: Temple University Press.

4

Walking through Contemporary North American Barrios

Hispanic Neighborhoods in New York, San Diego, and El Paso

ERNESTO CASTAÑEDA, KEVIN BECK, AND JOSUÉ LACHICA

*B*arrio means neighborhood in Spanish—although the word has different connotations and varying specific uses across Spanish-speaking countries and communities. In the United States the term *barrio* signifies an area with a visible Hispanic population—often presumed as the majority population in that neighborhood. But as this chapter shows, barrios in different American cities have different residential histories and compositions; some are forgotten and neglected, and others are threatened by gentrification.

In this chapter we look at the representations, visual feel, and spatial semiotics (Shortell and Krase 2010) of Hispanic neighborhoods in the Southwest and in New York City. We walk the reader through these neighborhoods through descriptions of place, accompanied by maps and photographs. We contrast what one encounters by walking these neighborhoods with census data and insights from surveys carried out by the authors. The particular places discussed are El Barrio in Manhattan, New York; El Segundo Barrio and Chihuahuita in El Paso, Texas; and Barrio Logan in San Diego, California. While these neighborhoods could be considered Hispanic barrios, there are important differences across these three sites. Rather than having intrinsic properties, barrios are shaped by the larger metropolitan areas of which they form a part. This chapter shows how, even if potentially deceiving, walking the city is a great complement to quantitative understandings of urban demographic dynamics.

All these barrios provide a sense of community, collective history, and relatively affordable housing to their residents. They act as important transition neighborhoods for new immigrants. All of them are places of stigma, areas avoided by many locals. They are stigmatized by outsiders as dangerous and dirty places (Castañeda 2012). Yet data on crime show that they are objectively safe, and their run-down conditions are an effect of poverty, divestment, and government retrenchment. The conditions of the streets should not be seen as caused by the neighborhood inhabitants, who, to the contrary, improve the physical conditions of the area through private home repairs, opening businesses, and cultural centers (Fuentes 2007; Serra del Pozo 2006; Thompson 2007).

El Barrio or Spanish Harlem in New York City has undergone a number of demographic transitions or ethnic successions (Bourgois 2003). At the end of the twentieth century, El Barrio had established itself as a Puerto Rican neighborhood (Dávila 2004). Yet in the last decades a new wave of mainly Mexicans and Central Americans combined with gentrification have changed the demographics of the area. Walking through East 116th Street, one has the feeling that one is in a little Mexico, yet survey and census data show that Mexicans in New York are spread throughout the city (Bergad 2013; Lobo and Salvo 2013). Original ethno-surveys of El Barrio conducted in 2009 and 2010 show that most people working in Spanish Harlem commute in, while many of El Barrio's inhabitants work elsewhere (Castañeda 2010). This goes against the idea of the "Venice ghetto," the self-contained urban village, or an ethnic enclave (Castañeda 2012; Gans 1962; Hutchison and Haynes 2012; Wilson and Portes 1980). This is also the case in El Paso; the Segundo Barrio is predominantly inhabited by people of Mexican origin but so are most neighborhoods in El Paso. Barrio Logan is a cultural symbol of the Mexican community, but many Mexicans also live in other neighborhoods of southeast San Diego and across San Diego.

This chapter discusses methodological and epistemological implications of walking, seeing, living, and studying a particular neighborhood. It uses a comparative perspective on Hispanic ethnicity, ethnic succession, gentrification, visual semiotics (through photographs and ethnographic descriptions), and lived experiences (walking, touring, photographing, surveying, and living) through particular present-day American neighborhoods that are often misunderstood by the larger public.

East Harlem or El Barrio, Manhattan, New York City, New York

One of the side effects of the extensive subway network in New York is that it allows residents to transport themselves from their places of residence to their places of work, or recreation, while blocking from sight most of the in-between areas. Therefore, people spend most of their time in the neighborhoods where they live and work. Subway riders are able to ignore whole areas of the city, and thus may have never visited El Barrio, the neighborhood just north of the Upper East Side of Manhattan, also known as East Harlem or Spanish Harlem.

In contrast to riding the subway, when one drives, and particularly when one walks, it is impressive to see the transition from the many luxury shops along Fifth Avenue or Madison Avenue when one arrives in El Barrio and observes a steep decline in luxury retail and a large numbers of public housing buildings. One can also see many brown and dark-skinned faces in Spanish Harlem, reproducing the false idea of a homogenous community since a mix of ethnicities lives in East Harlem (New York City Department of City Planning 2012).

In contrast with Texas and California, where Spanish-speaking people have historically been present, in New York the term *Hispanic* used to denote Puerto Ricans. Later it meant Dominicans, and now Mexicans and Central and South Americans, as these groups of immigrants have arrived in important numbers in the last two decades (Aranda 2008; Bourgois 2003; Dávila 2004; Fuentes 2007; Grasmuck and Pessar 1991; Jones-Correa 1998; Kasinitz, Mollenkopf, and Waters 2004; Kasinitz et al. 2008; Loveman and Muniz 2007; Marwell 2007).

This area has served as a landing pad for multiple waves of immigrant groups: from Dutch Calvinist farmers in the 1600s to German and Irish Catholic construction workers laying down subway and train tracks in the late 1880s to Central and Eastern European Jews at the beginning of the 1900s to African Americans, Finnish and Norwegian immigrants, and Greek Orthodox immigrants in the 1920s to Southern Italians in the 1930s, who were able to recreate many of their social and religious practices on these streets (Orsi 2002), to Puerto Ricans in the 1940s (Bourgois 2003) to Mexicans from Puebla around the 1990s, followed by Mexicans from La Mixteca area, including indigenous peoples. In the 2000s Central American and Muslim West African immigrants arrived in East Harlem.

While this neighborhood has offered a home and a sense of community for many groups, it has often been a place of concentrated poverty. Many immigrants and their children wished to leave East Harlem, because leaving was a clear sign of upward social mobility. Most people eventually manage to move out, if only to remember the days of community life in the neighborhood with nostalgia (Dávila 2004).

When one starts walking through El Barrio, it initially appears as the center of the Mexican community in Manhattan, if not in New York. In the early 2000s the number of Mexican inhabitants and businesses grew at high rates. Some landlords reported preferring Mexican renters because they say that Mexicans pay the rent on time and because many of them are undocumented, they do not cause any trouble nor demand too much. Mexicans show a do-it-yourself attitude when it comes to apartment repairs and dealing with emergencies (Fuentes 2007; Thompson 2007). Some academics call this demographic change in the neighborhood "ethnic succession"; black and Puerto Rican neighbors call it an invasion; and others see it as gentrification paving the way for students, artists, and other middle-class Americans to move in.

Despite the reality that many Mexican working men may live "ten to a room" in crowded shared quarters, as soon as they start forming new families they rent their own apartments. And in contrast to some of the Puerto Ricans of El Barrio, most Mexican workers do not live in public housing because (1) they may be undocumented and thus not eligible, (2) if eligible they have a hard time figuring out how to put their names on the waiting lists, (3) other local ethnic groups with longer tenure in New York and better political organization may engage in opportunity hoarding (Tilly 1998) of public housing and other public benefits (Marwell 2007), and (4) compared with other groups, Mexicans rely less on welfare (Van Hook and Bean 2009). The latter may be partly because of their tradition of sending remittances due to the meager size of the welfare state in Mexico.

A Little Mexico?

The blog "Walks of New York" dubs El Barrio as Manhattan's "Little Mexico" (Dobbins 2012). Naomi Fertitta also calls El Barrio "Little Mexico" (Fertitta and Aresu 2009). This labeling makes sense for branding and touristic reasons, yet it hides the heterogeneity of El Barrio and the fact that Mexicans and other Hispanics live in many neighborhoods of New York.

El Barrio is not a self-contained space; Mexican families spend leisure time in public parks and wherever it is fashionable at the time for New Yorkers of all ethnicities to be. And despite the real decrease of Puerto Rican residents, El Barrio is still the cultural heart of the Puerto Rican community in the New York metropolitan area. For example, the Camaradas Bar and Restaurant is still a place of reference for Puerto Rican cultural and political life in the area. There are still Puerto Rican *cuchifrito* restaurants in El Barrio. Thus any resident of El Barrio experiences Puerto Rican culture just by spending time on the streets and in the public spaces there.

New York Data

For three consecutive semesters (from spring 2009 to spring 2010), a group of around thirty students from Castañeda's course "Qualitative Studies of Communities" at Baruch College, of the City University of New York, conducted a collective study of El Barrio and other immigrant neighborhoods in New York. They carried out nonparticipant observation, ethno-surveys, in-depth interviews and shot video as part of the course.

Students were given the option to opt-out and before starting the project, many students initially refused to participate in the study, saying that although they had never been to El Barrio, they had heard it was a dirty and dangerous place. Many said that as they were growing up their parents had explicitly prohibited them from going there. Yet most of the area, especially along East 116th, is very busy and heavily patrolled by police; most importantly people know each other, and there are many eyes on street (Jacobs 1961). The students in the classes who had lived in the neighborhood stressed its overall safety. I mention these negative views of El Barrio because even though many students were immigrants or children of immigrants, and many were Hispanic, they had internalized the stigmas associated with El Barrio. This is an example of symbolic violence as described by Bourdieu (1991). It shows the generalized stigma attached to El Barrio, given that even the students living in objectively similar communities in Queens and Brooklyn had an initial reluctance to go there. But after we did a few field visits together, and as the students started interviewing people in El Barrio in pairs or small groups, their views changed. While they kept noting the dirty streets and the high levels of poverty, they lost their fear and came to appreciate the neighborhood and looked for structural explanations rather than cultural ones. For example, it appears that the city allocates less resources and sanitation employees to clean this area as compared with other neighborhoods south of it. As they experienced the neighborhood more and more, their negative expectations and stereotypes decreased.

Not a Ghetto or Bounded Community

While El Barrio is a strategic site to study Mexican immigration in New York, one must note that the Mexican population is not concentrated in any one area of the New York metropolitan area. So while, 116th Street and Lexington would appear to be the heart of a New York Mexican enclave or even a "Little Mexico," the reality is that most Mexicans living in New York do not live in El Barrio.

The overall increase of the Latino population in New York City in the last decade of the twentieth century was impressive. This increase has continued in the first decade of the twenty-first century. The overall increase in Latino population has occurred throughout New York City except for areas of Manhattan and Brooklyn undergoing gentrification. Manhattan keeps losing its Latino population as areas in the Bronx and Queens gain it (Lobo and Salvo 2013).

Because of new immigration, return migration, and migration within the United States, as well as overcrowded housing and undocumented status, it is an impossible challenge to enumerate all Mexican-origin residents in the New York metropolitan area at any given time. According to the latest decennial census, there were 319,263 Mexican-origin individuals living in New York City (U.S. Census 2010a). According to the five-year average of the American Community Survey, there are 308,952 (plus or minus 8,753) Mexicans in New York City (U.S. Census 2013). Data from the 2011 American Community Survey for New York City and Northeastern New Jersey count 525,000 Mexicans (Brown and Lopez 2013). Using IPUMS data for 2010 for all New York City boroughs, plus Long Island and northeastern New Jersey, the count goes to 607,503 (Bergad 2013). Yet scholars with ground-level information data estimate higher numbers; some estimated the number of Mexicans in New York to be more than 750,000 in 2008 (Hellman 2008). According to the Mexican Consulate, there are around 1.2 million Mexicans in New York City (Semple 2010). There is evidence showing that some migrants went back to Mexico after the financial crisis of 2008. So for us a good estimate, including the undocumented, would be around one million Mexicans in the New York metropolitan area. Regardless of the exact current numbers, nativity rates in New York City are highest for Mexican mothers, so much that if the current pace continues, Mexicans will be the biggest Hispanic group in New York City by 2025, surpassing Puerto Ricans, Dominicans, and South Americans (Bergad 2013). But despite their significant number, Mexicans often remain relatively hidden, relegated to the back rooms of stores and restaurants, and heavily undercounted in official censuses (Thompson 2007).

Latinos make up around a third (28.6 percent) of New York City's population (U.S. Census 2010b). Yet the image that New York projects outside its city limits is not that of a city where between a third to a half of its residents speak Spanish. A symbolic boundary underplays much of the culture produced by New York Latinos; the exception that confirms the rule could be salsa music, which was born in El Barrio (Dávila 2004).

So, is El Barrio sociologically a ghetto (Hutchison and Haynes 2012; Small 2008)? The answer is no. The people who come in and out of its boundaries and its residents are rather diverse with no one group able to claim an absolute majority. White residents of El Barrio made up around 12 percent in 2010, Puerto Ricans 27 percent, Mexicans 10 percent, Asians 6 percent, and black residents 32 percent; only 26 percent of all residents were foreign born (New York City Department of City Planning 2012). It is true that cheap rents make it a landing pad for many immigrants who spend the night there and work elsewhere. The storefronts on East 116th Street house an ethnic business enclave. The products and services offered in these businesses cater to the needs and nostalgia of the newcomers; weekend street festivals provide opportunities for positive ethnic pride and help develop a sense of belonging. But the look of El Barrio does not represent a community that is closed into itself or opposed to cultural assimilation or structural integration, as a superficial snapshot of the neighborhood could show. Rather, looking at the population change that takes place every few decades, it is clear that this is a place of passage and not one of permanent settlement for any ethnic community. The same is true for Central and West Harlem, which in the last years have seen an influx of West African immigrants, as well as middle-class African Americans, Latinos, and white people.

Manhattan's El Barrio is not a ghetto or a closed ethnic enclave, since, as we found from the hundreds of ethno-surveys conducted there, most of the business owners and employees do not live there but commute from all over the city. In the same way, most of the residents of El Barrio work in other neighborhoods and boroughs. Most Mexican children and teenagers stay close to home as their parents see the streets of New York as dangerous and thus limit the idle time that their children, especially young women, can spend in the streets.

The businesses selling Mexican products are what stands out the most when walking through Spanish Harlem and other affordable neighborhoods where some Mexicans live. While not necessarily living in enclaves, Mexicans in New York are able to keep watching many Mexican TV shows, listening to Mexican music, and eating Mexican food, thus they maintain many elements of their Mixteco, or local Mexican, culture at the same time that they are becoming New Yorkers.

Quotidian Experiences in Border Barrios

Barrio Logan

As of 2013, downtown San Diego's cityscape reflects more than twenty years of intense capital reinvestment. At the center of downtown is the Gaslamp Quarter with its long avenues boasting trendy restaurants and bars. The neighboring district, known as the East Village, now hosts the San Diego Padres baseball stadium and is surrounded by high-rise condos designed to attract middle- and upper-class residents. Next to the ballpark, a towering, egg-shaped public library is nearing completion and the ever-expanding conference center draws crowds from around the country. Much like in other large American cities, the past two decades were periods of intense gentrification and revitalization, including in the Gaslamp Quarter and parts of the East Village. The poverty and homelessness that once represented quotidian life in the city center has been pushed farther inland in order to enhance commerce on properties along the San Diego Bay. The relocation of poverty is visible to the east of the Gaslamp Quarter, where the social scene is strikingly poor and seemingly chaotic. The homeless congregate near Father Joe's, one of the city's largest providers of food and shelter for the homeless, and in the streets and vacant lots where homelessness is currently tolerated but always under the watchful eye of a mobile police surveillance station.

San Diego's changing urban forms are perhaps best observed on bicycle. As in other West Coast cities, San Diegans from all economic and social strata cycle for everyday commutes, for exercise, and for pleasure. However, not everyone takes the five-minute ride south of the Gaslamp Quarter to the ostensible border between downtown San Diego and peripheral neighborhoods. After pedaling past Father Joe's and the city's small skid row, one reaches Commercial Street, a road cut up by active trolley lines running down its center. The absence of homes and businesses has made the edges of this street a de facto graveyard for abandoned cars and a refuge for the homeless. Drugs are consumed openly, trash abounds, and rows of shopping carts lining the sidewalks contain the sum of local denizens' possessions. Commercial Street reveals the impoverished edge of downtown San Diego, an area not yet touched by the city's redevelopment agency. Crossing Commercial Street and riding south on Newton or National Avenues one enters Barrio Logan, a low-income Latino neighborhood in the process of renewal and gentrification. Upon entering the neighborhood, a bike rider takes a closer inspection of what motorists can easily bypass. To the southwest, there is the winter homeless shelter—a large tent that is seasonally pitched a few blocks from Barrio Logan's Perkin's Elementary School. As one heads deeper into the barrio, and up a short incline, the factories and warehouses come into view. Between faded signs and deteriorated storefronts sit tiny homes similarly in need of repair. Yet scattered throughout the neighborhood are new coffee shops and condos that stand out to draw the cyclist's attention. Reinvestment has arrived to the barrio.

Reinvestment is reaching Barrio Logan's empty lots through a twofold process: endogenous redevelopment efforts spearheaded by local residents, as well as rekindled interest from outside entrepreneurs and housing developers. While coffee wholesalers, a Northgate González supermarket, and professional firms surface in once-vacant properties, the neighborhood's many deteriorated houses continue the decades-long wait for renovation. Local residents attempt to reconcile the commercial reinvestment they are witnessing with the years of economic marginalization they have grown accustomed to. Indeed, the degree to which reinvestment causes gentrification is not only a matter of perspective but also a question that will only be clear when and if displacement pressures fully manifest.

After a ten-minute cycle from downtown, the rider reaches Barrio Logan's epicenter—Chicano Park, nearly eight acres of grass, murals, and historic icons located underneath the Coronado Bay Bridge. Since the 1970s, Barrio Logan has been a focal point of the Chicano Movement and an exemplar of successful grassroots movements aimed at securing local public space. In the late 1960s, the California Department of Transportation began the construction of the Coronado Bay Bridge and Interstate 5, both of which cut through the heart of Barrio Logan and displaced residents, demolished houses, and disrupted local commerce. In response, residents staged a three-day occupation of the area underneath the on-ramps to the Coronado Bridge, contesting the state's plans to construct a highway patrol station. The protests resulted in the state conceding the land below the bridge to local residents, who dubbed this space Chicano People's Park. The pylons supporting the Coronado Bridge were then symbolically appropriated; to this day, large murals depicting Chicano pride and the Mexican Revolution are ubiquitous on the bridge's support beams, making the park an icon of the Chicano Movement and bestowing on it wide recognition. Local residents, San Diegans, and many from Tijuana, Mexico, California, and the American Southwest, flock to Chicano Park to partake in yearly festivals commemorating the park's founding. For those living in San Diego, Chicano Park serves a more regular function of hosting rallies, speeches, celebrations, and even biweekly *Danzas Aztecas* on what is called the *kiosko*—the park's center stage.

The observant cyclist can almost read Barrio Logan's cityscape like a text—a history of social struggle and economic marginalization is observable everywhere. However, Barrio Logan is now starting to mirror the signs of redevelopment apparent in the East Village. Its small population of approximately thirty-five hundred residents is growing and, according to the 2010 Census, is becoming racially more diverse. A quick *tour-del-barrio* is sufficient to see the stark contrasts between the past and present. One-story Craftsman homes dating back to the early 1900s now sit next to immense affordable housing complexes erected in the 2000s. Famous Mexican eateries like Las Cuatro Milpas (the four cornfields), whose owners have been serving tortillas, tacos, beans, chorizo, and rice since 1933, now have as many local as nonlocal customers.

Chicano Park has returned to tourist maps as decades of gang conflict, drug use, and violence have tapered off. And of crucial importance to local residents, Barrio Logan may soon be rezoned to end more than fifty years of "mixed-use" zoning. Since the 1950s, heavy industries have been permitted to set up shop adjacent to residents' homes, causing severe pollution and leading to high asthma rates among children. New zoning proposals seek to establish buffer zones that separate residencies from industry in order to create a healthier living environment. In this barrio there is a swirling of poverty and wealth, diverse cohorts of newcomers and old-timers, historic icons, new grocery stores, an emerging art scene, and affordable housing complexes. In short, changes are taking place that challenge traditional understandings of barrios along the border.

Daily social practice among the local Latino population has also changed. Perhaps most significantly for a border barrio, the residents of Barrio Logan are now less likely to be recent immigrants. Although Barrio Logan was once a destination for Mexicans, in a non-probability sample survey we conducted of 112 Barrio Logan residents, only 35 percent were first-generation immigrants. The neighborhood's geographic proximity to the Gaslamp Quarter and the East Village no longer allows it to be the destination for immigrants that it once was because housing in Barrio Logan is now comparatively expensive. While most survey respondents maintain some connection with Mexico, and Tijuana in particular, many describe this connection as fading. On the Mexican side of the border reside family, friends, and preferred grocery shopping, but they are not as easily accessible as they once were. Barrio Logan residents cite the long lines at border crossings, the mandatory presentation of passports to reenter the United States (where driver licenses were once sufficient), and concerns for security in Tijuana as reasons for limiting the number of trips they make to Mexico each year. Most residents claim to have crossed the border more frequently in years past but for the reasons mentioned are less inclined to do so today.

Latino residents also notice that public life in Barrio Logan no longer looks as it once did. Residents' daily strolls through Chicano Park, or lunch breaks on the park's picnic benches, are now accompanied by what many claim is an indicator of the changing times: white people walking their dogs without concern for their safety and camera-toting tourists from around the globe snapping shots of the murals. Barrio residents make fewer trips to corner stores and small markets for groceries. In 2012, a Northgate González supermarket became a magnet for pedestrians and, according to many, marks the beginning of a new era in the neighborhood. These daily scenes suggest that even once highly isolated barrios along the border are susceptible to the broader economic changes occurring in the cities where they reside. Local Latinos with deep roots in Barrio Logan, and who value the neighborhood's symbolism of the Chicano Movement, debate who will benefit from the social and economic changes taking place. While many herald the prospect of increased neighborhood diversity, there is simultaneously apprehension over who will assert ownership over the neighborhood in years to come.

The effects of reinvestment and gentrification especially resonate among the barrio's longtime homeless population. To meet those who live in Barrio Logan's public spaces one must dismount the bicycle and spend time on the street corners and in the parks. The denizens of Chicano Park, for example, are tightly networked into the neighborhood's social life and maintain strong sentimental connections to Barrio Logan. Ironically, many of these men and women spent their childhoods in houses located only blocks away from their current residency in the park's nooks and shaded corners. After falling into financial trouble, usually due to unemployment, some of the homeless find living in Chicano Park a satisfying alternative. Several have assumed roles as its caretakers and are known and respected as such throughout the local community. One denizen, with more than ten years of sleeping in Chicano Park, has taken it upon himself to regularly water the small rose garden and pick up trash around the picnic tables. Others police the park to ensure it is delivered back to local families after years of gang activity prevented children from safely using the small jungle gym and swing set. Indeed, some are former gang members who are excited that families feel safe in the park once more. One park resident named Raul says that the arrival of new homeless people from the East Village threatens Barrio Logan's rising reputation. Raul explained that the homeless from downtown come to Chicano Park but are clearly identifiable by their unfamiliarity with this social space; they violate the informal codes of conduct that the park's dwellers strive to uphold. The following example is illustrative.

On one summer afternoon in 2012, a homeless man from downtown sat near the children's playground and solicited passersby to gamble by rolling dice. Raul and others viewed this as transgressing at least two locally established norms. The first is that families are granted priority access to the park, especially areas designed for children. During the day, the homeless defer to families by moving to the park's fringes and into spaces that are out of sight. Second, Raul and others view gambling as a public sign of disorder likely to keep families away and attract unwanted attention. Raul decided that the best way to handle the gambler was to call the police, who promptly ameliorated the situation. Although the homeless are not fond of the police, they are not afraid to instrumentally use the police to maintain the informal code of conduct they helped establish. Although the homeless use the police to prevent gambling, other illicit activities such as drinking in public are considered a local right. The homeless of Chicano Park maintain a unique understanding of neighborhood space in terms of who belongs and which activities should be permitted therein; they have a distinct vision for the neighborhood's future.

Similar to East Harlem, and El Segundo Barrio, Barrio Logan is only one of many well-established Latino neighborhoods to be stirred by the tide of structural changes like gentrification and renewal, whose effects shape street life for the homeless, longtime residents, and newcomers. How Latino residents in neighborhoods like Barrio Logan will be able to maintain their well-defined social space in the years to come is an ongoing question. Activists work to keep Chicano Park under local supervision and management. Community leaders run help centers and after-school programs to keep local support networks strong, especially for children. And still others have been active for years in the planning and construction of affordable housing complexes to provide much-needed options for low-income families. As decades of work by these leaders are finally coming to fruition, structural changes in the greater city of San Diego cast doubt over whether Barrio Logan will remain a Latino community in the future. Indeed, the changing form of barrios along the Mexico-U.S. border begs the question as to whether barrios will serve the same functions and hold the same meanings as they once did for longtime residents. Whether Barrio Logan is destined for historic district status like the "Little Italy" of San Diego or San Francisco and will thrive as a neighborhood with distinctly Mexican and Chicano identities or will become a touristic "Little Mexico" like some Chinatowns (see Chapter 3 in this volume) remains uncertain.

El Segundo Barrio and Chihuahuita Neighborhoods in El Paso, Texas

On any given morning the streets are alive on both sides of the border—people are conversing on street corners; neighborhood stores and restaurants are beginning to swing their doors open; and the hustle and bustle of a local economy, family shopping, and urban street life pour between the city centers along the streets that end on the Paso del Norte and Stanton International Bridges. Every day thousands of people cross international bridges by foot, car, bus, or bicycle to move between Ciudad Juárez, Mexico, and its twin city, El Paso, Texas. Crossers slowly move at whatever pace the U.S. custom agents decide is appropriate—in most cases cars move at a crawl.

From the U.S. side of the border one usually heads south on Stanton Street, heading toward Ciudad Juárez through the avenue that cuts through two of the oldest neighborhoods in El Paso, Texas—El Segundo Barrio and neighboring Chihuahuita. The relatively dense urban area of south El Paso straddles the U.S.-Mexican border and has been witness to centuries of geopolitical changes. From land disputes that resulted from war and the changing course of the Rio Grande to a temporary base of operations for Pancho Villa during his exile from Mexico and onto the birthplace of the zoot-suited Pachuco, El Paso's south side continues to play a crucial role for Mexicans and Mexican Americans alike. There is a rich history in these two neighborhoods that has often been left out of the official history in both the United States and Mexico.

The borders of these barrios are drawn by the railroads lining the entire western side, the border wall to the south and a four-lane Paisano boulevard to the north. But like most barrios, Segundo Barrio's exact boundaries are dependent on who is making the observation. Here we use the term Segundo Barrio to include the historical Segundo Barrio, the neighboring Chihuahuita neighborhood, and the peripheral Segundo Barrio in Central El Paso.

A walk across the international bridge from Mexico and into El Paso leads you through the supermajority Mexican neighborhood. These area was historically a residential starting point for newly arrived Mexican immigrants, and thus for a while they were the segregated neighborhoods set aside for Mexicans by the El Paso government. This area has transformed into multigenerational Mexican neighborhoods, yet the socioeconomic profile of the area residents has changed little. Residents have low levels of education, live in poverty, and are chronically unemployed, underpaid, and partly rely on the informal economy. Many of the local men work as agricultural workers and day laborers.

As of 2000, Segundo Barrio's population was around eight thousand with 96.2 percent of the population being Hispanic. According to the 2000 U.S. Census, Segundo Barrio's median household income was $10,240, with 62.1 percent of the population below the poverty level. Close to 79 percent (79.3) of Segundo Barrio residents reported having no high school diploma (City of El Paso 2010).

To best understand the complexities of Chihuahuita and Segundo Barrio, one must first address the interconnectedness and porous companionship between the city centers of both El Paso and Ciudad Juárez. Thousands of people cross back and forth between the two cities on a daily basis. "In 2010, over 60,000 passenger cars and nearly 22,000 pedestrians used these crossings each day. Overall, border-dependent businesses and travelers contributed over $1 billion to the regional economy and supported nearly 700,000 jobs on both sides of the border" (Texas Department of Transportation 2011). Taking an aerial view of the entire Paso del Norte region (El Paso/Ciudad Juárez metropolis), one quickly notes that the cities are in fact one and the same, albeit the mostly dry Rio Grande and the international border do split the two cities. One only needs to take a slow-paced walk from Ciudad Juárez over the Stanton Bridge north into El Paso to experience the little to no change of people, spoken language, shop signs in Spanish, and architecture. If not for the militarized border (Dunn 1996), a person would find it difficult to distinguish what side of the border they are on. To be sure there are signs of differences, although subtle, between the infrastructure of roads, street signs, amount of *puestesitos*—street kiosk vendors—and far fewer bars on the El Paso area close to the border.

Although the presence of *la migra*—border patrol and customs—reaches far and wide throughout most regions of El Paso, Chihuahuita and Segundo Barrio are two of the few neighborhoods in El Paso that are truly on the front line of the militarized border. This militarization has made life harder for people who conduct their daily lives in both sides of the border (Campbell and Lachica 2013; Heyman, Núñez, and Talavera 2009; Lachica, Castañeda, and McDonald 2013). While the majority of the El Paso border is lined with highways, which essentially act like a "no-man's-land," widening and separating nearby neighborhoods from the physical border, these barrios have no barriers besides Paisano Street and the customs check points. On the U.S. side, the high levels of transnational border crossing and the ubiquity of the bridge create a normalization of the ever-present border patrol. At the same time residents that cross back and forth experience and internalize the presence of a Panopticon-like militarized border.

One only has to begin to get near the Stanton Street International Bridge to experience the multitude of cameras lighting up a significant radius beyond the actual bridge and into the streets of Segundo Barrio and Chihuahuita. Whether you drive, walk, or ride a bike across the bridge, you will hear the clicking of still cameras and then feel the keen eyes of video cameras documenting your every move until you reach the Ciudad Juárez side of the bridge only to come face-to-face with Mexican soldiers caring MP5 submachine guns and M4 assault rifles.

On the way back from Ciudad Juárez into El Paso the intensity and invasiveness begins once again. A person can consider themselves lucky to not get asked to pull over for a full auto check by the U.S. customs agents. A person's rights, U.S. citizen or not, mean little in this zone. You may pass by with a simple question of "What's your citizenship?" and a quick wave to move on. Or if one of the eighty-pound German shepherds being led around each car decides to bark at your car, then you may just find yourself staring at your car as it is completely stripped of everything from your seats to your trunk.

Although living in such close proximity to this militarized zone can bring a type of numbness compared with what a tourist may experience, the clear power dynamics of "them" (customs and border patrol) versus "us" (everyone else, including Mexican nationals and U.S. citizens) is ever present.

Transnationalism

If transnationalism is ever present in immigrant neighborhoods, is it even more so in border neighborhoods? El Paso's south side neighborhoods line up right next to Mexico's Ciudad Juárez. People in Segundo Barrio and Chihuahuita do not simply practice transnationalism by speaking both languages, visiting Mexico, remitting, or by eating Mexican food and practicing Mexican cultural norms; many also live a daily form of transnationalism. Many people may live on one side of the border and attend school or work on the other side. Some may even have homes and employment on both sides of the border. Some homeless individuals may panhandle in the United States and sleep in Juárez (Campbell and Lachica 2013; Comar 2011). Such a mixture of daily transnational practices creates a continuous presence of Mexican culture and Mexican residents throughout El Segundo Barrio.

A number of important religious and secular institutions can be spotted as you walk through Segundo Barrio. Just a quick four blocks north of the Stanton Bridge stands the first Roman Catholic Church in the city of El Paso—Sagrado Corazón. As the church's website states, "We are a border community with roots both in Mexico and in El Paso's 'Segundo Barrio.' Our community is mostly made up of immigrants who have a host of needs and challenges which are directly related to their being uprooted" (Sacred Heart Church 2014). Like much of the community, the church and many of its parishioners are border transnationals (Castañeda, Morales, and Ochoa 2014) linked to both Mexico and the El Paso

Segundo Barrio. The Sagrado Corazón church is actually situated in the middle of both neighborhoods. In many ways the lines that border Segundo Barrio and Chihuahuita are blurred as they are neighboring communities that share many characteristics, business ties, people, and institutions.

The Lydia Patterson Institute is another example of a transnational institution in El Segundo Barrio. Lydia Patterson is a junior high and high school that was originally designed, a hundred years ago, as a school for neighborhood monolingual Spanish-speaking boys who, until it opened, did not have any options of formal schooling in El Paso. The institute thus began to fill the void helping Mexican children receive an education with a program far ahead of its time that specialized in English as a second language (ESL) students, prior to the rest of the nation adopting Spanish-language ESL pedagogical programs. The school continues to exist as a private Methodist high school, specializing in ESL, and continues to serve both students from the surrounding Segundo Barrio and those who cross from Ciudad Juárez (Grinberg 2009).

Segregation and Gentrification

As with many stories of gentrification of urban Mexican neighborhoods, El Paso is currently in the midst of a battle between varying factions of city government. Some are backed by heavy investors looking to develop downtown El Paso, while others are backed by local residents and neighborhood business owners that fear that gentrification will lead to displacement.

The high density of Mexican immigrants and Mexican Americans in these neighborhoods is in part attributed to the proximity of the ports of entry into Mexico, making for a logical residential location if one wants to be able to cross back and forth between countries. Yet structural influences have historically been at play since the initial years of neighborhood development. At the turn of the century, the town of El Paso began to industrialize and grow and the white political powers enforced segregation of the poor, who were mainly Mexican and Mexican American blue-collar workers whose meager wages forced them to remain in south El Paso tenements. Largely ignored by El Paso's white government elites, barrios were left in ill repair and poverty. Although the racialization of neighborhoods has largely changed in recent decades as El Paso's population has moved to a majority Mexican American population, class segregation has continued to proliferate within these south El Paso neighborhoods.

Much like San Diego's Barrio Logan, El Segundo Barrio has been central to the historical and present-day Chicano Movements. Chicanos have been actively involved in the social development and pride of neighborhood residents. From the early days of the Zoot Suit Pachuco movement to more recent ventures among local organizations, the Chicano Movement has been subtle but always alive in these neighborhoods. The community along with the University of Texas at El Paso's Borderlands History Program are attempting to revive the neighborhood's history with various ongoing publications and projects including the Museo Urbano, where the oral and physical histories of this Mexican

American neighborhood are being collected and prepared for public viewing (Hall 2011; Romo 2005).

Homelessness, Housing, and Agricultural Workers

The cinder-block, brick, and stucco architecture remains similar throughout both Chihuahuita and Segundo Barrio. Many of the buildings within the vicinity of Chihuahuita are two-story tenement-style brick buildings that are visibly dilapidated and in need of repair. Although the tenement housing is not up to par with most of the rest of El Paso's housing, this neighborhood is very affordable and arguably plays an important role in housing many people that would otherwise have few to no housing resources available to them.

Many of El Paso's homeless shelters are located within the peripheral Segundo Barrio, which may account for much of the visibly homeless population that can be found throughout the neighborhood. There is one shelter within the boundaries of the historical Segundo Barrio, El Centro de los Trabajadores Agrícolas Fronterizos (the Border Farmworker Center), that was designed specifically to server as agricultural workers' temporary housing.

Agricultural workers are often seen outside the El Centro de los Trabajadores Agrícolas Fronterizos and a few blocks north on a major avenue that cuts through downtown El Paso and Segundo Barrio—Paisano Avenue. Day laborers and agricultural workers unable to find steady work are often on the corners of a neighborhood KFC waiting to be picked up for day labor. Although a local resident may be able to pick up the slight nuances between average barrio residents, agricultural workers, day laborers, and the homeless, the reality one would see by walking these streets is that all of these populations live side by side. Although Juárez, Mexico, has historically been a tourist destination for many Americans, the past years of violence have brought on a tourist drought, and many Anglos, tourists, and middle-class Mexican Americans tend to avoid the neighborhood.

Conclusion

While the term *barrio* is used to describe the three neighborhoods discussed in this chapter, there are important historical, geographic, and symbolic differences between them. Each one has a different feel when one walks its streets. One can buy tacos and hear music in Spanish in all of them, but they are otherwise very different. Being so physically close to Mexico, and indeed having a large majority of Hispanic residents, El Segundo Barrio and Chihuahuita are indeed extensions of Mexico under the political jurisdiction of the United States. Barrio Logan is farther away from the border, and the connection with Mexico is there but it is less immediate. As Chicano Park represents, Barrio Logan has more of a Mexican American feeling than a Mexican neighborhood. New York's El Barrio has many storefronts along 116th Street that signal the place as a Mexican neighborhood, but it is not the center of the Mexican diaspora in the New

York metropolitan area, the border is far away, and transnationalism is more sporadic and long-distance (Castañeda, Morales, and Ochoa 2014).

The message broadcast by public spaces in American barrios is deceiving if viewed only superficially: despite appearances after a quick stroll, New York City's El Barrio population is ethnically and culturally heterogeneous, and the neighborhood is not a Mexican ghetto. San Diego's Barrio Logan simultaneously shows evidence of marginalization and gentrification with unique effects rendered onto the local culture. In El Segundo Barrio, one is not simply in El Paso or Ciudad Juárez but in both, and, as a result, certain features of social life pivot around the border's militarization.

Structural changes taking place across the United States and the globe are affecting all these barrios, which were marginalized for much of the twentieth century. Economic and urban growth is affecting where and how all urbanites live, and we describe some of these effects on the lived and cultural experiences in barrios. But because barrio residents are more heterogeneous than conventional wisdom would suggest, barrios cannot be described through a singular quotidian experience, and their gentrification or ethnic succession is not an issue of purely local nature. Thus there is a need to compare change across barrios and through time.

REFERENCES

Aranda, Elizabeth M. 2008. "Class Backgrounds, Modes of Incorporation, and Puerto Ricans' Pathways into the Transnational Professional Workforce." *American Behavioral Scientist* 52:426–456.

Bergad, Laird W. 2013. *Demographic, Economic and Social Transformations in the Mexican-Origin Population of the New York City Metropolitan Area, 1990–2010*. New York: Center for Latin American, Caribbean and Latino Studies, Graduate Center, City University of New York.

Bourdieu, Pierre. 1991. *Language and Symbolic Power*. Cambridge, MA: Harvard University Press.

Bourgois, Philippe. 2003. *In Search of Respect: Selling Crack in El Barrio*. Cambridge: Cambridge University Press.

Brown, Anna and Mark Hugo Lopez. 2013. *Mapping the Latino Population, By State, County and City*. Washington, DC: Pew Research Center's Hispanic Trends Project.

Campbell, Howard and Josué G. Lachica. 2013. "Transnational Homelessness: Finding a Place on the U.S.-Mexico Border." *Journal of Borderlands Studies* 28:279–290.

Castañeda, Ernesto. 2010. "Exclusion, Inclusion, and Everyday Citizenship in New York, Paris, and Barcelona." Ph.D. dissertation, Department of Sociology, Columbia University, New York.

———. 2012. "Places of Stigma: Ghettos, Barrios and Banlieues." Pp. 159–190 in *The Ghetto: Contemporary Global Issues and Controversies*, edited by Ray Hutchison and Bruce D. Haynes. Boulder, CO: Westview.

Castañeda, Ernesto, Cristina Morales, and Olga Ochoa. 2014. "The Relationship between Immigrant Integration and Transnationalism: Comparative Research in New York, El Paso, and Paris." *Comparative Migration Studies* 2(3):305–334.

City of El Paso. 2010. "El Segundo Barrio: Neighborhood Revitalization Strategy." City of El Paso, El Paso. Retrieved June 1, 2015. http://www.elpasotexas.gov/~/media/files/coep/community%20and%20human%20development/elsegundobarrio_neighrevit alizationstrategy.ashx?la=en.

Comar, Scott. 2011. *Border Junkies: Addiction and Survival on the Streets of Juárez and El Paso.* Austin: University of Texas Press.

Dávila, Arlene M. 2004. *Barrio Dreams: Puerto Ricans, Latinos, and the Neoliberal City.* Berkeley: University of California Press.

Dobbins, Jeff. 2012. "Manhattan's 'Little Mexico.'" In *Walks of New York.* New York. Retrieved June 1, 2015. https://www.walksofnewyork.com/blog/manhattans-little -mexico.

Dunn, Timothy J. 1996. *The Militarization of the U.S.-Mexico Border, 1978–1992: Low-Intensity Conflict Doctrine Comes Home.* Austin: University of Texas Press.

Fertitta, Naomi and Paul Aresu. 2009. *New York: The Big City and Its Little Neighborhoods.* New York: Universe.

Fuentes, Norma. 2007. "The Immigrant Experiences of Dominican and Mexican Women in the 1990s: Crossing Boundaries or Temporary Work Spaces?" Pp. 94–119 in *Crossing Borders and Constructing Boundaries: Immigration Race and Ethnicity,* edited by Caroline Brettell. New York: Lexington Books.

Gans, Herbert J. 1962. *The Urban Villagers: Group and Class in the Life of Italian-Americans.* New York: Free Press.

Grasmuck, Sherri and Patricia R. Pessar. 1991. *Between Two Islands: Dominican International Migration.* Berkeley: University of California Press.

Grinberg, Emanuella. 2009. "El Paso School a Haven along Violent Border." CNN.com. Retrieved June 1, 2015. http://www.cnn.com/2009/US/05/20/elpaso.juarez.school/index.html.

Hall, John. 2011. "Museo Urbano Opens: Museum Dedicated to El Paso's Segundo Barrio." *El Paso Times,* 9 May, pp. 5, 9. Retrieved June 1, 2015. http://www .elpasotimes.com/ci_18019051.

Hellman, Judith Adler. 2008. *The World of Mexican Migrants: The Rock and the Hard Place.* New York: New Press.

Heyman, Josiah McC., Guillermina Gina Núñez, and Victor Talavera. 2009. "Health Care Access and Barriers for Unauthorized Immigrants in El Paso County, Texas." *Family and Community Health* 32:4–21.

Hutchison, Ray and Bruce D. Haynes. 2012. *The Ghetto: Contemporary Global Issues and Controversies.* Boulder, CO: Westview.

Jacobs, Jane. 1961. *The Death and Life of Great American Cities.* New York: Random House.

Jones-Correa, Michael. 1998. *Between Two Nations: The Political Predicament of Latinos in New York City.* Ithaca, NY: Cornell University Press.

Kasinitz, Philip, John H. Mollenkopf, and Mary C. Waters, eds. 2004. *Becoming New Yorkers: Ethnographies of the New Second Generation.* New York: Russell Sage Foundation.

Kasinitz, Philip, John H. Mollenkopf, Mary C. Waters, and Jennifer Holdaway. 2008. *Inheriting the City: The Children of Immigrants Come of Age.* New York: Russell Sage Foundation.

Lachica, Josué, Ernesto Castañeda, and Yolanda McDonald. 2013. "Poverty, Place, and Health along the US-Mexico Border." Pp. 87–104 in *Poverty and Health: A Crisis among America's Most Vulnerable,* vol. 2, *Place and Health among the Vulnerable,* edited by Kevin Fitzpatrick. Goleta, CA: ABC-CLIO.

Lobo, Arun Peter and Joseph J. Salvo. 2013. *The Newest New Yorkers: Characteristics of the City's Foreign-Born Population.* New York: New York City Department of City Planning.

Loveman, Mara and Jeronimo O. Muniz. 2007. "How Puerto Rico Became White: Boundary Dynamics and Intercensus Racial Reclassification." *American Sociological Review* 72:915–939.

Marwell, Nicole P. 2007. *Bargaining for Brooklyn: Community Organizations in the Entrepreneurial City.* Chicago: University of Chicago Press.

New York City Department of City Planning. 2012. "Profile of Manhattan Community District 11."

Orsi, Robert Anthony. 2002. *The Madonna of 115th Street: Faith and Community in Italian Harlem, 1880–1950.* New Haven, CT: Yale University Press.

Romo, David. 2005. *Ringside Seat to a Revolution: An Underground Cultural History of El Paso and Juarez: 1893–1923.* El Paso: Cinco Puntos Press.

Sacred Heart Church. 2014. "Sacred Heart Church Mission Statement." El Paso. Retrieved June 1, 2015. http://sacredheartelpaso.org/who-we-are/mission.

Semple, Kirk. 2010. "Immigrant in Run for Mayor, Back Home in Mexico." *New York Times,* 1 June.

Serra del Pozo, Pau. 2006. *El Comercio Etnico en el Distrito de Ciutat Vella de Barcelona.* Barcelona: Fundación la Caixa.

Shortell, Timothy and Jerome Krase. 2010. "On the Visual Semiotics of Collective Identity in Urban Vernacular Spaces." Paper presented at the 17th ISA World Congress of Sociology, Gothenburg, Sweden.

Small, Mario Luis. 2008. "Four Reasons to Abandon the Idea of 'The Ghetto.'" *City and Community* 7:389–398.

Texas Department of Transportation. 2011. *El Paso Regional Ports of Entry Operations Plan.* El Paso: Texas Department of Transportation.

Thompson, Gabriel. 2007. *There's No José Here: Following the Hidden Lives of Mexican Immigrants.* New York: Nation Books.

Tilly, Charles. 1998. *Durable Inequality.* Berkeley: University of California Press.

U.S. Census. 2010a. "DP-1-Geography-New York City, New York: Profile of General Population and Housing Characteristics: 2010." In *U.S. Census 2010.* U.S. Census Bureau.

———. 2010b. "U.S. Census Bureau State & County QuickFacts, New York (City), New York." U.S. Census Bureau.

———. 2013. "Hispanic or Latino Origin by Specific Origin, New York City." In *2008–2012 American Community Survey.* U.S. Census Bureau.

Van Hook, Jennifer and Frank D. Bean. 2009. "Explaining Mexican Immigrant Welfare Behaviors: The Importance of Employment-Related Cultural Repertoires." *American Sociological Review* 74:423–444.

Wilson, Kenneth L. and Alejandro Portes. 1980. "Immigrant Enclaves: An Analysis of the Labor Market Experiences of Cubans in Miami." *American Journal of Sociology* 86:295–319.

II

Gender

As mentioned in Chapter 1, walking in modern cities presents itself as an activity of expression from "below," empowering the average citizen to create a sense of place through daily routinized activity. For the chapters in this part, such vernacular landscapes are circumscribed by gender, which makes motility, or access to potential forms of mobility and routes, a relevant topic of discussion.

It was originally the male walker as urban wanderer who practiced *flânerie* as a way of seeing and interpreting the city. Such a procedure involved subverting the prevailing everyday quotidian practices of the city to interpret and understand its multilayered potential meanings ascribed to space. Jenks and Neves (2000:1) argued that *flânerie*, like ethnography, "involves the observation of people and social types and contexts; a way of reading the city, its population, its spatial configurations whilst also a way of reading and producing texts." Nuvolati (2014) argued that these two practices, *flânerie* and ethnography, produce different kinds of texts: poetic and academic, respectively. The complex multilayered characteristics of the urban environment are revealed as that which is familiar and taken for granted that becomes strange as it is conferred multifaceted meaning. This leads to raising questions via the process of answering old ones. The city is rediscovered and redefined through the ethnographic *flâneur* as the method permits reflexivity between perception and knowledge as alternative social realities of spatiality are explored.

If this exploration was the practice of the premodern lone male *flâneur*, then the postmodern female *flâneuse* may adopt the same principle as a wanderer without the stigma of exploring alone as her predecessors. Now the contemporary *flâneuse* can explore, discover, and rediscover elements of urban life that would otherwise be overlooked in the grand narrative. The city can now be presented through the female voice as wanderer. This can be added to Michel de Certeau's (1984) argument that walking provides a sanctuary for invisible every-day meanings of the city as the "female view" is one that warrants exploration.

Nazgol Bagheri's discussion of the *flâneuse* in Chapter 5 is conceptual-ized and applied to two shopping malls in Tehran, Iran. Bagheri articulates the Westernized notion of mall life as sterile, privatized areas where movement is controlled and behavior regulated. In contrast, the malls in Iran (Tandis and Golestan) have removed the restrictions of sharia law, freeing its female shop-pers with an opportunity for authentic self-expression. Bagheri argues that in Tehran such spaces are less restrictive of identity practices than is the case out-side of them. This empowers the women to more freely use the shopping malls as places of consumption and otherwise elusive identity expression. In doing so, Bagheri contributes to the understanding of motility and the spatial produc-tion of gender. It is in the privately owned "public" space where the freedom of expression is allowed, pointing to gendered limits of motility in urban envi-ronments, a characteristic not limited to countries with strict gender-defined religious practices (Cresswell and Uteng 2008).

In Chapter 6, Marlese Durr applies Kristin Larsen's (2005) concept of the doughnut hole, the geographic center of a poverty-ridden city surrounded by prosperous suburbs brought about by gentrification, to Dayton, Ohio. In her chapter, Durr's "doughnut hole" represents a public transportation hub located near gentrified sections of the city that brings poorer residents in close contact with their upwardly mobile and predominantly white neighbors. While being less explicit, she appears to embrace the act of a *flânerie* without deploying the term and expresses a form of attachment and detachment to the behavior of commuters. As a *flâneuse* she presents a complexity of relations otherwise ig-nored by city authorities. Their attempts to manufacture socially hygienic space obscure the richness of experience a metropolitan city has to offer.

REFERENCES

Cresswell, Tim and Tanu Priya Uteng. 2008. "Gendered Mobilities: Towards an Holistic Understanding." Pp. 16–27 in *Gendered Mobilities*, edited by Tanu Priya Uteng and Tim Cresswell. Burlington, VT: Ashgate.
de Certeau, Michel. 1984. *The Practice of Everyday Life*. Berkeley: University of California Press.
Jenks, Chris and Tiago Neves. 2000 "A Walk on the Wild Side: Urban Ethnography Meets the Flâneur." *Cultural Values* 4(1):1–17.
Larsen, Kristin. 2005. "New Urbanism's Role in Inner-City Neighborhood Revitalization." *Housing Studies* 20(5):795–813.
Nuvolati, Giampaolo. 2014. "The *Flâneur*: A Way of Walking, Exploring, and Interpreting the City." Pp. 21–40 in *Walking in the European City: Quotidian Mobility and Urban Ethnography*, edited by Timothy Shortell and Evrick Brown. Burlington, VT: Ashgate.

5

The Emancipated *Flâneuse* in Tehran's Shopping Malls

NAZGOL BAGHERI

Located in the far north end of Tehran and on the southern slope of the Alborz Mountains, Tandis shopping mall was opened to the public in 2005 after five years of construction. Since then, it has been repeatedly ranked as the most popular shopping mall in Tehran. Although finding a parking spot in its nine-story underground parking structure is time-consuming and exhausting, the shopping mall's four stories offer top European and American brands, including Armani, Versace, Tommy Hilfiger, and Gucci, and are always packed with all kinds of people. Among them, there are many young women (aged eighteen to thirty-five) who come to the mall not only to shop but more often to window-shop, hang out, watch, and, of course, be watched.

The aim of this study is to explore how women use the shopping mall's space and, more specifically, how the modern mall in Tehran has become something more than a space of consumption, facilitating the experience of freedom, equity, and self-expression for Iranian women. To do so, I use the concept of *flâneur* and review its geohistorical origin in mid-nineteenth-century Paris. I then follow the concept's changes to its new version in twenty-first-century postmodern landscapes, including shopping malls. This study offers a fuller understanding of women's consumption *of* space, the social construction of space, and latent ethno-cultural meanings, as well as the class values women attach to such a seemingly simple practice. I will illustrate this by drawing on fifty-three interviews with women accompanied by behavioral mapping of the Tandis and Golestan shopping malls in Tehran. Findings address the variety of women strollers and add a new dimension to the predominant critical studies of modern and privatized public spaces by urban design scholars in the North America.

Introduction

Walking in Tehran can be seen as a sustainable mode of transportation, an exercise activity, or a political gesture, but many Tehranian women think of it as something similar to what Walter Benjamin calls leisure walking or *flânerie*. Although the concepts of *flânerie* and *flâneur* are not widely used in Iran, they can explain a diverse range of "spatial practices" (de Certeau 1984; Lefebvre 1991) and also the "social lives" (Appadurai 1996) of postmodern spaces, particularly in the constantly emerging modern-looking shopping malls in Tehran.

Despite the higher population density in the south and central parts of Tehran, the majority of shopping malls are located in the north and northwestern parts of the city (Figure 5.1). This concentration can be understood through the city's urban form. Tehran, home for more than fifteen million people of diverse ethnicities and social classes, is known for its omnipresent tension between "deep-seated tradition and wild modernity" (Bayat 2010:99). Tehran is a socially and spatially divided city to Bala Shahr (high city) and Paeen Shahr (low city). Besides the physical and environmental advantages, such as better water supplies, a newer built environment, and visual dominance over Paeen Shahr, Bala Shahr has also been associated with dominant class-related values and preferences. Paeen Shahr is associated with old-school, traditional ideology, religious conservatism, and a premodern built environment.

Unlike the Paeen Shahr, Bala Shahr evokes images that associate it with higher classes, progressive liberal ideology, religious openness, Westernized modern architecture, and public spaces. Although the distinction is vaguely defined, geographically fuzzy, and changing, the pairing of Paeen Shahr–Bala Shahr survives symbolically in residents' everyday lives and indirectly influences individuals' housing, shopping, and transportation preferences. Besides the high demand for shopping malls that often carry Western and fashion goods, the associated meanings to Bala Shahr make these malls more attractive to the masses. It is a common practice that if a woman is shopping for fashion and Western brands, she goes to the malls, and if she is considering more affordable choices of clothing and goods, she would consider Tehran bazaar (Grand Bazaar) or other retail discount stores mostly located in the central or southern Tehran.

Tandis and Golestan shopping malls (see Figure 5.1) were selected for this study based on three unique characteristics: First, they were ranked the most popular shopping malls according to popular Iranian shopping websites.[1] Second is their specific geographical location. Tandis mall is located in one of the major squares in Tehran, Tajrish Square, and Golestan is located in Shahrak-e-Gharb in the northwest of the city and is also accessible by the subway and other public transportation options, as well as personal automobile. They are

---

[1] This is based on statistics published in Farsi on www.dabi.ir and selected articles found on www.tehranmalls.org.

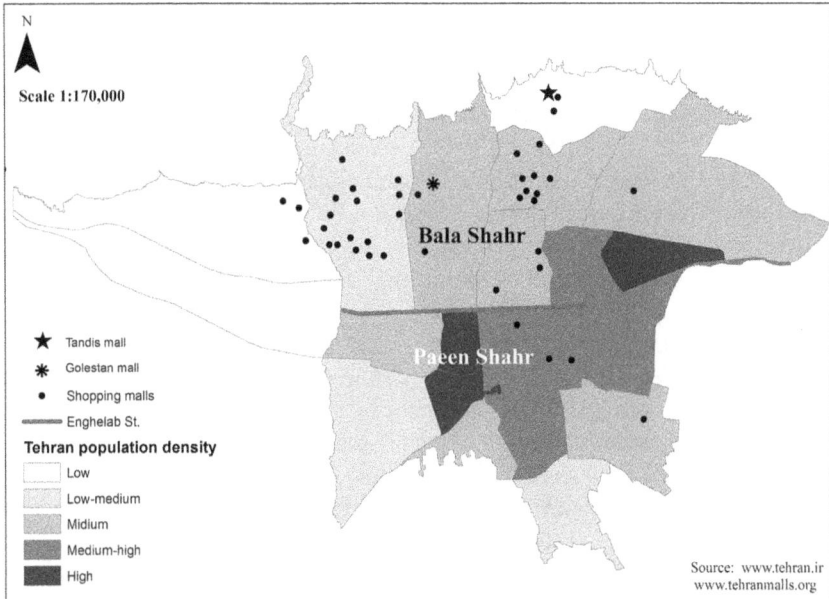

Figure 5.1 Shopping Mall Spatial Distribution in Tehran and the Locations of Selected Case Studies. (www.tehranmalls.org; image created by author)

located in a free traffic zone, which makes it easier to drive. In order to control the high air pollution in Tehran, the city is divided into different traffic zones. For example, the central parts of Tehran are in a *Tarh-e-Traffic* zone, and personal automobiles are not allowed to enter it between 7:00 A.M. and 5:00 P.M. Therefore, the selected shopping malls' automobile and public transit accessibility attracts a wider range of users and visitors, which was significant for this research. Third, they offer a combination of retail stores, fast-food restaurants, video game stores, coffee shops, and other services (such as hair and nail salons).

Using the concept of the *flâneur* and its specific emphasis on wandering, watching, and being watched was particularly helpful not only in explaining the wide range of types and activities of women in the shopping mall but also in connecting the findings to the broader critics of shopping malls in the West. Many urban planners and human geographers (see Banerjee and Loukaitou-Sideris 1992; Crawford 1992; J. Shields 1990; Soja 2003; Sorkin 1992; Zukin 2003) have warned us of the loss of authentic *public* spaces and the danger of overtly controlled designs and behaviors in privatized public places such as shopping malls. The critics emphasize the lack of sense of place based on the boxy and boring designs of shopping malls, the potential of segregation through target audiences and controlled behavior, the systematically designed notion of consumption and leisure, and finally depoliticizing the space through confining the user's democratic rights. Although there have been a few efforts (Day

1999; Salcedo 2003) to include more diverse experience into these criticisms, the literature still lacks the inclusion of examples from non-Western contexts where the shopping malls, like other features and forces of modernity, are developed, perceived, and used in significantly different ways.

Participant observation and fifty-three semistructured interviews with women who were (walking) in Tandis and Golestan shopping malls are the main sources of ethnographic data in this research. Interview participants were randomly chosen in the mall representing diversity in age (all over eighteen), occupation, hijab style,[2] and home location. Except six women I approached, all the other fifty-three women openly answered my questions and shared their experiences. Although the majority of women in the mall dressed less conservatively compared with other parts of Tehran, I tried to pay extra attention to women's appearance (hijab style and makeup) to talk with both traditional and modern-looking women evenly. In the interviews, I asked women why they were walking in the malls, where they were coming from, how often they come, and how long they usually stay. Women discussed their feelings toward and activities in the shopping malls. Interviews were collected during 2011 and 2012. They were tape-recorded, translated to English, transcribed, and discourse analyzed.[3]

Following the feminist approaches and based on my unique status as an Iranian woman and researcher, I situated myself as an insider, both the researcher and the researched. This way, I was able to reduce the distance between myself and the female users in the shopping malls by establishing a relationship based on our commonalities (Bondi 2003; McDowell 1992). Such a relationship made it possible for me to draw on my own experiences and also to give voice to women with similar challenges and opportunities in the malls. In addition to the interviews, I prepared social behavioral mapping (SBM) in the selected spaces in the malls. SBM is a type of systematic observation research often used by architects, urban designers, and anthropologists to track behavior over space and time. SBM was conducted in twelve one-hour segments at each location, evenly representing the days of the week (weekday and weekends) and the time of day (morning, afternoon, and evening). At twenty-minute intervals, I recorded women's activities and locations and characteristics that are readily observable, such as approximate age, sex, and whether the individual was alone or in a group. These spatial representations illustrate the walking patterns and the spatial concentrations of women in the mall.

The chapter proceeds in three main sections. First, I situate the *flâneur* in its contemporary context through exploring its old and new representations. I examine how the concept of nineteenth-century *flânerie* and its postmodern version are related. Given this research's focus on women, I also review the

---

[2] Since the Islamic Revolution of 1979 in Iran, hijab, or covering the hair and body, has been compulsory for women in public spaces. However, women's hijab styles vary depending on their faith, class, age, geographical locations, and so forth.

[3] The interview interpretation was drawn upon a poststructural approach to discourse analysis.

feminist contributions to the subject. Second, I conceptualize the *flâneuse* in shopping malls through reviewing the critical perspectives of urban scholars on the mall and "mall rats" (youth who regularly socialize in malls without any shopping goals) in North American contexts (Bauman 1994). Finally, drawing on the ethnographic data I collected in the field, I argue that Iranian women's experiences challenge the homogenizing aspects of the theory on contemporary *flâneurs* in the mall. It is suggested before we evaluate or categorize the *flâneurs* in postmodern public spaces, including shopping malls, we must consider the experiences by a more diverse population as well as the ethno-cultural meanings people attach to those places.

From the Nineteenth-Century *Flânerie* to the Shopping Mall's *Flâneuse*

A *flâneur* is the male urban stroller and observer who first emerged on Paris's streets in the mid-nineteenth century. As presented in Honoré de Balzac's *Physiologie du Mariage* (1837) and Victor Hugo's *Les Misérables* (1884), the *flâneur* is associated with a specific time and place. For Walter Benjamin (1999), *flâneur* is defined as an iconic character of modern city walking, wandering throughout the city, watching people and places, and experiencing simultaneous attachment and detachment to modern life's complexities and contradictions. In Benjamin's "articulation of Baudelaire's hero of modernity . . . the *flâneur* appears as a symbol of modernity, at first acting as its critical observer, only to become its victim, and eventually, its agent, whose cynical detachment has fallen prey to the overarching commoditization of everyday life" (Trivundža 2011:71–72).

Ilija Tomanić Trivundža (2011:73) suggests "four discursive elements" (gaze, knowledge production, textual production, and time) for explaining the concept of *flâneur* that are quite useful in capturing the concept's elusive nature both in its specific geohistorical and more contemporary contexts. Central to the concept is the act of observing; therefore, the *flâneur* does not aimlessly stroll around the city. Instead, he attentively watches the urban scenes, people, and places, and discovers the signs; in other words, he "*reads* the city as if it were a book" (Trivundža 2011:74).

In *The Painter of Modern Life and Other Essays*, Charles Baudelaire (1995) emphasizes that the *flâneur*'s gaze goes beyond the surface of the city and seeks latent meanings behind each scene. As a solitary urban stroller, the *flâneur* enjoys a sense of anonymity and freedom of societal constraints even when he is among an urban crowd throughout the day. Such anonymity, or even sovereignty, gives the *flâneur* "an ability to make for himself the meaning and the significance of the metropolitan spaces and the spectacle of the public" (Tester 1994:4). Rob Shields (1992:68) describes the *flâneur* as the opposite of Georg Simmel's stranger in modern society: "the stranger is the foreigner who becomes like a native, whereas the *flâneur* is the inverse, a native who becomes like a foreigner." Keith Tester (1994:3) also reminds us that "Baudelaire's poet [the *flâneur*] is the man *of* the crowd as opposed to the man *in* the crowd."

The second element of the *flâneur* is his eagerness to interpret the signs, to translate the images he gathered into social meanings and/or aesthetical beauty. His focus is not merely people (social) or places (built environment); instead he integrates both dimensions in order to discover social and artist phenomena. The *flâneur*'s discursive characteristic as a knowledge producer results in his third constitutive element, text production either in its visual or reading materials (poetry, photography, critical article, and so on). While it is also important to remember that what the *flâneur* produces is so little compared with what he accumulates, this discursive element, knowledge/text production, can become challenging in including or excluding the shopping mall rats into the category.

The last defining element of the concept of *flâneur* is his connection with time, or, in fact, his disconnection with utilitarian time. Trivundža (2011) suggests that it is the concept of "non-utilitarian time," not the commodity that links the *flâneur* to capitalism. He (2011:79) contends that the "*flâneur* exists outside the disciplining power of time that is linked to capitalist productive relations, to confinement of productive work time and functional leisure."

The discussed characteristics of the *flâneur* help to partially capture the elusive nature of the concept; however, this conceptualization in its original geohistorical context offers little insight in understanding the fast-growing emergence of new generations of the *flâneur* in Tehran's shopping malls. So, how does exploring the specific social type that emerged in the mid-nineteenth century have any relevance today? Gluck (2003:53) highlights, "The contemporary critical discussions have produced as many images of the flâneur as there are the conceptions of the modern." Therefore, as modernity and its features can be developed, defined, and perceived in different ways across temporal and spatial boundaries so does the concept of the *flâneur*.

Meanwhile, Balzac's division of the concept to artist-*flâneur* and ordinary-*flâneur* becomes helpful in understanding the relationship between the geohistorical definition of *flâneur* and its contemporary version in shopping malls. For Balzac, the artist-*flâneur* is of the privileged elite who critically watch the social and aesthetic dimension of urban modern life. The artist-*flâneur* creates new knowledge in the form of a cultural critique, photograph, poem, or painting. The latter category of ordinary-*flâneur*, which constitutes the majority of *flâneurs*, is a group of "passive readers of urban text, taken up, and taken in, by the surface agitation" (Ferguson 1992:29).

Perhaps the contemporary journalists, artists, and bloggers who use the cities for inspiration can be included in the former category, but who are the shopping mall's strollers? Are they *the passive readers of urban text* completely controlled by the neoliberal political economy of capitalist market? Or are there other reasons beside consumption of goods for these strollers in Tehran's malls?

As women make up the majority of strollers in Tehran's shopping malls (see Tables 5.1 and 5.2), it is necessary to briefly examine feminist approaches to the existence of women *flâneurs*. There are contrasting perspectives about the existence of the *flâneuse*. Feminist scholars like Janet Wolff (1985) and Griselda Pollock (1988) suggest the *flâneur's* anonymity in cities and accessibility to public life was unavailable to women at the time; therefore, the female version of *flâneur*, the *flâneuse*, was invisible. In this model, the city was seen as a white masculine space where men enjoyed the public and women had to be protected in the private/domestic space of home. Others (see Wilson 1995) argue that she existed but in different ways that were ignored by male-dominant history writers of the time. The Victorian era's sexual division of public versus private spheres has been criticized by the next generation of feminist scholars.

Although the actual lived experiences of women during the nineteenth century present "a tremendous variety spatial practices across different genders, classes, and ethnicities" (D'Souza and McDonough 2006:2), it was not until the 1850s and 1860s that the establishment of the department store opened new doors for women to legitimate public life (Wolff 1985). According to Morawski (1994:189), the new *flâneur's* strolling has relocated to the shopping mall, telling a story of "scanning the determinants of the consumerist civilization and culture." Bauman (1994:146) emphasizes that "the right to walk curiously was to be the *flâneur's*, tomorrow the customer's, reward. Pleasurable display, fascinating view, the enticing game of shapes and colors." In what follows, I shall show how the shopping mall's spaces are socially and culturally produced based on Iranian women strollers.

The Emancipated *Flâneuse*

Many believe that a neoliberal political economy along with capitalism and its inherent consumption culture have turned the *flâneur* into its new modern/postmodern version, idler, loafer, lounger, or shopping mall rat. Often, the shopping mall rat is associated with women while the *flâneur* represents a male figure. That is directly related to the social construction of women as consumers and objects of consumption in capitalist societies. Shopping malls—sometimes called artifacts of globalization—have been highly criticized by urban scholars (see Banerjee and Loukaitou-Sideris 1992; Soja 2003; Sorkin 1992). They are seen as a serious threat for authentic public spheres, degrading the agency's role and encouraging consumption and sameness in North American cities. Critics emphasize the uninteresting "standardized" copy-and-paste architectural design, the overtly controlled behavior through complete surveillance, and potential homogenization and social segregation (Crawford 1992; Judd 1995). Although these criticisms are valid in many cases, particularly in their North American contexts, they do not include the variety of experiences by diverse populations in different countries and cultures. For instance, Day (1999) makes an effort to introduce gender to the critique of privatized public spaces and studies how private spaces, including a regional shopping mall in Orange County, California, are experienced by women in different ways from those included in the predominant critique of malls. In "When the Global Meets the Local at the Mall," Salcedo (2003:1084) comments how "urban scholars" mistakenly "have assumed that the mall is an outpost of the globalized economy that diminishes locality and human agency" and such criticisms are only based on "the ideological construction of the mall and the tendency toward a preoccupation with surveillance and social exclusion [that] may merely reflect particular aspects of U.S. culture and politics."

The late 1980s mark a significant time in shopping mall history, both in the United States and Iran. By then, the American suburban market was saturated by shopping malls (Crawford 1992; Salcedo 2003), and many malls were either demolished or abandoned. By the end of the 1980s and the early 1990s, Tehran witnessed a great change in its postwar reconstruction and urban development under the pro-market government of President Hashemi Rafsanjani. The new president left the dark years of the Iran-Iraq War behind, "scaling back the command economy and replacing rationing with increased opportunities for consumption" (Bayat 2010:109). Tehran's parks and boulevards were planted with flowers and new highways and increased public transportation decreased the north-south social and spatial distance. New cultural complexes were constructed to provide morally safe public spaces for the youth's recreation, and modern high-rise shopping malls were added to the capital's horizon. The first structure close in design and function to a Western shopping mall was the Golestan complex originally constructed by the Bonyad-e Mostaz'afin (the Foundation of the Dispossessed, associated with the government) and later transferred to the private sector. Unlike the traditional bazaar where different products are spatially separated along *rasteh bazars* (narrow corridors specializing in certain goods), the malls brought together varieties of mass-produced clothing and household goods.

Today's Tehran has some forty shopping malls, including Tandis located in Tajrish Square, one of the major transportation, recreation, religious, and commercial centers in northern Tehran, well known for carrying the latest fashions of Paris and New York. Tandis and Golestan are among the most visited malls in Tehran, and between five thousand and seven thousand people visit them each day. Table 5.1 summarizes the malls' general characteristics. While American malls attracted people to a "repackage of the city (what we lack in suburban areas) in a safe, clean, and controlled form" (Crawford 1992:23), malls attract Iranians for quite different reasons. Malls in Iran attract people because they are less controlled compared with other public spaces such as streets and squares.

The modern and Western-looking malls opened new doors for Tehranians, allowing them to go beyond the socio-geographic boundaries of their own neighborhoods to the whole city. People started exploring the city and its new malls through the city's affordable public transportation. In addition, the malls

TABLE 5.1 GENERAL CHARACTERISTICS OF TANDIS AND GOLESTAN
SHOPPING MALLS

Shopping Mall	Location	Year Built	Number of Stores	Parking	Number of Floors	Visitors per Day	Number of Interviews
Tandis	North, Tajrish Square	2005	185	Yes	4	5,000–7,000	27
Golestan	West, Shahrak-e-Gharb	1989	149	Yes	6	5,000–7,000	26

provided a climate-controlled environment not only for shopping but also for wandering around and social meetings. In contrast to the American case, the shopping mall in Tehran has become a place of gathering for a diverse range of people from different parts of the city, different socioeconomic classes, and for different reasons.

In the first few days of my participant observation, along with other *flâneuses* I strolled in the malls' halls full of small stores that offered European and American brands. One would think these high-end fashion products would attract a very narrow type of consumer, that is, those of the high-income class who probably live around the mall in the northern neighborhoods of Tehran. But after a day or two, I noticed that was not the case. This raised the question: What is the relationship between the kinds of products the mall offers and the type of people who use the space? In *Distinction: A Social Critique of the Judgment of Taste*, Pierre Bourdieu (1984) argues that people use their aesthetic taste to distinguish their class from others, which holds true in Tehran's malls, as well. The malls located in more affluent neighborhoods, such as Tandis and Golestan, often offer higher-end goods and brands. While the rich elite in Tehran strive to assert their class distinction through fashion and consumption habits, Tehran's subway made the malls accessible for people from other parts of the city. The mall was turned into to "an almost classless space." Women were not there merely for shopping but for getting ideas of the latest fashions, window-shopping, gathering in the mall's coffee shop, or just strolling. When I asked a young woman who was wandering around with her girlfriends what they were doing, she responded:

> We are here to have fun. . . . Of course, I would not buy anything here [Tandis]; it is superexpensive for me, and I think you can find something similar enough but much cheaper somewhere else. . . . But we like it here, we come and [laughing] watch people and stores. (18–25)[4]

I agree with Bauman's (1994) observation that postmodern *flâneurs* make daily or weekly visits to shopping malls. There were different groups of women I met many times while I was gathering data.

---

[4] The range in parentheses shows the interviewee's age category.

I come here [Golestan mall] to check out the fashion; you know I might not
buy all my clothes here, but I like to see what color is in fashion or what
shoes are in fashion. (18–25)

Security is one of the most important characteristics of malls, both in American and Iranian cases. Unlike the case with an American mall that can cause
social segregation through overt surveillance, Tandis appeared to invite a diverse group of women. The women I talked with came from all over the city and
even from smaller cities around Tehran. While I agree with Crawford (1992:11)
that "the ethos of consumption has penetrated every sphere of our lives," there
is something more than simple consumption that attracts these women to the
mall.

I am coming from Amireh [neighborhood in southern Tehran] and it takes
me a little more than an hour to get here [Tandis] by the subway . . . I feel
comfortable here. I am here because nobody knows who I am and where
I am coming from. (26–35)

Malls are the only places where my boyfriend and I feel safe to go . . . we
can hang out without being worried about being seen or caught with the
fashion police. (18–25)

According to the law, women have to cover their hair and bodies in public,
but that did not stop women from innovatively creating new ways to represent
themselves and show their beauty. The fashion police are mostly located in the
main squares in Tehran (and other larger cities) and the entrance/exit of major
subway stations, and they oversee women's hijab observance and the relationship between opposite sexes. The fashion police claim to *educate* what they call
"Western dolls" about Islamic dress codes, but in their actions, they have gone
further and often arrest women whose dresses are too tight or who do not cover
their hair completely. Although malls have their own security guards, the presence of the fashion police is much less tangible there. In fact, as the malls are
semipublic spaces, it is not that easy for the fashion police to get in.[5]

I chatted with a female security guard who was curious about what I was
doing in Golestan mall. I asked her what she thinks about the frequent users,
and she replied, "We have all kinds of people, and that is one of the reasons I
can stand my boring job here, walking around the mall and watching people."
The decreased presence of the fashion police in the malls made a lot of women
feel more comfortable.

---

[5] The inside of the malls in Iran are semipublic as they are partially owned by the store owners; however, because it is the Islamic Republic of Iran, the fashion police (in general any government-related
agency) has access to it. But, compared with streets and squares, which are more public, access to
malls is often more difficult for the fashion police.

I like to look good and fashionable and I feel less watched . . . and free here in the enclosed space of Tandis mall . . . When I am ready to leave the mall, I run into the bathroom to make sure my hair is covered up . . . There might be some police just outside the mall or on Tajrish Square. (18–25)

The sense of freedom she was describing was not unfamiliar to me or other women I talked with. The following narratives are illustrative.

There is something in the space, in its clean, bright, colorful settings . . . or there is something in the people here that I very much prefer walking in the mall than on polluted streets in my neighborhood [central Tehran], where even the shopkeepers give us [her and her boyfriend] a bad look. . . . Like it is his business that I have a boyfriend! (18–25)

I go down to the bazaar [the Grand Bazaar] and I buy what I need and get out . . . but when I am here, I do not mind wandering around the mall after I am done shopping. I just feel safer as a woman in the mall rather than the mazelike bazaar complex. (35–46)

Malls in North America typically tend to exclude the poor, particularly because of their strategically selected locations in middle- and higher-middle-income neighborhoods and the lack of sufficient public transportation. But since Tehran's subway runs all the way from the north end of the city in Tajrish Square to Kahrizak, in the south boundaries of Tehran, shopping malls are more inclusive and accessible to the poor, of course not for shopping but for leisure walking or *flânerie*. They provide a place for self-expression and self-representation. Almost 60 percent (Table 5.2) of women I talked with were coming from the central and southern parts (south of Enghelab Street) of Tehran.

Women coming from lower-income classes did not see the mall as a merely commercial space but rather a recreational space. A young conservatively dressed women in a black silk chador with a bright purple *rosari* (head cover under the chador), who claimed to have her own style, had come from Qom, the most religious city in Iran with the highest concentration of mosques and *Hozeye Elmieh* (Ayatollah training schools). She stated "my fiancé and I have

TABLE 5.2   WOMEN'S CHARACTERISTICS BASED ON THE BEHAVIOR MAPPING IN THE MALLS

Shopping Mall	Gender of Users		Women's Home Location		Women's First Goal	
	Women (%)	Men (%)	Northern Tehran (%)	Central and Southern Tehran (%)	Shopping	Not Shopping
Tandis	59	41	41	59	7	20
Golestan	53	47	46	54	9	18

come here every Thursday evening since our official engagement two months ago. We enjoy being in the modern mall; it is like a break for us from our everyday life in Qom."

In other words, there is more emphasis on the consumption *of* space in Tehran's malls than the consumption *in* space. It is not only the European and American brands and fashion goods that attract women to the mall; the mall's space, itself, is consumed as a commodity. Malls are often more than commercial spaces and indeed can provide their users with places of self-representing, exploration, social interaction, and relaxation (Zukin 2003). Women repeatedly mentioned that they were in the malls "because of its environment or ambiance." The mall also offers a classless place, blurring the distinctions of prosperity and poverty.

One good thing about Tandis is that I come here and I dress like everybody else! I put on more colorful clothes and more makeup than if I were going to neighborhood's stores [located in central Tehran]. (26–35)

I do not have to spend any money in the mall, so I come here with my friends on Thursdays and Fridays [Iranian weekends] to have fun and get out of the house. (18–25)

The latter comment is in line with Zukin's (2003) conclusion in *Point of Purchase* that the shopping is often not the goal, rather the walking, the watching, and the daydreaming about how it would feel to be able to afford or buy a fashionable item. Although there is no doubt that consumerism has long penetrated Iranian society, particularly the rich elite residing in Bala Shahr, the shopping mall strollers were not what Crawford (1992:12) calls "impulse shoppers" or "unstable subjects." The role Tehran's subway and other forms of public transportation plays in the mall's ease of access is significant. The spatial and social distinction of Bala Shahr and Paeen Shahr is slowly blurring as more people get to experience other parts of the city, beyond their own neighborhoods.

These women were not completely aimless, but rather were similar to the old version of *flâneurs*; some were watching and enjoying the contradictory combination of tradition and modernity.

Honestly, I feel I have to become or I just become somebody else when I am here [Golestan mall]. You feel the pressure on you to dress better, look better, and be somebody else whom I am not sure I like or dislike yet [smiling]! So I guess that is why I keep coming to watch others and know myself. (25–36)

I never thought about the names of these malls until one of the women who happened to be a sociology student brought it up.

*Tandis means statue! Right? That is why I feel everybody can be a statue
and have a mask on, wearing a mask to either exaggerate who they
are and what they have or conceal who they are and what they do not
have . . . See they even sell those masks! Those made-in-China American
brands!* (18–25)

Her response reminded me Erving Goffman's (1959) dramaturgical approach in
studying self-presentation in everyday life: people resembling actors in a theater.
I asked her what she was doing, and she replied "I am walking . . . walking and
watching." I agree with Michel de Certeau (1984:100) that walking in the city
has its own "rhetoric" and provides a haven in which those invisible everyday
meanings that are often overlooked by modernists can reemerge. "The act of
walking is to the urban system what the speech act is to language or, to the
statements uttered" (de Certeau 1984:97). I was amazed to find out that of fifty-
three women with whom I talked, thirty-eight (see Table 5.2) were not there to
shop but rather to consume the mall as a semiprivatized safe place to hang out.
Indeed, I agree with Zukin (2003:52) that learning from people's experiences in
public spaces can be "a humbling experience, for it upsets many of the assumptions and values on which a critical understanding of modern society is based."
Similar to North America's commercial spaces, the cultural sphere has merged
with the economic in Tehran's shopping malls.

*The mall is my favorite place to walk. First, it is less polluted than streets
and even parks, and, second, I get a chance to watch other people and
their styles. I get my everyday exercise and enjoy the mall's scenes. It is
just fun!* (45–56)

*It is entertaining and kind of relaxing. I stop by the mall before going
home to just take a moment for myself and walk around.* (36–45)

The design issue came up couple of times when women were discussing
what they like or dislike about the mall. As an architect, it was very important
for me to know how women think about the so-called modernist boxy design
of the malls.

*I like the design! It is colorful and new . . . Plus they all have public bath-
rooms something that bazaar and retail stores do not have.* (36–45)

*I wish the design was more Iranian, but I do not think it really matters. If
you are here and enjoying looking at Gap and Gucci's brands, you probably do not mind the different architecture as much.* (26–35)

Based on my interviews, women did not consider the architecture of the
malls important. They mostly emphasized the sense of freedom and equality

they felt in them and counted them as recreational spaces rather than merely shopping places. They enjoyed getting lost, becoming strangers, getting ideas for future shopping, walking and chatting with their boyfriends outside the fashion police's watch, and even merely hanging out.[6] More importantly, unlike malls in North America, Tandis and Golestan malls provide women and youth with less controlled public spaces than more traditional public spaces, including streets and squares. The findings highlight the significance of the contextualizing of consumption culture, like any other culture, in a fuller understanding of the act of strolling by Iranian women in shopping malls. It is suggested that the individual subjectivity/agencies vary by culture, something that was ignored by modernists. In North America, what is perceived as a freedom of expression does not exist at all inside shopping malls. This study shows, in Tehran, malls have become women's favorite places to walk and spend time because of the sense of freedom and self-expression they offer.

Conclusion

This study seeks to enhance our understanding of the relationships among the sociocultural construction of modern public spaces and human agencies using the figure of the *flâneur* contextualized in Iranian shopping malls. Women's leisure walking, or *flânerie*, was the subject of this study, and I also used it as a research method to collect data in the malls. In these two examples of Tehran's shopping malls, I showed how shopping and leisure are mixed together and create a new form of spatial practices through the symbolic and cultural values associated with the space. These are meanings and values that change the dynamics of commercialized privatized public spaces and convert consumption *in* space to consumption *of* space. The goal is not to compare the Iranian mall with the North American one; rather I would like to emphasize how the specific written religious laws enforced by the government (that is, compulsory hijab and the presence of the fashion police on Tehran's streets) and unwritten societal norms (that is, the conservative approach to women's role and presence in public in specific neighborhoods in Tehran) can change the consumption culture and overall ambiance of shopping malls in an Islamic country. The Iranian *flâneuse* is, indeed, emancipated in the shopping mall, the same place that has been criticized for segregation and exclusion because of its control over behavior in the North America mall.

The act of walking in the city, as de Certeau (1984:99) contends, "creates a mobile organicity" and offers "unlimited diversity." The act of strolling in the shopping mall, as women in this study expressed, becomes a means to relax, have fun, watch and be watched, and, more importantly, enjoy a sense of free-

---

[6] As women now have access to go beyond their immediate neighborhoods, they can become strangers in the city. Nobody knows them, so the possibility to gossip about them decreases as they go farther from their place of residency.

dom, self-expression, and self-representation. The ethnographic analysis highlights the sociopolitical forces and the roles they play in the spatial practices by women and the symbolic construction of the shopping mall.

Iranian women traditionally have been limited to the private sphere, but their presence dramatically, and surprisingly, increased after the Islamic Revolution of 1979. There are three important factors that contributed to this change and invited more women into public spaces. First was the change in societal norms and the compulsory hijab that allowed many traditional women to feel comfortable and use public spaces. Second was the Iran-Iraq War period (1980–1988) when women had to come to the public life to compensate for the losses in the male workforce. Third was the postwar urban development that added many new public spaces and an increased opportunity for consumption. The latest factor is still happening and is relevant to this study. The increased women's presence and participation in public spaces has changed the women's roles and the definition of "a good Muslim woman" in Iranian society. Therefore, it is critical to understand the role of modern public spaces, such as shopping malls, in this change.

Women's narratives suggest that they use the modern commercial spaces as places of recreation, self-expression, and relaxation. In short, this perspective on the shopping mall posits that consumption culture has to be contextualized in a specific time and space. Unlike many North American malls that have been demolished or abandoned, the malls in Iran are still popular and, indeed, rapidly growing, not because the Iranians' socioeconomic and technological advancement may be behind North America's, but rather because of unique ethno-social meanings associated with their enclosed quasi-private spaces, providing women with a sense of freedom and equality. The findings also challenge the homogenizing dimensions of Anglo-American theory on authenticity of postmodern public spaces and highlight the opportunities in learning from international studies.

ACKNOWLEDGMENTS

This research was supported by generous grants from the University of Missouri–Kansas City, the American Association of University Women, and the Association of American Geographers.

REFERENCES

Appadurai, Arjun. 1996. *Modernity at Large: Cultural Dimensions of Globalization.* Minneapolis: University of Minnesota Press.

Balzac, Honoré de. 1837. *Physiologie du Mariage, ou Méditations de Philosophie Éclectique, sur le Bonheur et le Malheur Conjugal.* Brussels: Meline, Cans et Compagnie.

Banerjee, Tridib and Anastasia Loukaitou-Sideris. 1992. *Private Production of Downtown Public Open Space: Experiences of Los Angeles and San Francisco.* Los Angeles: University of Southern California.

Baudelaire, Charles. 1995. *The Painter of Modern Life and Other Essays*. London: Phaidon.

Bauman, Zygmunt. 1994. "Desert Spectacular." Pp. 138–157 in *The Flâneur*, edited by Keith Tester. London: Routledge.

Bayat, Asef. 2010. "Tehran: Paradox City." *New Left Review* 66:99–122.

Benjamin, Walter. 1999. *The Arcades Project*. Translated by Howard Eliland and Kevin McLaughlin. Cambridge, MA: Harvard University Press.

Bondi, Liz. 2003. "Empathy and Identification: Conceptual Resources for Feminist Fieldwork." *ACME* 2:64–76.

Bourdieu, Pierre. 1984. *Distinction: A Social Critique of the Judgment of Taste*. Cambridge, MA: Harvard University Press.

Crawford, Margaret. 1992. "The World in a Shopping Mall." Pp. 3–30 in *Variations on a Theme Park: The New American City and the End of Public Space*, edited by Michael Sorkin. New York: Hill and Wang.

Day, Kristen. 1999. "Introducing Gender to the Critique of Privatized Public Space." *Journal of Urban Design* 4(2):155–178.

de Certeau, Michel. 1984. *The Practice of Everyday Life*. Berkeley: University of California Press.

D'Souza, Aruna and Tom McDonough, eds. 2006. *The Invisible Flâneuse?: Gender, Public Space and Visual Culture in Nineteenth Century Paris*. Manchester, UK: Manchester University Press.

Ferguson, Harvie. 1992. "Watching the World Go Round: Atrium Culture and the Psychology of Shopping." Pp. 21–40 in *Lifestyle Shopping: The Subject of Consumption*, edited by Rob Shields. London: Routledge.

Gluck, Mary. 2003. "The Flâneur and the Aesthetic: Appropriation of Urban Culture in Mid-19th-Century Paris." *Theory Culture and Society* 20(5):53–80.

Goffman, Erving. 1959. *The Presentation of Self in Everyday Life*. Garden City, NY: Doubleday.

Hugo, Victor. 1884. *Les Misérables*. New York: Carleton.

Judd, Dennis. 1995. "The Rise of the New Walled Cities." Pp. 144–165 in *Spatial Practices*, edited by Helen Ligget and David Perry. Thousand Oaks, CA: Sage.

Lefebvre, Henri. 1991. *The Production of Space*. London: Blackwell.

McDowell, Linda. 1992. "Doing Gender: Feminism, Feminists and Research Methods in Human Geography." *Transactions: Institute of British Geographers* 17:399–416.

Morawski, Stefan. 1994. "The Hopeless Game of Flânerie." Pp. 181–197 in *The Flâneur*, edited by Keith Tester. London: Routledge.

Pollock, Griselda. 1988. *Vision and Difference: Femininity, Feminism and the Histories of Art*. London: Routledge.

Salcedo, Rodrigo. 2003. "When the Global Meets the Local at the Mall." *American Behavioral Scientist* 46(8):1084–1103.

Shields, James W. 1990. "The American Mall: Towards a Corporate Control of 'Public' Space." *Urbanism* 3:34–39.

Shields, Rob, ed. 1992. *Lifestyle Shopping: The Subject of Consumption*. London: Routledge.

Soja, Edward W. 2003. *Postmodern Geographies: The Reassertion of Space in Critical Social Theory*. 8th ed. New York: Verso.

Sorkin, Michael, ed. 1992. *Variations on a Theme Park: The New American City and the End of Public Space*. New York: Hill and Wang.

Tester, Keith, ed. 1994. *The Flâneur*. London: Routledge.

Trivundža, Ilija Tomanić. 2011. "Dragons and Arcades: Towards a Discursive Construction of the Flâneur." Pp. 71–81 in *Critical Perspectives on the European Mediasphere*, edited by Ilija Tomanić Trivundža, Nico Carpentier, Hannu Nieminen, Pille Pruulmann-Venerfeldt, Richard Kilborn, Ebba Sundin, and Tobias Olsson. Ljubljana, Slovenia: ECREA.

Wilson, Elizabeth. 1995. "The Invisible Flâneur." Pp. 59–79 in *Postmodern Cities and Spaces*, edited by Sophie Watson and Katherine Gibson. London: Blackwell.

Wolff, Janet. 1985. "The Invisible Flâneuse: Women and the Literature of Modernity." *Theory Culture and Society* 2(3):27–46.

Zukin, Sharon. 2003. *Point of Purchase: How Shopping Changed American Culture*. New York: Routledge.

6

The Doughnut Hole Experience

Using a Discerning Eye while Walking in Cities

MARLESE DURR

The Café au Lait City and Neighborhoods

Walking is an activity that reveals and isolates emergent forms of stratified, segregated, and gendered social interaction and/or locations in our daily routines. Citizens are able to see changes in city neighborhoods and downtowns that possess walkable café au lait neighborhoods, localities near the "doughnut hole," the geographic center, of a poverty-ridden city surrounded by prosperous suburbs, brought about by gentrification (Larsen 2005). Walking through such neighborhoods there is a realization that cities are no longer molded by deindustrialization or divided by race and structural poverty of the 1970s (Birch and Wachter 2009). American cities have taken on a new face as public transportation (the bus line) runs adjacent to new walkable neighborhoods. However, in many instances, as we walk we casually note, then dismiss, this social phenomena. We admire the beauty of such neighborhoods and changes in the city center, and often questions are not raised or triggered about the character of contemporary social life in such spaces. As gentrification has become the established way to revitalize neighborhoods and downtowns, walking presents the opportunity to examine the interface between municipal urban development and citizen revitalization of neighborhoods. Dayton, Ohio, is not unlike many American cities where gentrification has taken place and may be still ongoing despite the economic recession. It is the sixth largest city in Ohio, according to the U.S. Department of Census in 2012, has a homeownership rate of 48 percent, and boasts fourteen historic districts within the confines of the city. Most neighborhoods surround or have a bus line that runs adjacent to the city.

Yet Dayton is unlike the Portland community spoken about by Drew (2012). There are no cross-racial discussions about social or racial problems, nor does antiracist place making occur. Residents' concern and sentiments are about their living spaces expressed through manicured streets and pristine blocks of housing in the city's urban core. Despite the beautification of such neighborhoods, walkers see residents' feelings about safety, minus bars or gates on windows and doors, but plenty of dogs and surveillance camera signs. The neighborhoods have become havens for many to the exclusion of others, despite their link to public transportation.

As citizens walk through these neighborhoods to bus stops in the "doughnut hole," despite the locals' smooth complexions and transforming sexual orientation, walkers notice an almost nonexistent racial blending, signaling residents are fearful. For some, walkers, especially if they are African American, are intruders if their dress, language, and deportment are a mismatch to what residents believe to be appropriate. Although not openly spoken, they are concerned the walkers are not white and middle to upper middle class. Nevertheless, as neighborhood development matures, citizens' sentiments regarding safety, public space, and city-neighborhood revitalization are embraced and manifested through their apprehension centered on public transportation—riding the bus—possibly because of the loss of the center city's loss of vibrancy. Many local specialty businesses have closed, because they believe black people standing at bus stops are running away potential customers. Thus, many of Dayton's historic neighborhoods have built distinct boundaries around their residences in the city through via elements of defensible space, that is—plush natural landscaping, low iron fences, a series of one-way entry and exits, and speed bumps.

Massey, Rothwell, and Domina (2009) argue that class segregation has increased while race desegregation is improving alongside housing discrimination. This is an engaging and cogent point, given that most of these neighborhoods have bus lines running through restored neighborhoods with Victorian, Tudor, Colonial, Foursquare, and Cotswold Cottage–style homes dating back to the 1800s. Gentrification, America's newest form of residential segregation, reverses the twentieth-century geographic diffusion of racial/ethnic minorities and uses spatial organization of cities and residents to determine citizens and interaction based on race, class, gender, and sexuality. Another thread of this argument is that class and race segregation will increasingly reflect "political decisions about land use" (Massey, Rothwell, and Domina 2009). Political land use decisions will continue to contribute to place-based stratification and inequality (Lobao, Hooks, and Tickamyer 2007; Massey, Rothwell, and Domina 2009), but also of local growth machines as well as the economy of place (Logan and Molotch 1990) where economic regions and labor markets compete with political and economic interests (for example, local businesses, municipal governments, school districts, and planning districts) designing the local growth of cities. The real estate interests of the occupants of such neighborhoods are important in shaping the city neighborhoods as the homes gain value.

Possibly influenced by Robert Putnam (2000), citizens within these neighborhoods are engaged politically from voting to neighborhood cleanups and picnics to attending public land zoning meetings, serving on city government committees, and working within political parties. They are civically engaged. Such citizens and their neighborhoods are gaining social capital based on their social interactions with one another.

I live in one of these neighborhoods. For me, walking through my and other nearby historic districts to the bus stop has allowed me the opportunity to pay close attention to the social interaction and development of such neighborhoods. It was a good thing to a new member of the community. It was beautiful and also walkable like upstate New York. As many women walked as men did, in twos and sometime threes, segregated by race but not always by gender as I made the morning trek. Although not quite one of them yet, I was happy for the company.

For weeks, from late August until early September, I walked alone. However, I heard snippets of conversation and found that many walkers lived on my street or on the two streets contiguous to mine. I had recognized many from the neighborhood, even one or two persons who worked where I did, and I was particularly surprised that the women who had seen me in the neighborhood never spoke, smiled, nodded, or acknowledged my existence. If women walked alone during the early morning, they hurried rather than walked leisurely. I was speechless. I always felt that women were more personable. If men walked alone, they maintained their regular walking pace, but, like the women, they never smiled, nodded, or spoke despite my smiles and nods when I thought I could be seen. I thought, *Speaking costs nothing*, as my grandmother would say. But it appeared there was cost from these walkers. I thought, *So much for integration and getting to know one another.* Still, I wondered, *I am clean, don't look drugged or "feened" out; my hair is neatly pressed; I speak good English and work at a university, but nothing—even from colleagues.* Then my thoughts turned to the feminist alliance between white women and women of color, in which they worked together as confederates in a purposeful and deliberate fashion for social change. But, I decided, the 1980s changed that. Only later did I find out that my neighborhood was composed of a majority of same-sex partners, many of whom worried about gay bashing. Nevertheless, just as I made these observations, the African American walkers, first women and then men, began to wait for me and we all became walking partners. We made sure to speak and laugh softly, no outbursts of surprise or excitement. We wanted to fit in and make sure our behavior fit our social space and location. I wondered why but never questioned further because I enjoyed the comradery. More importantly, the exercise was good.

An additional benefit was that I made friends, learned more about the city, and assisted fellow walkers and riders with queries about paying their bills online or who to call in city hall about water bills. Often I conversed with several riders about how to get energy (utility) assistance or about their vacations (family reunions) in New York City, Atlanta, Newark, or Philadelphia, where many have relatives. I looked forward to hearing, "Hey, Doc, can you help with this?" or "What do you know about shopping in New York City?" Where many riders used to be surprised that I walked and rode the bus, it gradually became a given, and many asked where I had been when they did not meet me on our walk to the bus stop or if I did not ride the bus for a day or two. The camaraderie filled me with joy because I was one of them. Many times I said to myself, especially after hearing the virtues of driving and the woes of parking, *This service is great. It's as quick as a subway and almost always on time. Walking and riding the bus is fine with me.*

As I took my twenty-minute walk at 7:00 A.M., from my neighborhood to the city center, Third and Main, to catch the bus to work, I found myself in the middle of scores of people. The crowd was divided between high schoolers and people going to work. George, my walking partner, a man of Bahamian descent, said, "Walking saves me parking expenses" as he talked to me and a few others he had come to know. He never spoke about the neighborhoods we walked through except to say, "They are too expensive for my blood." As we walked, I wondered aloud why so many students were at a series of the bus stops. Marva, the third member of our group, replied, "They get here as early as 6:30 A.M. because Dayton is a school desegregation city and they travel throughout the city to school." I said, "OK" and wondered what this was like since I attended school in the Northeast and this was not part of my experience. I walked to a neighborhood school. In fact, I thought about the scores of people I knew in upstate New York who walked to work along with students. I thought, *What happened to a 9:00 A.M. to 3:00 P.M. school day?*

Getting off the bus and walking about four blocks, huddled next to the façades of local business, were multiracial groups of Jehovah Witnesses Pioneers giving away, rather than getting, a donation for *Watchtower* magazine. Next to them were African American men selling incense and oils, and sometimes jewelry, books, and articles of clothing. I always smiled when I saw this and thought, *It reminds me of the city, New York City* (Duneier 1999). The people were vibrant and full of life. They talked, laughed, joked, sold, and made the best of their day as they moved from one segment of their lives to another. For example, many started the day by "funking through the morning," listening to music on iPods. Others told loudly spoken amusing stories, while local missionaries and self-appointed prophets regaled the crowd with scriptures from the Bible and the Lord's return. Still others took on the role of the local "Black Dispatch," providing the riders with news in the lives of the citizenry who may or may not be personal acquaintances, by highlighting who had been arrested, relationships that had ended, who was sick, and who to watch out for. As I walked by, "good mornings" abounded.

Another group subtly mixed in with commuters: homeless men and women—usually more men than women, often asking for a cigarette or money for coffee or to catch the bus. They were never rude or belligerent. When I said, "I do not have any change," they would say, "Thank you" and move on.

Once I knew their names and got used to their daily appearance, I inquired about their whereabouts if they were missing for more than a few days. It was common to hear, "Have you seen Joe or Sandy? It's been a few days." Finally, businessmen and businesswomen strolled past, never saying good morning or giving a smile. I thought, *This is because some homeless people are in the crowd*, and just shrugged it off. But when talking to Bebe, our hub transfer partner, I learned that citizens feel this corner is dangerous, and most never use "public transportation." She stated, "I and most people prefer private transportation." She continued, "Aren't you afraid 'they' will mug you? I mean, you catch the bus so early. You wear nice clothes and sometimes carry cash. Girl! You need to get a car." I thought, *She might be right, because my briefcase is beginning to get heavy*, but never did it occur to me to stop catching the bus. I was at home with the people who dotted the four corners that walked to and waited for the bus.

Others would ask me the same thing when they found out where I worked and took the bus. I responded, "I don't mind taking the bus. I am not nervous or scared." Invariably, the conversation would turn to driving. Joe, another hub transfer partner, would start with, "Driving, it's a different kind of independence. You can come and go as you please." I asked my neighbor Terry why people look at you strangely when you say you take the bus. He responded, "It's like not being a man or a woman. It says a lot about you and who you are. When I didn't have a car for a while, I did not feel like a man." I was puzzled by this statement. I thought, *Owning a car has nothing to do with self-worth or who you believe yourself to be*. I said, "OK" and left it at that, but I silently thought, *It is the Midwest, actually the Mid-Atlantic, but maybe this is a regional thing—not to use public transportation if it can be helped*. What was clear for me was that the commuters lived in the time and space in which they were located. But things changed, slowly, to the detriment of many but to the delight of others.

The Alley: Invisible but Present

In fall 2008, the Greater Dayton Regional Transit Authority (RTA) announced changes in service, with the most significant modification being a raise in the fare and transfers no longer being free. At first the changes were small and unnoticed. But soon benches placed at or close to bus stops were removed. Complaints from local business owners about the students on the corners became louder and louder. Despite the elevated bemoaning, the four corners where I and others had waited for the bus remained the same, for a while. Riders on the corner made disparaging comments about changes and shook their heads. The transfer would cost an additional twenty-five cents. To avoid the cost of a transfer, which could get expensive, riders who took more than two buses could buy a forty-dollar monthlong bus pass. They could ride all day and night using the pass. Riders with steady jobs paid, since public transportation was reliable, for this amenity. Around this time, discussion about building a "hub" began to circulate among the riders via company workers, with promises of even better service and safer and cleaner spaces.

However, before the hub was built, the interior hallway of the bus company offices was turned into a space where riders could wait. It would help eliminate the clutter on the four corners. To many, it sounded as if they were cluttering up Main Street, but they also heard they were scaring customers away from the local businesses. However, many riders would say, "What business? It's a ghost town downtown. They have closed up all the businesses or the businesses have moved to the suburbs." They continued, "There is nowhere for us to shop in this city, no grocery stores, coffee shops, no cleaners, restaurants, or video stores, just banks." Others discussed how the bus stops were moved: "They moved the bus stops to keep us off the street to keep the business owners happy. But we frequent these stores. Are they complaining about us? Are we scaring them?" The riders were predominately, but not exclusively, African American.

However, for almost six months or more we walked to the bus stop and waited in the interior of the RTA building lobby, the temporary hub, which had become the area to wait while waiting on the bus. I noticed how benches were placed in an oblong room that was quite spacious and had several policemen walking around. Many of the walkers and riders complained that the space was cramped and smelled. The homeless had become residents of the temporary hub. Throngs of youth, not necessarily high schoolers, began to mingle through the crowd. It was noisy, but drug sales could be recognized, despite the presence of the police. Patrons became extremely nervous about the tight fit. They felt they had nowhere to run if trouble broke out, or no one to assist them if their purses were snatched or they were pickpocketed. They complained it was too close to the hub. I would hear the complaints of the patrons as they grumbled about the changes causing even more safety problems. I would overhear people say, "Somebody is going to get hurt in here" or "Watch your pocketbook—he is getting too close with you." Many persons known to have addictions were also laced in the crowd, which frightened them. I would hear that so and so was "on that stuff. Watch them . . . Don't let them get close to you."

Then the conversation would turn to young people, especially during the spring and summer months, concerning appearance and decorum, for example, loud and angry discussions on cell phones, the use of four-letter words, the "N" word, tight dresses, pants, and skirts for women, and sagging pants for the men. Mabel often said to me, "Where is their pride? Skirts too short, pants too tight, I can see their draws, if they are wearing any. Black girls and women use to have pride. My mother would have skinned me alive for dressing like that." Scat preached to the young men (and anybody listening) about pride in their dress by saying, "You look like a thug! Pull up your pants and act like you got some pride. Be a man! In my day, black men prided themselves on looking their best. I will buy you a belt if you need one. Take that rag off your head." For the most part, teens listened, spoke respectfully, and complied, but once out of eyesight, they returned their clothing to its original state. This brought about more pleas and discussions about dress and decorum. Once on the bus, male regular riders spoke sharply and loudly when teens did not relinquish seats to seniors. Jason often excused himself from conversation with us by saying, "Let me step to this kid." Then he would say, "Let this person have the seat; remember, you will be that age one day." Often I would hear, "I wonder if I was like that when I was young." They would end up smiling and saying, "Probably." For many of these riders, they were educating old-school style, and they were talking at and to the young people, praying they heard them.

In January 2007, unknown to the riders, sociologist Richard Florida spoke at a local university at the invitation of the Southwestern Ohio Council for Higher Education, who brought together a Creative Class Taskforce to form a Creative Communities Leadership Project in the greater Dayton area. It was called Dayton CREATE, an effort to revitalize the region's economic competitiveness using Florida's creative class theory to build on existing strengths and open source planning with the community. Most riders had never heard of Florida, the "creative class," or his visit to the city. But I had. I thought, *Oh, Sugar, Honey, Ice Tea, or Shit, here it comes.* I thought, *How does Florida's assertion that metropolitan regions with high concentrations of technology workers, artists, musicians, lesbians and gay men, a group he describes as "high bohemians," exhibit a higher level of economic development to these residents of the city. More important, how to explain Florida's reference to these groups of people collectively as the "creative class"?* The bus riders would see this as a signal their race was a problem and their presence was not wanted. Florida theorizes that a "creative class" cultivates an open, dynamic, personal, and professional urban environment, which attracts more creatives, as well as businesses, and capital to attract and retain high-quality talent rather than municipal government and city movers and shakers focusing on projects like sports stadiums, iconic buildings, and shopping centers, and he posits that this is a better use of a city's resources for regeneration and for long-term prosperity. Although I knew Florida's premises were a source of commendation and controversy as critiqued from social, cultural, and political perspectives by scholars, together with newspaper and magazine columnists, the city residents would not. But by the fall of 2009, the hub was built and, in advancing this project, talks had begun in earnest. All bus stops from First and Main to Fourth and Main Street were removed and riders were directed to the hub. Once again, service was cut, schedules changed, and fares rose from $1.50 to $2.00 depending on whether you purchased a bus pass or transfer. "We're in an alley. A damn alley," screamed Jerri, a sometime hub transfer partner. It brought to mind *Superfly*'s theme song performed by Curtis Mayfield: "I'm your mama, I'm your daddy; I'm that nigga in the alley . . . I'm your pusherman."

Jerri, along with others, began to speak forcefully about being seen as riffraff, rather than persons going to work and schoolchildren. They wondered out loud about businesses' claims that "they" caused a decline in their businesses, and many argued no businesses existed along the strip where they waited for their buses. Riders resented this silently spoken message. To them the one-block island was barely big enough for them to get on and off the bus. There was and is constant yelling to move to the side so that others can board the bus, but if you do not watch your step, you are run over or pushed by the group of people trying to follow the directions being yelled at them. Riders had a difficult time reading the new GPS bulletin boards. More importantly, the GPS boards announcing the arrival and departure of the buses in some instances were wrong, and buses coming and going were always late.

Evelyn said, "Its 3:33 P.M. Where is the bus? It's minus three degrees out here." Bobby replied, "It's on the way. You know it's always late." Yet fifteen minutes later, the bus still had not arrived and several of the patrons began to complain and called the RTA Ride Line to inquire where the bus was. Sarah said, "I pay fifty-five dollars a month, and the bus is always late. They promised changes would make the service better. But it's worse than it was before. By the time I get downtown, I will have missed my connection for the third time this week." Susie cried, "They treat us like trash! As though we are not responsible adults with jobs and need to be there on time." Then Jerri asserted, "This shit has got to change!"

Still every morning, Sarah, Susie, Jerri, and I walked to and waited for the bus and watched the bright blues, greens, yellows, and reds fill the sidewalk before us in the latest in fashions. As I enjoyed the fashion show and listened to discussion about hairstyles, children, and the latest events in the riders' and their friends' lives, I thought, *I hope I haven't missed my bus.* In most instances buses were on time, but often riders grumbled about the ever-changing schedule, which was either too late or too early for their purposes. But almost always there was a subtle form of anger about being subjected to the attitudes of the local public transportation service. Although it was explained to riders these changes were due to declining revenues, riders were upset about not having the timely service that they paid for. Many would walk to the next bus stop, two blocks down at a transfer point, to catch the bus. Jackson, Richard, and Lacey, among them, saying, "We don't want to be pushed and stepped on to get on the bus."

They felt ripped off by the local transit company, because fifty-five dollars a month is a lot for poor service. Kiesha said, "I pay my money and money for my two daughters; that's $165.00 a month. Something has got to change." For many, the drivers added insult to injury. They were slow, sullen, and did not care about passengers' schedules, especially if they had two or more disabled passengers in wheelchairs on the bus. Drivers were given two minutes to load wheelchair riders. If they had two, instead of four minutes it took ten or more minutes, causing serious time problems for the other passengers. For example, some buses only ran once an hour, so if you missed it by a minute, you would be late by an hour or two. This caused some of the riders to have their pay docked.

Often I heard women add up the time they walked and waited on the bus after missing their connections. One woman said:

I missed my bus to work, which meant I had to wait another forty min-
utes for the next bus after getting up at around 5:00 A.M. to walk three
blocks just to catch the bus on time. Then later that evening, the bus was
again late and I waited another forty minutes. This is happening at least
three times a week, so I am losing eighty minutes a day for three days or
240 minutes or four hours (a week) or sixteen hours a month, which is
two days' worth of sleep. If you multiply that sixteen hours across three
months, it is equal to forty-eight hours.

Sometimes I heard the riders complain that the drivers were too slow. "They
are driving very slow, and they are going to make me miss my connection, no
matter what the schedule they are working under says, I am going to be late."
But, the most angrily spoken words by some riders referred to the new regulations associated with the new hub that directed drivers on pulling away from the
curb with closed doors instructing them to not open them even if they saw customers coming to the bus after getting off one of the slow-arriving buses. Most
people screamed after missing this bus, "What happened to customer service?
They saw me coming, and they know the walkway is very crowded. I have to
push to get to the bus. They are ridiculous!" This almost always caused gnashing
of the teeth and many four-letter words. As I listened, I heard a conversation regarding these changes. Many citizens discussed the new entertainment complex
and how its owner wanted them moved off the streets as well as the Greyhound
bus complex moved to comply with business owners' wishes. Often they would
say, "Who does he think he is? Why should we be treated so shabbily?"

As I watched the many men and women run from bus to bus, I was struck
by the class of the workers. They were not white and black and middle class, like
those who use New York City subways and buses in Manhattan and Chicago;
they were black and white working poor. For many, this was their only way to
work, and they seemed to understand their circumstances. With quiet dignity,
they waited for transport, despite grumbling about being late at times. Some
even used buses to go shopping for food and other necessities. The better grocery stores and shopping centers are located outside the predominately chocolate
(African American) center. The major shopping malls do not allow the buses to
drop citizens off at the mall entrance or near the front doors. In most instances,
buses stop on streets outside the mall or on major thoroughfares that boast
heavy traffic. Potential customers, along with the workers, have to walk from
the street into the mall. Those persons employed in the malls have to take earlier
than usual buses to not be late, since their walk may be substantial. I asked a bus
company official, Jack, "Why doesn't the bus stop inside the mall near an anchor
store business?" He replied, "It's private property, and they do not want the bus
coming on the property." Bus riders vehemently argue, "They do not want black
people on the property." A recent federal court decision reported in the *Dayton
Daily News* by staff writer Doug Page in October 2013, made way for RTA to
build bus stops at the Mall at Fairfield Commons in Beavercreek, Ohio, a city

in Greene County, Ohio, but second largest suburb of Dayton. In 2011, the City Council of Beavercreek denied RTA's request to build three bus stops near this mall, despite the transit authority meeting the city's 2000 bus stop ordinance. However, in the council request denial, the council inserted additional criteria alongside a statement saying they believed that the city needed to ensure public safety and to prevent the city from incurring added costs. Leaders for Equality and Action in Dayton (LEAD) appealed this decision with the Federal Highway Administration (FHA) in 2011 and won. LEAD's success was grounded in the municipality violation of the 1964 Civil Rights Act. The federal suits findings cited the city as denying minority access to jobs, education, and medical services in the mall.

In a 5–2 vote, the Beavercreek City Council accepted the federal recommendation that the council revisit RTA application and revising its bus stop policy based on the possible loss of 10 million in FHA funds. Plans for bus stops on Pentagon Boulevard began immediately. Needless to say, the bus riders were very happy. They would no longer have to walk across a busy highway four or maybe five files away from where they worked after being dropped off the bus, miles away from the mall. Most of the bus rider were African American and worked in the local restaurants and stores in the mall. Many times I had heard in addition to they do not want black people on the property with "You know how they are. Always think we gonna steal or break into their houses or cars." This victory was talked about by many for a while. Since it made the local paper and WHIO (Channel 7 News) charged the city of Beavercreek with discrimination against the RTA, whose customers are mostly African American.

Wheelchairs and Making Your Connections

Although today buses are equipped to provide service to the disabled, a love-hate relationship exists between the regular riders and the "wheelchairs" as they are called. Riders complained that the bus was almost always late when wheelchairs ride. Most riders inwardly groaned, but Sherri cried, "Oh, shit! I am going to be late again. I am going to miss my connection. Let me call my sitter." Most times the wheelchairs caught the bus from 10:00 A.M. through the early afternoon. Their ridership was especially heavy during the first through the fifteenth of each month, check days. The riders were upset because it took the drivers so long to get these riders on the bus and in place before other riders were allowed to enter and pay their fares. These riders, like those already on the bus, complained because they also were aware that wherever they were going, if a transfer connection was involved they would be late catching their bus. Alice cried out, "Why don't they use Project Mobility? We are constantly late or missing our connections."

One of the riders on the bus, who was new to our group, stated, "They have the right to ride. It's the law." But then Robert cried, "Is it the law that they ride for a lower cost? Is it the law that the company and the drivers do not consider the other riders?" This anger was based on the fact that most riders had to pay for a monthly pass and wheelchairs were allowed to ride at a reduced rate, despite having a provision that would give them door-to-door service for where they want to go, but it costs seven dollars for a round-trip appointment. No one had any information as to why the "wheelchairs" were given a pass to ride free, but this along with their making the other riders late was very upsetting for the other passengers.

Some wheelchair riders had persons available to assist them on and off the bus. This usually made their entrance and exit go a little more smoothly. But still it ate up time. According to one driver, they were given two minutes to get the wheelchairs on the bus and strapped in place. But often it took five minutes or more depending on the size of the chair and the person. If there were two wheelchairs, which appeared to be all the bus could hold, it took ten minutes and then another five for riders waiting for the driver to finish with the wheelchairs to collect their fares and provide them with transfers. I asked Robert, a regular wheelchair, "Why don't you use Project Mobility?" He replied, "I don't get a subsidy and it costs seven dollars daily every time I use the service. It is cheaper to use the card allowing me to ride free since my income is limited." I said, "You can't argue with that!" He stated, "I know people don't think it's fair that they pay and we hold them up. But we can't afford to pay what they ask. If you have to go to three doctor's appointment is one week, that's twenty-one dollars, and if you need to go to two more appointments next week, that is fourteen dollars or twenty-eight dollars. It adds up." Still, a love-hate relationship exists between the paying riders and the wheelchairs. Where Robert was very aware of the costs to other riders, others like Nancy shouted at riders who groaned about missing their bus or being late, "It's too damn bad. You will have to wait until I get on and off. Take an earlier bus, and then you won't be late. " Her words made the riders angrier.

Street Vendors and the New Hub

Vendors used to be part of the pleasure of walking to the bus stop downtown. They were always there with a smile and bit of conversation to lure in customers, but no longer. The hub and its managers no longer allow direct contact with the people to sell their wares. Before construction of the hub, RTA managers did not have control of the space where vendors sold their wares. Unlike New York City, they did not have tables of products, but walked up and down the crowd asking if you wanted to purchase oils or incense. Now they sit on benches across the street from the hub. These venders range in age from thirty-five to sixty and feel that their way of making money has been taken away with the building of the hub and the various private property signs posted in the hub area. When talking with Zafir, a man about sixty-five, he says:

I can only go in the hub when I am catching the bus to go home or to come downtown. They will not allow me to sit on the benches inside the prop-

erty and sell incense. They say its private property and I am not allowed to be in there unless I am using the services. So, I send out the word I am sitting across the street. But because of the new schedules and rules for the drivers, many of my former customers don't come over. They are afraid they will miss their bus.

Others were angry at the aggressive stance taken by the RTA, which requested policemen to patrol the area along with RTA ambassadors (mostly African American males), who provided direction, but mostly security to move the crowd through the hub.

Hub Central's Plaza Customers

Within the hub there are a couple of convenience stores and eateries, and an ample amount of benches and tables for customers to sit and eat. Yet most of the time, people just sat at the benches and talked. Few, if any, people purchased food, except when they thought they were going to be asked to leave the hub, or seniors who populated this short-term gathering place to enjoy each other's company. I noticed that a store that was a favorite of early morning walkers to the bus stop was gone. Dottie, a rider who knew the owner well, said, "Dick says RTA is trying to run him out of business. They did not offer him a chance to bid for the space close to the door where the buses arrive, nor did they offer to let him sell the bus passes." I thought this could be because they had made a decision to close off part of the building, the part that his store was located in, but one entrance was left open, so people could enter that way. I wondered about Dottie's comments.

One of the stores now sells the monthly bus passes, since RTA for a time no longer has a cashier at a window to purchase passes. Recently they put in a machine where you can buy a bus pass, but many people are concerned that if the machine malfunctions, they will be out their money as well as a pass. Others are concerned about using the machines because of the number of people who mill around and feel they may have their wallets or purses snatched or become the victims of pickpockets. Senior riders have become accustomed to teens ignoring the signs posted throughout the buses that the front seats should be given to them or the handicapped. The teens don't move, and the bus drivers do not ask them to. Despite these problems, RTA feels that they have the situation under control. Within the hub are several small businesses that sell coffee, pop, lottery tickets, cigarettes, pizza, and submarine sandwiches. However, they are cash-and-carry businesses.

You could not use a credit card in some stores because of the fear of crime. Most of the businesses were frequented by teens and most of them were white-owned. This caused the riders to question why no black businesses had been able to purchase space in the hub, especially when the majority of the customers were black. Yet they remained calm about the situation, since they were unable to do much about that.

Fear of the Hub

The new hub has been touted as being the solution to the problem of students on the street fighting, yelling, using foul language, and the like. The construction of the hub makes it difficult for anyone other than the riders to eliminate problems if heavily crowded. Police have to struggle to part the crowd as arguments among teens frequently escalate into fights. The police seemed to be missing in action as bus company employees (mostly African Americans) rushed in to break up fights. For many it was ironic that most of the bus company employees controlling the traffic flow and the crowd were African American. One employee, a black woman, patrolled the crowd of "kids," as they were referred as, to keep order. She would yell, "Stop blocking people's path" or "Break it up" when an altercation appeared to be in the making. Although most students complied, some grumbling occurred. Many times I saw this woman break up disputes and pull the teens aside, at least those who would listen. Over the years, around 4:00 P.M., it has always been her who has taken charge of the corner, now the hub. This woman displayed an aggressive "I'm your mama," moving her head and shaking her finger attitude. She used this same bravado when she went up against the hard-core students who felt she was a nuisance. In some instances I saw men accompany her, but most of the time it was her who held the line. Until recently, when she was threatened.

Like Nicole Fleetwood (2004), Elijah Anderson (1990), Michel de Certeau (1984), and Erving Goffman (1973) posit, places such as public transit are noted as a particular site where black youth engage with adults' fears and with media representations of youth and racialized bodies as threats to the social order and safe spaces. How are adults' perceptions and black youths' actions and responses shaped by a social construction of racialized youth as deviant? The media stereotypes continue to portray black youth as criminals. The public arena becomes a material space for youth to reify and contest through social performance the construction of youthful and racialized identities as deviant and threatening. I continue to watch and listen since the more things change, the more they stay the same. Despite riders paying a higher fare, the service they receive is still poor. They are spoken to in a brusque manner and remain hostage to the bus company.

Conclusion

Walking has provided me the opportunity to watch the interaction, social segregation, and isolation that takes place at the center of the city. What I have found is that as the city becomes a more beautiful place to live, more frustration is brought about by the municipal changes that are part of the gentrification and retrofitting of the city. The working poor, black and white, seem to be caught in the malaise of social change. I now drive, and it would be impossible to see the problems associated with public transportation and individual discomfort.

Despite the location of the hub, it is clearly part of the changing neighborhood in which I reside. At the nexus of these problems is the "undesirable men and women," who many feel are making the core of the city uninhabitable, just going to work.

REFERENCES

Anderson, Elijah. 1990. *Streetwise: Race, Class, and Change in an Urban Community.* Chicago: University of Chicago Press.

Birch, Eugénie L. and Susan M. Wachter. 2009. "The Shape of the New American City." *Annals of the American Academy of Political and Social Science* 626(1):6–10.

de Certeau, Michel. 1984. *The Practice of Everyday Life.* Berkeley: University of California Press.

Drew, Emily. 2012. "'Listening through White Ears': Cross-Racial Dialogues as a Strategy to Address the Racial Effects of Gentrification." *Journal of Urban Affairs* 34(2):99–115.

Duneier, Mitchell. 1999. *Sidewalk.* New York: Farrar, Straus and Giroux.

Fleetwood, Nicole. 2004. "'Busing It' in the City: Black Youth, Performance, and Public Transit." *Drama Review* 48(2):33–48.

Goffman, Erving. 1973. *The Presentation of Self in Everyday Life.* Woodstock, NY: Overlook.

Larsen, Kristin. 2005. "New Urbanism's Role in Inner-City Neighborhood Revitalization." *Housing Studies* 20(5):795–813.

Lobao, Linda M., Greg Hooks, and Ann R. Tickamyer. 2007. *The Sociology of Spatial Inequality.* Albany: State University of New York Press.

Logan, John R. and Harvey L. Molotch. 1990. *Urban Fortunes: The Political Economy of Place.* Berkeley: University of California Press.

Massey, Douglas S., Jonathan Rothwell, and Thurston Domina. 2009. "The Changing Bases of Segregation in the United States." *Annals of the American Academy of Political and Social Science* 626(1):74–90.

Page, Doug. 2013. "Beavercreek Council Approves RTA Bus Stops." 14 October. Retrieved May 30, 2015. http://www.daytondailynews.com/news/news/beavercreek-council -approves-rta-bus-stops/nbNpj/.

Putnam, Robert D. 2000. *Bowling Alone: The Collapse and Revival of American Community.* New York: Simon and Schuster.

III

Social Class

U rban researchers and theorists have much discussed the ways that social class manifests differences and distinctions in public space, including how people across class groups act and interact in public spaces and the extent to which urban public spaces are open to people in different class locations, as well as differences in mobility patterns and practices. Although there are differences in the structure of class stratification in different contemporary societies, all capitalist societies contain class distinctions that manifest significant differences in ways of living and substantial inequalities of power. These differences and inequalities differentiate urban public space.

Both Charles Suchar (1988, 1993) and Judith DeSena (2009, 2012) note that in gentrifying neighborhoods there are signs of multiple groups in uneasy coexistence. Suchar photographed gentrifying neighborhoods in Chicago and Amsterdam. Speaking of residents in these changing spaces, he observes, "Their identities as groups are colored by how they view members of other resident groups . . . but also how they view the changing material and physical transformations made to the community by members of such groups" (1993:50). DeSena arrives at the same conclusion, using the concept of "parallel play" to explain how the gentry and working class get along, for the most part, without assimilating. She observes, "The gentry create a parallel culture that coexists with the established local culture of immigrant and working-class residents" in Greenpoint, Brooklyn (2012:82).

Another important indicator of the social class status of urban spaces concerns the built environment and the ways that it mediates social interaction. Jerome Krase and Timothy Shortell (2013) demonstrate the visibility of the recent financial crisis in New York City by examining signs of distress in neighborhoods most affected by foreclosure. Changes in the physical space, such as boarded-up buildings and abandoned lots, communicate distress and therefore class location. But the housing crisis produced indirect effects, as well, in the ways that residents reacted to the foreclosures. "Foreclosures stress neighborhoods more than just the financial distress of the families affected. Abandoned and boarded up buildings become signifiers of poverty, which stigmatizes the surrounding area. . . . Neighbors often try particularly hard to undo the stigmatization by maintaining and beautifying their own property" (Krase and Shortell 2013:200).

The built environment and social interaction are equally important aspects of the experience of everyday social class. When urban dwellers become aware of differences in spaces, they perceive stratification, whether or not they understand it explicitly in those terms. Some spaces are exclusionary for ordinary (especially poorer) urban dwellers. Others are nominally public but are designed, whether officially or by the patterns of usage of dominant groups, to discourage interclass interactions. We might think of these spaces as the opposite of the "cosmopolitan canopies" that Elijah Anderson (2011) discussed, played out on the class dimension.

Everyday mobility is an important, though too often unexamined, part of how class stratification is experienced in the vernacular urban landscape. The use of private or public transportation is one important sorting mechanism. As a result, the public spaces around forms of transportation themselves become effectively segregated by class. Being a pedestrian in certain neighborhoods at certain times of the day is also a visible indicator of class. Looking out of place is possible, in fact, only to the extent that urban dwellers expect particular public places to be dominated by particular classes (and, of course, the other dimensions that intersect with social class). This kind of everyday mobility can prompt the explicit exercise of power, as when police question pedestrians who look "out of place."

The chapters in this part use walking methods to explore gentrification and how it relates to various aspects of urban space. At the same time, the research describes how class is manifest, in part, in the ways that people use and move around and through particular urban spaces. Michelle Hall uses a walking method to investigate a residential suburb of Melbourne in Chapter 7. She employs walking as a means of experiencing the "throwntogetherness" of two particular places. This quality, applied from Massey (2005), creates the conditions in which urban dwellers form an attachment to place that is specifically a neighborhood-based community. The places of anchoring and of exposure refer specifically to the ways that mobility relates to sociability; it calls to mind the notion of fixed points and flows identified by the Situationists in their explorations of Paris (Shortell and Aderer 2014).

In Chapter 8, Judith N. DeSena describes the link between quotidian mobility and gentrification in Greenpoint, Brooklyn. She demonstrates how parallel play in the neighborhood results in what we might call "parallel mobility." There is a different form of sociability in the walking patterns of gentry and working-class residents.

In Chapter 9, Kristen A. Williams brings tools from cultural anthropology, planning, and performance studies to investigate a development of public space in Providence, Rhode Island, in terms of "walkability." Despite the optimism of the public relations materials for the development, the space falls short of its goal of creating a democratized public place. This failure represents an important quality of urban public space, the ways that inequality differentiates—encouraging some kinds of accessibility for some groups and discouraging others.

Interestingly, these three chapters reveal some of the variation in auto-ethnography. There is a clear connection between walking and ethnographic observation, and especially reflexive observation (Carabelli 2014; Krase 2014). It is also a warning, of sorts, to interested urban researchers: Walking is a good way to get to know urban space, but the meanings of places and practices is fully revealed by familiarity and intimacy, and these require time—and a lot of walking.

REFERENCES

Anderson, Elijah. 2011. *The Cosmopolitan Canopy: Race and Civility in Everyday Life.* New York: Norton.
Carabelli, Giulia. 2014. *"Gdje si?* Walking as Reflexive Practice." Pp. 191–206 in *Walking in the European City: Quotidian Mobility and Urban Ethnography,* edited by Timothy Shortell and Evrick Brown. Farnham, UK: Ashgate.
DeSena, Judith N. 2009. *Gentrification and Inequality in Brooklyn: New Kids on the Block.* Lanham, MD: Lexington Books.
———. 2012. "Gentrification in Everyday Life in Brooklyn." Pp. 65–88 in *The World in Brooklyn: Gentrification, Immigration, and Ethnic Politics in a Global City,* edited by Judith N. DeSena and Timothy Shortell. Lanham, MD: Lexington Books.
Krase, Jerome. 2014. "Walking in Search of Migrants in European Cities." Pp. 153–172 in *Walking in the European City: Quotidian Mobility and Urban Ethnography,* edited by Timothy Shortell and Evrick Brown. Farnham, UK: Ashgate.
Krase, Jerome, and Timothy Shortell. 2013. "Seeing New York City's Financial Crisis in the Vernacular Landscape." Pp. 188–217 in *Cities and Crisis: New Critical Urban Theory,* edited by Kuniko Fujita. London: Sage.
Massey, Doreen. 2005. *For Space.* London: Sage.
Shortell, Timothy and Konrad Aderer. 2014. "Drifting in Chinatowns: Toward a Situationist Analysis of Polyglot Urban Spaces in New York, Paris, and London." Pp. 109–128 in *Walking in the European City: Quotidian Mobility and Urban Ethnography,* edited by Timothy Shortell and Evrick Brown. Farnham, UK: Ashgate.
Suchar, Charles S. 1988. "Photographing the Changing Material Culture of a Gentrified Community." *Visual Sociology* 3(2):17–12.
———. 1993. "The Jordaan: Community Change and Gentrification in Amsterdam." *Visual Sociology* 8(1):41–51.

7

"Just Going Down the Street"

Constructing Community through Everyday Movements

MICHELLE HALL

his chapter focuses on the experience of walking through the ordinary public spaces of a neighborhood and considers the ways these often mundane and routinized patterns of movement may be layered into a construction of a sense of place. The chapter explores the manner in which everyday movements may operate as a locus for what Doreen Massey (2005) has termed the throwntogetherness of space. Drawing on this theorization, and Ash Amin's (2007, 2008) related application to collective culture, the aim of this chapter is to explore the relation between the throwntogetherness of ordinary public spaces as experienced when moving through them, and identification with neighborhood-based community.

To do so, I draw on my everyday movements in and through the main street and shopping center of my inner-city Melbourne neighborhood, Northcote. Both include a series of quasi-public spaces that connected into a larger public space by footpaths, roadways, and the movement of people through them. Separately these spaces seem to appeal to, and communicate, different elements of the neighborhood's diverse population and fragmented identity. However, when viewed through the trajectories of my movements, the physical, social, and symbolic elements of these spaces can be seen to be thrown together in ways that build layers of emplaced meaning into these ordinary "just going down the street" experiences.

Throwing Together the Situated Multiplicity
of Exposure Realms in Public Space

This chapter draws on research that explored the ways we experience neighborhood-based community within the contemporary city, and that had a particular focus on the manner in which this experience of belonging is held together by imagination, communicative acts, and emotional responses. As argued by theorists such as John Urry (2000), and Amin and Nigel Thrift (2002), within contemporary cities our human relations are entangled with visible and hidden flows: of objects, history, symbolism, memories, and time. This confluence is well captured in Massey's (2005) concept of space as a throwntogetherness, a term that describes the ways the trajectories of these elements come together in a moment of negotiation, and are then dispersed, at different times, speeds, and directions. For Massey this throwntogetherness means that places are not fixed; instead, they are best understood as a collection of stories-so-far whose meaning is generated through these moments of negotiation. That is, it is the manner in which we make sense of the coming together of these varying spatialities and temporalities that emplaces meaning (Massey 2005). In this chapter, I explore what this may mean for the way we understand neighborhood-based community.

To do so I draw on Amin's (2007, 2008) exploration of the collective potential of the throwntogetherness of public space. Drawing on Massey's theory, Amin (2008) argues that when visibly manifest as an unconstrained circulation of multiple bodies in shared space, our negotiations of throwntogetherness may generate a social ethos with potentially strong civic connotations. To examine the ways that this multiplicity is experienced, and could be supported, Amin (2008) describes a series of elements, termed resonances, which condition social action in ways that he calls social reflexes. These resonances include the situated multiplicity, territorialization, emplacement, emergence, and symbolic projection. According to Amin, these can generate reflexes that include tolerance of the multiplicity, spatial ordering, and symbolic compliance. For example, through resonances such as territorialization and emplacement, we pattern and domesticate public space, both spatially and temporally. As previously noted in relation to norms of public space interaction (for example, Goffman 1963; Lofland 1998), the spatial ordering this reflexively generates reduces (or tames) some of the threats associated with the surplus, such as the anxiety and confusion long associated with the urban crowd. The civic potential of this kind of domesticated ordering has been demonstrated in research on light touch sociality, or "rubbing along," which has been shown to support the habituation of difference in ways that build tolerance between cultural and ethnic groups (for example, Watson 2006; Wise 2011).

Conversely, spatial ordering also allows for an appreciation of the disruptions or surprises that continually emerge from the multiplicity. These emergences can work to create novelty, even in familiar spaces, by introducing the possibility of new rhythms and unexpected encounters that stimulate our senses and contribute to the vibrancy of the multiplicity. Such emergences can include physical disruptions, those arising through everyday sociality, as well as more performative expressions of identity, such as festivals and flash mobs (for example, Stevens 2007; Watson 2006). Finally, the symbolic projections of physical and aesthetic elements, such as architecture, advertising, and the cultural displays of users, can subtly shape patterns of behavior, and attributions of identity (Amin 2008).

However my research is interested not only in fleeting moments of public space sociality but also the manner in which these may come together over time to represent an experience of neighborhood-based community. That is, how these processes of spatial ordering, tolerance of multiplicity, and symbolic compliance are thrown together into an evolving story of place. To do so, I draw on Veronique Aubert-Gamet and Bernard Cova's (1999) exploration of the ways consumption spaces support the development of community, and their argument that shared consumer experiences offer opportunities for the development of shared identifications. Drawing on established notions of spaces as closed and open, Aubert-Gamet and Cova proposed quasi-public spaces may operate as sites of anchoring and exposure. Anchoring sites are those in which established communities reinforce their connections—the shops, bars, and cafés that Ray Oldenburg (1999) celebrates as third places. Exposure sites are more open, but still safe spaces, where similar to Amin's situated multiplicity, individuals are exposed to the identification practices of others in ways that involve limited risk. In sites of exposure the individual is neither exactly at home nor in the home of others (Aubert-Gamet and Cova 1999), suggesting the potential for openness to the kinds of disruptions and emergences that Amin (2008) argues may activate the social ethos of the throwntogetherness. Returning to Massey (2005), who argues that the meaning of *here* that is generated through such negotiations is both spatial and temporal, I suggest that the mundane and repeated use of exposure spaces can support a kind of layered emplacing of such moments in ways that can come to be experienced as neighborhood-based community.

To demonstrate this, the chapter focuses on my everyday experiences of being in and moving through two ordinary spaces in my neighborhood: its shopping center and its main shopping street. Both are open and lightly regulated spaces that offer potential as exposure sites. However, because of the differences in the ways the physical, social, and symbolic are thrown together in these spaces, the exposure they offer takes on distinct forms and communicates different elements of neighborhood identity. I explore the ways these experiences are thrown together through the trajectory of my regular walking route—from my house, through the shopping center, and down the main street—and consider how these movements construct moments of exposure that are experienced as neighborhood-based community. The following section provides a brief background of the neighborhood, its public spaces, and the methodology of this research. I then invite you to take a walk with me, to share in my interactions with people, objects, and symbols as they work together to construct my experiences of my neighborhood, and my sense of my place within it.

A Partial History of Northcote's Public Spaces

Northcote is a gentrifying residential suburb of approximately twenty-three thousand people in inner-city Melbourne. As with many gentrifying areas, Northcote's shifting identity is writ large within its built form and public spaces. It can be seen in the repurposing of historical buildings, the renovation of old houses, the development of new apartments on old industrial sites, and the increasing number and diversity of cafés, bars, and restaurants. These shifts are particularly evident within Northcote's two key public spaces: High Street and Northcote Plaza. These two spaces have been the focus of my research and my experiences of this neighborhood.

The High Street shopping area is the lifestyle and entertainment precinct of Northcote. It is also an important arterial road and public transport route through Melbourne's northeast. In this chapter I focus on a section of approximately seven hundred meters known as Ruckers Hill. At the time of writing, this section of around two hundred different businesses included four live music venues; five bars; and at least thirty restaurants and cafés, including those serving food from Japan, India, Sri Lanka, Vietnam, Thailand, Nepal, Mexico, Italy, and Greece. There is also designer and vintage clothing, gift and homewares stores, bookstores, children's clothing and toy stores, alternative and mainstream health services, beauticians, and hairdressers. The area also includes a pawn shop and short-term money lender, a national brand pizza takeaway, takeaway food shops selling kebabs and fish and chips, chemists, dry cleaners, an alterations shop, a small supermarket, a number of professional services such as accountants and lawyers, health services targeted at the Indigenous population, and employment services for those with disabilities, as well as a number of long-term vacant and somewhat derelict shop fronts. High Street operates as a day and night economy, with the last bar closing as late as 5:00 A.M., and the cafés opening from seven.

This diversity of architecture, business types, and hours of operation means that High Street does not project a coherent identity through its appearance and consumption offering. Instead High Street's identities are expressed through spatial and temporal clusters formed around specific landmark businesses or precincts, and times of the day and week. While some sections appear gentrified, others target particular ethnic groups or a geographical demographic. That is, while High Street displays the clearest expression of the neighborhood's gentrification, it combines this with representations of the area's broader diversity, by offering a broad range of consumption-based identification opportunities.

High Street's business offering is also shaped by its proximity to Northcote Plaza. This eighteen-thousand-square-meter enclosed shopping center was built on an old brickworks site in the early 1980s. The adjacent clay pit first served as a rubbish dump, and it is now a large park. Northcote Plaza contains more than sixty different shops, including two supermarkets; a discount department store; services such as banking and the post office; and a range of other food and retail stores, including bakeries, chemists, a newsagent, a butcher, a health food store, a key cutter, a travel agent, a pet shop, takeaway food outlets, and telecommunications retailers, plus some low-cost clothing and homewares stores and generic "two-dollar" shops. The center is open from 6:00 A.M. until midnight, with restricted access after 10:00 P.M. This allows access to the late-night supermarket, but limits the doors customers can use. It is only at these later hours that a security presence is evident.

The Plaza's everyday offering is reflected in its usage. It is consistently well patronized by a broad range of people: families, couples, people by themselves, the elderly, schoolchildren, and those from a range of ethnic backgrounds. On Saturdays, when it is cold, or raining (which is common in Melbourne), the center is bustling—often in stark contrast to the quiet High Street just beyond it. However, Northcote Plaza is not a destination mall, and it is best described as an ordinary neighborhood shopping center.

In many ways, then, the everyday consumption offering of the Plaza is complementary to the lifestyle-focused consumption offering of High Street. Indeed, these two spaces could be said to be evolving together; the Plaza's offering concentrates provisioning activities within its walls, leaving High Street businesses to target specific demographics and cultural groups. It is the interplay between the anchoring and exposure sites created within these two spaces, and the ways these may be thrown together into a construction of neighborhood identity that is of interest to this chapter.

To do so I draw on auto-ethnographic data collected from 2008 to 2010. The purpose of that investigation was to explore the relation between consumption spaces and practices, and experiences of neighborhood-based community. Following the methods of auto-ethnography described by Carolyn Ellis (2004), I recorded research memos focusing on my actions, interactions, and emotional responses, as I moved through the public and quasi-public spaces of Northcote. These memos generated a wealth of observational and experiential data that has enabled me to not only explore the ways such spaces may support or constrain neighborhood-based community but also to consider how the interplay between different spaces contributes to that process.

In this chapter I draw on these experiences to construct what Ellis (2004) calls a composite or telescoped narrative. These are used in auto-ethnography to provide insight into personal experiences whilst managing for erroneous details or repetition. In this case I am throwing together my experiences from thousands of walks down the street—a trip of twenty minutes or so—into a story of one journey. The aim of the narrative is to focus on the manner in which the physical, social, and symbolic elements of these spaces are brought together through my ordinary patterns of movement. That is, how—when moving in and through these spaces—I am constructing realms of exposure, which are themselves thrown together over multiple journeys into an evolving experience of neighborhood-based community. My story of my journey through these spaces begins, as it always does, with Northcote Plaza.

Ordinary Consumers Rubbing Along in the Plaza

The Plaza is just down the road from my house, and is a space I visit many times a week for everyday goods and services or to pass through on my way to High Street. This ordinary consumption space has become a fundamental part of the way I understand the identity of my neighborhood. It is also a site to which I now feel a great deal of attachment, as I have territorialized and emplaced the Plaza's spaces, routines, and people into my patterns of moving through my neighborhood.

Within the first few weeks of moving to the area in May 2008, I established a habitual walking route to the Plaza: down the residential streets and through one section of the adjacent park. From there I follow a footpath that leads past a basketball court and skate ramp down to the shopping center entrances. Even when I am heading to High Street beyond, I still follow this route through the park and the Plaza. It is more visually pleasing and safer than cutting through the car park that surrounds the center, and faster than following the main roads down to High Street. Mostly, however, this route is just habit: an ordering reflex that was established at a time when I was shedding the patterns of a different city and making them anew in Northcote. As noted above, spatial ordering can serve as a means of taming the uncertainty of the urban environment. In my case it also helped to re-create structure in an unfamiliar environment, one in which I had no established social networks to guide patterns of behavior or consumption space preferences.

As I enter the Plaza my wandering mind returns to the task at hand—or at least to the environment in which I am undertaking it. As is often noted of shopping centers, the design is intended to deemphasize time and climate and mask their commercial intent within a sanitized version of public space (for example, Auge 1995; Langman 1992). Despite its ordinariness, the Plaza is no different. The wide passageway I follow has a ceiling of clear glass, offering a regulated experience of the weather outside. Piped music subtly captures my attention and has me silently singing along to songs from the 1980s and 1990s that I still remember the words to as I stroll past benches, rubbish bins, potted plants, and permanent and temporary business stalls that punctuate the Plaza's public spaces. School holidays feature performances from Elvis, a magician, and Santa. However, the plans of a local musician to run performances of local independent music are less likely to come to fruition.

While these passageways may be privatized and their usage constrained, they are also full of people: walking, waiting, loitering, and people watching (see Figure 7.1). Rides and games encourage children to stop and play, forcing

Figure 7.1 Ballet of the Plaza. (Image by author)

their parents to linger while their children try to work the machines. Nearby bank automatic teller machines allow users to watch the people watchers and the children while they wait in line. Sometimes I see people I know or recognize, and we pass with a waved hello or stop for a brief chat before moving on with our shopping. Indeed this ballet of the Plaza seems to mimic what is idealized as public space sociality (for example, Jacobs 1961), where established principles of public space interaction support diverse demographic mingling and a toleration of the mostly banal multiplicity of this shopping center. And despite recognizing the superficiality of this ballet, it does not stop me from experiencing it as a meaningful display of public sociality or appreciating this as the most consistently active public space within the neighborhood.

As I continue down the passageway in the filtered sunshine, I glance into the Chinese massage shop, where customers on fold-up plastic seats receive clothed massages in full view of passersby. At times I stop for a twenty-minute neck and shoulder massage, one of the many pleasures of the Plaza that my friends and I make affectionate jokes about. Other times I try to smile at staff I think I recognize. But I am not confident I am familiar to them and feel fleetingly embarrassed because I know that I do not always sufficiently look at their faces. The smile comes out thinly. Urban theorists concerned with power relations in public spaces may argue that this attempted engagement could be read as a middle-class privilege that reduces cross-cultural engagement to a fleeting transaction (for example, Butler and Robson 2003; Valentine 2008). Yet the reduction of such a personal service to a shopping center transaction makes familiarization feel odd, and my attempts at pleasantries or to establish a practitioner-patient relationship feel awkward within that context. However at the same time, the low cost and convenience increase the frequency of my patronage, and thus also my exposure to the cultural symbols and practices that remain: the map of the body's acupuncture meridians, the plastic lucky cat with the waving hand, the business owner playing in the passageway with his grandson. Today I do not stop; however, I am pleased when one or two of the employees notice my glance and smile, and smile in response as I go by.

My passage through the Plaza also takes me past the group of elderly Greek men who regularly occupy some café tables positioned at one of the prime people-watching spots within the Plaza (see Figure 7.1). It was my growing awareness of this group of men that highlighted the importance of the Plaza to the public culture of my neighborhood, as well as my developing attachment to this space. For these men, the Plaza operates as an anchoring site where they come together to socialize and survey the comings and goings of other Plaza patrons. This type of anchoring behavior enables established communities to re-inforce social connections within public spaces, and has been recorded in shopping centers elsewhere, particularly in relation to teenagers and the elderly (for example, Sandikci and Holt 1998). However, what is less often considered is the manner in which this anchoring shapes its broader context, and the responses of those such as myself, who are exposed to but excluded from this process of collective identification.

For me, their seemingly constant presence operates as a slower-moving trajectory that symbolically marks this piece of space as something more than a site of instrumental consumption or fleeting public sociality. Their appropriation of this space—for purposes other than those projected by the decor, music, and advertising signage—is a juxtaposition that only serves to highlight the lack of hyperreality or spectacle in this overwhelmingly ordinary space. Furthermore, in their watching of me as I pass them by, I become a trajectory that moves through their world: another actor in the Plaza tableaux that is constructed through our looking. And thus in their gathering there, and in my passing by, we become objects in each other's patterning of space, which (for me at least) embeds a human element that further undermines the Plaza's symbolic inducements to consume.

Over time I have become quite attached to the Plaza's ordinariness and the sociality this supports. Through that attachment it has become more than a convenient location in which to access everyday goods and services, but also one that offers me a sense of connection to other residents of my neighborhood through our shared construction of this exposure realm. I would not claim, however, that this exposure provides me with any particular insight into the world of these Greek men whom I look forward to seeing when I pass; or of the Chinese who give massages and whom I care about being recognized by; or the parents and their children, the elderly women often sitting on benches, or any of the other types of people I see in the Plaza. Instead, as Wise (2011) similarly describes in a shopping center food court, this is mostly a banal sharing of space where all our otherness is domesticated because it is framed within the parameters of everyday consumption. However rather than lament this constrained sociality as evidence of an impoverished civic culture, or argue, as DeSena does in Chapter 8 of this volume, that this represents a kind of parallel play that limits integration, I instead suggest that this ordinary sharing of space is effective in constructing a site of exposure precisely because there is no real interaction to shatter the imagined connection that is created.

This is not to suggest, of course, that all Northcote residents bear this kind of affection toward the Plaza. I have spoken to many who disparage it for many of the same reasons that I am enamored with it. Significantly, however, this does not prevent them from using this space; this, I argue, is the key factor that underlies the Plaza's success as a space in which layered encounters can emplace a Northcote identity. That is, its instrumentality, which overrides many consumption preferences or cultural group identifications, creates an atmosphere of ordinariness that does not seek to bridge ethnic or social divides, but instead exposes us to the neighborhood's demographic diversity within a physical and symbolic environment that is designed to mask this differentiation with ordinary shopping practices. However, to appreciate the significance of this ordinary shopping center supporting everyday expressions of commonality and sociality, the Plaza needs to be considered in the context of the public space that is directly adjacent to it, Northcote's High Street. In the following section I continue my walk down High Street, to explore those differences and their cumulative effects for my experience of neighborhood-based community in Northcote.

Movement and Differentiation in High Street

Usually, after passing the group of Greek men, I would head into the supermarket for mundane necessities, and sometimes to the Italian delicatessen, or the chemist, or the health food store. Today, however, I am going to High Street, and thus continue through the Plaza and out the southwestern doors and toward Separation Street. This busy intersection marks the boundary between the Plaza and High Street, and there is little sign of Northcote's gentrification in its built form or business types. Instead the physical environment is dominated by warehouse-style buildings and discount retailers, including a discount chemist, a warehouse-style sporting goods store, an intermittently empty art deco building that is at present a twenty-four-hour gym, and the tired-looking shop space of a recently closed discount supermarket. This space is also defined by the constant flow of cars, trams, and people moving through the intersection. Occasionally I see and fleetingly smile at people I recognize. Or banter with someone who has followed the same path from the Plaza. But mostly I just wait for the traffic lights to change.

In contrast to the comforting predictability of the Plaza, High Street is a less coherent public space—one where the area's past and future unfold in fragments through its built form, consumption offerings, and range of uses. Heading from north to south, one passes through a series of areas that subtly represent different aspects of the suburb's culture and history and that offer significant contrast to the seemingly unchanging present of the Plaza. High Street communicates the ways that time and movement overlap in the production of this neighborhood in ways that the Plaza cannot. However, the representations of this identity are more likely to be expressed in built or symbolic form, as its public spaces are often devoid of people.

The lights change, and I cross the road, heading south. The business offering of this section contains little that appeals to me, and thus I rarely focus on the activities occurring within them. Instead, as I walk through this section of the street it is the physical manifestations of the area's shifting identities and temporalities that capture my attention. The slow escape of the tree from its planter box, changing the mosaic handiwork of an earlier attempt at place making into a safety risk, is made more apparent by the regular passing of trams, and the seemingly unending changes in business ownership and offering of the surrounding stores (see Figure 7.2). Three large two-story Victorian buildings, sensitively converted into offices and apartments, dominate this area. Their age, beauty, and seemingly unchanging presence is contrast with the mix of

Figure 7.2 High Street in the Past, Present, and Future. (Image by author)

late twentieth-century shop fronts that face renovation at each new business use. An organic bakery became a takeaway pizza shop and then a Vietnamese restaurant. A fashion boutique became a formal dressmaker and is now a bar. A Council notice tells me that these trees and their crumbling planter boxes will soon be removed, to be replaced with something deemed more suited to the street's current uses.

I wander onward, enjoying the rare sunshine, and enter into an area of the street that is dominated by businesses owned and patronized by the area's Greek community. The outdoor seating brings life to the footpath, and as I pass through I sometimes imagine these customers are the children and grandchildren of the men who gather in the Plaza. However these are not quaint ethnic establishments that offer opportunities to use food as a mediator between different cultural groups, as is associated with Butler and Robson's (2003) tectonic metaphor, but instead large cafés and restaurants with modern fit-outs that aim to appeal to the omnivorous nature of the Australian diner. In many ways, the ethnicity of these businesses appears secondary to their promotion of sociality as consumption based, reminding me that the Australian urban middle class is a broad demographic that shares a range of generalized consumption practices, with café culture being one of them. Yet the decor and atmosphere of these spaces don't appeal to me, and as I negotiate the footpath diners I am reminded of the specificity of my own tastes and the extent to which such preferences segment users of the street.

I continue down the street past takeaways, professional services, and a shop selling music posters. It replaced a business that, in what appeared to be a bet on the area's gentrification played too early, sold upmarket furniture and interior design elements. Nearby a small bar recently took on the name of an older pub that was knocked down for the construction of Northcote Central. The original Carters Arms served laborers from the brickworks that previously occupied the site where the Plaza now stands. The new Carters Public House seems to appeal to a relatively mainstream middle-class customer, with a mix of sports and live acoustic music and a subtly casual interior (see Figure 7.2). I wonder, as I pass, if these customers recognize this nod to history, and what the area's older residents who remember the earlier incarnation think of this reclamation. High Street is full of these moments of the future and the past coming together in this way; however, the effectiveness of these symbolic projections in constructing a broadly understood narrative of identity is less clear.

Layered over the slower-moving cycles of time created by the built form and the shifting commercial uses that give these buildings their current purpose is the daily movement of people. During peak hour, or as the nearby schools begin and end, the footpaths are alive with transiting pedestrians, while the road is a stream of trams and cars. The varying opening and closing times of the businesses add further layers, both temporally and spatially dispersing types of usage and users. During the daytime I see a group of middle-aged men gathered outside the sports betting shop to smoke cigarettes and drink beer from brown paper bags. Across the road during the evening, groups of younger men and women similarly gather outside bars and music venues to smoke cigarettes—*their* beers left inside at the insistence of the bouncer. The weather, of course, mediates all of these behaviors; this environmental imposition perhaps offering the most effective means of constructing connections between disparate groups of people as they huddle under awnings, and in limiting interaction altogether.

As I continue past the betting shop, I glance at, but do not acknowledge, a person I am familiar with from my patronage of my favorite café and bar. As I rarely see friends or acquaintances in the public spaces of High Street, one might expect I would welcome this disruption to the constrained sociality of this space. However, when removed from the identity cues and rituals of service that frame interaction within those familiar quasi-public spaces, I feel less certain of the basis of this acquaintance. This is because within the fragmented and mostly transitory space of High Street, the spatial and cultural anchors to these identifications are blurred. Is this acknowledgment based on our recognition of mutual acquaintances and shared consumption preferences established within anchoring realms? Can it be extrapolated to recognition of a broader sharing of neighborhood space? In this moment of uncertainty, I revert to norms of civil inattention and continue on my way.

This is not to suggest that High Street is devoid of interaction; instead, such interaction is more likely to reinforce its role as a space of consumption-based individual or cultural group-specific identity definition. High Street does generally feel like a space where the work required to uphold norms of public interaction seems to hover just below the surface. This is not an easy and freeing anonymity, such as offered by the Plaza, where I have little expectation of interaction with those with whom I share the space, and where I welcome it when I do. Instead, it is one that feels awkward and loaded with the expectation of primary and intimate secondary relations (Lofland 1998), both past and anticipated. Thus, as I glance into shop windows in a habit that has established routines of greeting with some businesses owners, I at times feel pleased both at the personal recognition and at its public expression. Yet at other times I consciously strive to break this habit of greeting, as if I am not certain of the altruism of my motives or feel that this public display is somehow out of place in this mostly socially expressionless space.

In part the lack of obvious sociality in High Street is due to the physical characteristics of the space itself. A busy road and rows of parked cars divide the narrow footpaths and separate pedestrian traffic in ways that can both enhance and decrease the visibility of pedestrians. Those on the other side of the road barely register, while those who share my path are difficult to ignore. However, this configuration also heightens the street's potential as one of personal display, such that patterns of movement can become markers of belonging. Simple activities such as crossing the road outside of regulated pedestrian crossings can be a moment of unintended impression management. This is because traffic flows often require pedestrians to pause in the middle of the road, displaying their presence to onlookers in cars, cafés, and on the footpaths. Sometimes it feels like a display of ownership, at other times an unwanted announcement of my movements and intentions. Nonetheless, as I pause there to wait for traffic and trams, I experience a momentary feeling of belonging, as the open space of the road allows for a more complete view of the High Street precinct and a more coherent sense of the places I have passed through. In many ways this experience sums up much of what the public spaces of High Street offer: oscillation between belonging and anonymity that is as much a product of the physical and symbolic environment as it is social.

I cross the street and enter my regular café, whose owner, staff, and some customers I have become familiar with over time. In doing so, I leave the shifting realms constructed by the multiple trajectories of this public space and enter into one that anchors me within this neighborhood, through commercial friendships, cultural group identifications, and consumption offerings that express my individual identity. It is such spaces that most clearly define the High Street experience: a collection of anchoring sites that frame its sociality according to their cultural group specificity or demographic target. This sociality is one that is mostly only glimpsed at—through shop windows, in footpath seating areas. This is less rubbing along of diverse people in public space and more reinforcing of established relationships and identifications in the sight of others. The value of High Street in this respect, then, is its ability to emplace these anchoring realms within a broader realm of exposure that offers its users the ability to continually renegotiate their relationship to its representation of the neighborhood's diversity as similar processes of differentiation. Whether that be through moments of recognition of shared practices of differentiation, embodied experiences of belonging afforded by visual cues, or of aloneness as the sole user of an empty footpath who has the knowledge that they have somewhere familiar to go.

Conclusion: Throwing Together Shared Ordinariness and Similar Difference

This chapter has drawn on my everyday movements in and through the public and quasi-public spaces of my neighborhood to explore the ways that negotiations of their physical, social, and symbolic elements may be thrown together into an experience of neighborhood-based community. To do so I have drawn on the work of Amin on the potential of multiplicity to support collective culture and Massey's theorization of space as a throwntogetherness, and sought to explore how this can be applied through Aubert-Gamet and Cova's concept of exposure sites. Research has recognized the potential for open and lightly regulated public and quasi-public spaces to support the light touch sociality of rubbing along, and civic culture in general. However, this chapter sought to explore the manner in which that exposure may construct links between different individuals or groups of people that specifically relates to a third identity—that of the neighborhood in which those spaces are situated.

In this chapter I proposed that mundane and repeated encounters with the physical, social, and symbolic elements of exposure sites may be thrown together as an evolving story of shared neighborhood identity. Then I explored the application of this through my own experiences of moving in and through my neighborhood's key public spaces, which both offer potential as realms of exposure, yet in very different ways. I sought to consider the ways that my everyday movements through these spaces supported the construction of an experience of neighborhood-based community by following the trajectory of my walking route from my house, through the Plaza, and down High Street.

As this chapter described, High Street communicates the diversity of the neighborhood through the symbolic projections of its built form, the shifting range of offerings of the businesses within it, and the ebb and flow of uses according to time of day. It is a space of movement at different speeds of time, not only because it is a busy road but also because it is in flux—like the neighborhood itself. This movement constructs geographic connections to other places, as well as to other times: older buildings are renovated, planter boxes crumble, and new business make references to the past and the future. In that respect, then, much of High Street's potential to operate as a realm of exposure relies on memory traces and symbolic projections.

High Street is also a space where the work of negotiating the throwntogetherness feels most apparent, highlighted by hoped-for disruptions that do not manifest, or that trigger a retreat into patterns of ordering, and where belonging is more likely to be experienced through embodied actions that reinforce connections to the physical and symbolic rather than the social. It is not surprising, then, that in such a context people seek to engage with people and places that are most like them, creating a series of fragmented anchoring realms that project the identities, consumption preferences, and gathering practices of the area's different demographic and cultural groups. Of course, unlike the Plaza, the diversity of High Street businesses allows this choice, supporting the expression of distinct cultural identities. At the same, this differentiation's location within specific businesses, rather than within the public spaces of the street, limits the potential for exposure in ways that may help to domesticate this diversity.

The Plaza, in contrast, provides space for a diverse range of people to be in, anonymously but together. Through its generic built form and consumption offering, it provides a stable, everyday shopping experience where ethnic and socioeconomic differences are reduced to that of ordinary Plaza consumer. As with many shopping centers, its design and symbolic projections are intended to enclose, yet in doing so the Plaza constructs a realm that is experienced as separate from the cars, parks, and weather that surround it. Instead one's senses are captured by the thoroughly ordinary situated multiplicity of this space, and the domesticated ballet of trajectories that this constructs.

Yet this space is not so constrained that it prevents breaches in its instrumentality, as the appropriation of one section by a group of elderly men for their own social purposes demonstrates. In doing so, they contribute to an experience of easy rubbing along in space that does not differentiate based on age, gender, or ethnicity, instead requiring only one's presence in the Plaza's never ending *now*. The power of this exposure realm is such that the Plaza has become a site to which I feel a great deal of attachment, as I have territorialized and emplaced its people and spaces into my construction of neighborhood-based identity.

By themselves, these spaces could be read as epitomizing the negative impacts of gentrification and the privatization of public space; they offer collective identification either in the form of the anonymity of consumption, or the specificity of a cultural group. Together, however, these public spaces communicate the area's diversity and the different cultural practices of its specific groups, while also providing a stable environment in which to share everyday behaviors and attachments. High Street provides a physical and symbolic anchor around which to build an individualized experience of Northcote, supported by the convenience of the ordinary consumption offering of the Plaza. At the same time, the Plaza's banality and lowest common denominator identification offers an experience of belonging that is contrast to the cultural group specificity of High Street consumption spaces—such that each can offer a respite from the other.

Thus rather than focus on the ways such spaces may segregate activities or people, this chapter has sought to foreground the interplay between these spaces and the ways experiences within them are combined through the habitual routes of residents, myself included. As Amin argues, our negotiations of the thrown-togetherness of the urban environment can create opportunities to construct tacit experiences of encounter and to embed meaning into place. Through my negotiations of the juxtaposition of different built forms, histories, consumption practices, and modes of gathering that are brought together through my patterns of movement, I create a series of connections: between the histories and trajectories of the Plaza and High Street, and between the different groups of people who use these spaces in the similar ways. In doing so I create my own Northcote exposure realm, manifest through a thrown together understanding of these distinct but related spaces, which I invest with a specific public culture that has come to define my experiences of and in this place.

REFERENCES

Amin, Ash. 2007. "Re-Thinking the Urban Social." *City* 11(1):100–114.
———. 2008. "Collective Culture and Urban Public Space." *City* 12(1):5–24.
Amin, Ash and Nigel Thrift. 2002. *Cities: Reimagining the Urban*. Cambridge: Polity.
Aubert-Gamet, Veronique and Bernard Cova. 1999. "Servicescapes: From Modern Non-Places to Postmodern Common Places." *Journal of Business Research* 44:37–45.

Auge, Marc. 1995. *Non-Places: Introduction to an Anthropology of Supermodernity.* London: Verso.

Butler, Tim and Garry Robson. 2003. "Negotiating Their Way In: The Middle Classes, Gentrification and the Deployment of Capital in a Globalising Metropolis." *Urban Studies* 40:1791–1809.

Ellis, Carolyn. 2004. *The Ethnographic I: A Methodological Novel about Teaching and Doing Autoethnography.* Walnut Creek, CA: Altamira.

Goffman, Erving. 1963. *Behaviour in Public Places: Notes on the Social Organisation of Gatherings.* New York: Free Press.

Jacobs, Jane. 1961. *The Death and Life of Great American Cities.* New York: Vintage.

Langman, Lauren. 1992. "Neon Cages: Shopping for Subjectivity." Pp. 40–82 in *Lifestyle Shopping: The Subject of Consumption*, edited by Rob Shields. London: Routledge.

Lofland, Lyn H. 1998. *The Public Realm: Exploring the City's Quintessential Social Territory.* Hawthorne, NY: Aldine de Gruyter.

Massey, Doreen. 2005. *For Space.* London: Sage.

Oldenburg, Ray. 1999. *The Great Good Place: Cafes, Coffee Shops, Bookstores, Bars, Hair Salons, and Other Hangouts at the Heart of a Community.* New York: Marlowe and Company.

Sandikci, Ozlem and Douglas B. Holt. 1998. "Malling Society: Mall Consumption Practices and the Future of Public Space." Pp. 305–341 in *Servicescapes: The Concept of Place in Contemporary Markets*, edited by John F. Sherry Jr. Chicago: NTC Business Books.

Stevens, Quentin. 2007. *The Ludic City: Exploring the Potential of Public Spaces.* London: Routledge.

Urry, John. 2000. *Sociology beyond Societies: Mobilities for the 21st Century.* London: Routledge.

Valentine, Gill. 2008. "Living with Difference: Reflections on Geographies of Encounter." *Progress in Human Geography* 32(3):323–337.

Watson, Sophie. 2006. *City Publics: The (Dis)Enchantments of Urban Encounters.* Abingdon, UK: Routledge.

Wise, Amanda. 2011. "Moving Food: Gustatory Commensality and Disjuncture in Everyday Multiculturalism." *New Formations* 74(Winter):82–107.

8

Encountering the "Old and New" Kids on the Block

Walking in the Neighborhood

T his chapter presents the process of gentrification as it is unfolding in Greenpoint, Brooklyn, in New York City. Walking, in all its forms, is a central local activity in this neighborhood. It is the means through which residents engage in social and public space. As a researcher, I too participated in this practice. Thus, data were collected by walking in the neighborhood through its streets, talking to residents and merchants, closely listening to their comments, and examining public expressions of both established and newer residents. Through walking, one investigates gentrification in everyday life. In this chapter, mobility is the backdrop of the analysis.

The Neighborhood

Greenpoint is a peninsula at the northernmost tip of Brooklyn. Greenpoint lies across the river from Manhattan. The Citicorp building on Manhattan's east side is visible from the tip of Greenpoint's major commercial center, looming far above the low-scale buildings in the community. Greenpoint is also connected to neighborhoods in Queens (Long Island City, Sunnyside, and Maspeth) by the Pulaski, the Greenpoint Avenue, and the Kosciusko Bridges. The Kosciusko Bridge also links the Brooklyn–Queens Expressway with the Long Island Expressway.

Adjacent to Greenpoint in Brooklyn, lying just across its southern boundary is Williamsburg. Greenpoint and Williamsburg share the administration of many municipal services, and together they make up Brooklyn's Community Board 1, an extension of New York City government in the community.

Gentrifying Greenpoint

Greenpoint is also home to people of a variety of social classes. Residents are poor, working class, middle class, and upper-middle class. Among the higher socioeconomic status groups are gentrifiers. Greenpoint has been a working-class community for most of its history. Greenpoint's poor and working classes are being displaced by a very expensive local economy driven by gentrification.

In 2010, the total population of Greenpoint was 36,091 (U.S. Bureau of the Census 2010). Like New York City as a whole, the population has exhibited small increases since 2000. There were few changes in the racial profile of the neighborhood in that a large majority of the neighborhood remained white. The formal education of Greenpoint's residents has increased from 2000 to 2010. By 2010, the largest group of residents held bachelor's degrees. This is a dramatic change since 1980. By 2010, the median household income in Greenpoint was $56,143, indicating an increase of income. In terms of occupation, in 2010, management and business, science and arts professionals constituted the largest group, followed by sales and office occupations and service. This is in contrast to 1980 when the largest occupational group was in technical and sales followed by operators and laborers. The persistence and growth of a mostly white community, coupled with an increase of formal education and income among the population, and a shift to significantly more professionals and less laborers than in the past are indicators supporting the growth of a gentrifying neighborhood (Mason, Morlock, and Pisano 2012).

In terms of housing in 2010, 80 percent of households in Greenpoint are renters, and about a quarter of these are not rent regulated (Scott 2003). Furthermore, "The percentage of affordable housing in Greenpoint is dropping faster than it is in New York City as a whole. The percentage of rental units in the most expensive category is skyrocketing" (Scott 2003:7). The notion of affordability is defined as being no more than 30 percent of a household's income going toward rental costs. In Greenpoint in 2000 "about 40% of households paid more than 30% of their income on rent" (Scott 2003:9). Market rate rents for a two-bedroom apartment in Greenpoint in 2002 ranged from $1,500 to $1,900 (Scott 2003:16). This represents a 50 percent increase since 1997. They continue to increase. In 2013, a renovated two-bedroom, two-bath rental apartment was advertised in a realtor's window for $2,800 a month. Additional indicators of gentrification within the housing sector are featured in articles in the local newspapers discussing "skyrocketing rents," and "loft regulations urged" (*Greenline* 2001a, 2001b). Houses are selling for $600,000 (for a building housing two families) and upward, especially in the historic district (Mooney 2009).

Greenpoint has been a sought-after community with a deindustrialized waterfront. It was historically white and stable, affordable, physically well kept, with high occupancy rates, relatively low crime, high levels of social capital, and a high degree of neighboring relative to other neighborhoods. Ironically, it is these very characteristics that attracted gentrifiers and developers. Its authenticity, as an industrial, ethnic, working-class enclave, and as seen through its nineteenth-century buildings and small-town charm, was appealing as a place of residence. At the same time, gentrifiers in Greenpoint segregate themselves from other working-class and immigrant residents, and they socialize and create community with other residents like themselves. As described by one resident gentrifier, "We liked that it was a neighborhood with other creative people like ourselves." In general, what has developed is a clash of lifestyles and social norms between working-class and immigrant residents and gentrifiers. This chapter indicates that in Greenpoint, the new gentrifying residents and established working-class residents exist as parallel cultures, living side by side but not integrating on a regular basis. Thus, these groups engage in parallel play (Parten 1932), forming individual communities within the neighborhood. They "play" next to each other but not with each other. The working-class residents (and immigrants) continue to engage in traditional, local institutions (church, ethnic organizations, PTA), while gentrifiers create new social milieus (bars with sidewalk seating, art galleries, new community organizations). These differences of lifestyle with conflicting social norms are played out in the course of everyday life.

Greenpoint is a "walking" community. For the most part, children attending local schools are escorted by walking adults. Elderly residents walk to stores, churches, and coffee shops. Residents in a rush often avoid walking on Manhattan Avenue in order to elude meeting and stopping to talk with others, and thus being late. Walking is a major part of the social fabric of Greenpoint. For a sociologist, walking in the neighborhood is also used as an approach to data collection. While walking, expressions of a parallel culture were observed visually and audibly. They are the focus of this chapter.

On Walking

In *The Practice of Everyday Life*, Michel de Certeau (1984) devotes a chapter to "Walking in the City." He begins by looking down at New York City from the top of the World Trade Center. Up there, one leaves the streets. "His elevation transfigures him into a voyeur. It puts him at a distance" (93). "Ordinary practitioners" are found below. They walk and use spaces that are not visible from far above. For de Certeau, "The act of walking is to the urban system what the speech act is to language or to the statements uttered" (98).

The practice of walking has a prominent place in sociology. Friedrich Engels ([1845] 1987) observed the conditions of the working class firsthand. Urban ethnographies have been organized, through the art of walking within physical and social space, with a focus on various groups and settings. From their historical origins with the Chicago School, Robert Park urged members of the Department of Sociology to go out into the city of Chicago and walk around! Urban ethnographies that followed involve living among and interacting with those ordinary people being studied (for example, Kornblum 1974; Liebow 1967; Susser 1982; Whyte 1955).

It is through walking that one encounters the urban landscape and "sees" social life. In *Seeing Cities Change: Local Culture and Class,* Jerome Krase (2012) analyzes social change in cities in the United Stated and Europe through a visual approach. Krase "sees" change by walking around and taking photographs of vernacular landscapes. For Krase, "We can photograph, film, or video ethnic enclaves to both document and illustrate how their new occupants change particular spaces" (10). Through walking in the city, Krase presents urban change that was brought about by ordinary people. This approach also assists scholars in reconciling demographic data with the population actually inhabiting a place. For Krase, "Seeing is the only way of knowing" (249).

Walking in the Neighborhood

This chapter presents the process of gentrification in everyday life through interactions between long-term working-class residents and new gentrifiers. By walking in the neighborhood, this researcher talked to residents, participated in informal groups, and noticed visual symbols of social class, ethnicity, and religion, which included representations of conflict, negotiation, and accommodation.

As a resident home owner in Greenpoint since 1985, I have walked in the neighborhood, frequenting its many stores, restaurants, and local institutions. I also participated in the community through the lives of my children. This project commenced for me as my son was enrolled at a preschool in Greenpoint for three- and four-year-olds. As we walked to and from school each day, interactions with "old and new" residents took place. During the school year and in good weather, time was spent frequenting play grounds in a variety of local parks, backyard gatherings, and birthday parties after school and on weekends. Parents also gathered as they chaperoned school trips. Weekends were largely spent in recreational activities for children, such as basketball, baseball, gymnastics, soccer, swimming, dance, art, and music. These were held at numerous parks, church gymnasiums, and the sites of community organizations. At times, activities would be held outside the neighborhood. Summers were often spent with parents chatting as children were brought to and from local summer camp programs and cooled off in sprinklers at local parks. As our children grew older and moved on to other schools, residents would walk in the neighborhood, meet others on the street or at a planned destination, and spend time talking and "catching up" on life. As a resident researcher, I was viewed as an "insider" of the groups being studied. I am perceived as a gentrifier by those new to the neighborhood and, at the same time, as a long-term working-class resident by that group. In this way, I easily moved from one group to the other. My research style was unobtrusive and centered on closely listening to statements and conversations of residents. I continue to walk around and collect data.

By using walking as a research method, this chapter analyzes the local everyday practices of each group, including school selection and recreation for children. These ways of everyday life create each group's culture, while also reflecting their social class differences. In the end, parallel play amounts to segregation by social class. Conclusions address the notion of mobility within the context of public space.

Aspects of Everyday Life

The concept of everyday life is embedded in the field of sociology. It is used to convey the "ordinary," our taken-for-granted interactions that occur in informal settings but remain a major part of social life. The investigations of theorists such as Robert Park, Erving Goffman, and Dorothy Smith are grounded in everyday life.

As head of the Sociology Department, Park's (1925) vision for the Chicago School was to study the everyday life of various groups and people in the city. Goffman (1959) viewed our actions in everyday life in one sense as theater, in which we are front stage or backstage delivering public or private behavior. Public behavior is for an audience, while private behavior entails being oneself. Goffman refers to the "face work" that we do in order to "save face." It consists of the work of deference for the purpose of impression management, adjusting one's behavior in order to control the impression one makes on others.

Smith's (1987) standpoint theory focuses on the everyday life of women. Unlike Smith, my research on gentrification in everyday life in Greenpoint analyzes social class from the standpoint of long-term working-class residents, including women. This is essentially an analysis of everyday life in "third places" (Oldenburg 1989). These are spaces and places within the neighborhood that are semipublic and add another "stage" to Goffman's analysis. Third places allow for the informal grouping and gathering of ordinary people in which the private home and public world meet, and social expectations are negotiated. As a neighborhood in Brooklyn, Greenpoint can be thought of as a "cosmopolitan canopy" (Anderson 2004). Elijah Anderson states that under the canopy are more intimate social settings. In moving around under Greenpoint's canopy, one encounters more intimate third places and investigates the informal interactions among neighbors and residents of the neighborhood that take place.

Neighboring

Neighboring occurs on a number of levels. For the working class, many residents grew up together, married friends, and presently live in another part of the neighborhood from their childhood homes. For these residents, neighboring takes place while trekking with children to and from local schools, shopping in local stores, and frequenting local establishments such as diners, restaurants, bars, laundromats, and religious services. Neighboring also occurs on one's street of residence. Mobility, by foot and on the street, is the activity that promotes neighboring. Once newer residents are established, they too practice neighboring.

Through neighboring, the parallel play and parallel cultures at work in Greenpoint are brought to the forefront. Differences are manifested while living together and sharing a neighborhood. Examples of neighboring examined include dog walking, bicycle parking, filmmaking, and noise.

Dog Walking

Dogs have a prominent place in Greenpoint. They serve as family pets as well as security systems for homes in lieu of alarms. Dog walking is very much a part of the neighborhood culture. Residents are required by New York City law to keep dogs on leashes, "curb your dog," and "pick up after your dog," or face a fine.

Dog walking is another area of everyday life that is approached differently by newer residents. Gentry residents walk their dogs on the sidewalk instead of in the street, and they allow their pets to urinate on trees and the iron gates in front of people's homes and drop their poop on the sidewalk. They do not "curb" their dogs as is customary in the neighborhood, and often do not "clean up" after the dogs. In some cases, home owners have installed fencing around trees and at the bottoms of iron gates in front of their homes to discourage dogs and their owners. When abuses are witnessed, long-term home owners confront violating dog walkers and articulate the local practice as well as the city's law.

Resident school personnel, who greet children and parents each morning at a local school, have also expressed concern about the dog-walking style of gentrifiers. The relatively few children of gentrifiers who attend this particular public school in Greenpoint are often accompanied by a parent and a dog to the school's entrance. One school aide said, "I told the principal about these dogs. God forbid a kid is bitten. You never know—they're animals!"[1] In addition, there are notices taped around light posts outside the school indicating city laws regarding dogs. The first reminds the public that dogs must be on a leash, and the second states the "pooper scoop" ordinance in which there is a fine for not cleaning up after your dog. The location of these notices directly around the school seems like a deliberate reminder to parents with dogs and dog walkers in general.

Bicycles

With an increase in gentrifiers comes an increase in bicycle use as a means of transportation within the city of New York. Gentrifiers use bicycles far more than other groups in Greenpoint do. One observes gentrifiers riding all types of bicycles, with or without protective helmets, moving in tow with vehicular

[1] Quotations from residents throughout this chapter come from field notes.

traffic. Residents now look both ways before crossing streets, since bicyclists are found riding both ways on one-way streets. In general, car drivers and pedestrians alike need to exercise more caution. They proceed with caution as traffic lights turn green because bicyclists often ride through red lights directed at them. In fact, on one street corner in Greenpoint stands a white painted bicycle with flowers laid across its handlebars, chained to a pole. This is a "ghost bike," which signifies that a cyclist was killed on that street. A plaque attached tells the story of a young woman killed by a truck. More recently, a delivery person of Chinese take-out food was killed on his bicycle while working. Negotiation is required for all moving transport vehicles, and also by pedestrians. One lifelong resident said as she crossed the street and was almost hit by a moving bicycle, "These bicycles, they're so arrogant!"

The parking and storing of bicycles by gentrifiers ignites additional tension in Greenpoint. Bicycles are often parked by attaching them to a pole by a chain and lock and then are left that way on residential property. Long-term home owners often leave notes on bicycles asking that they be removed and not parked there again. Similarly, one can observe signs on the entrance to subway stations indicating that chaining bicycles to the subway structure violates the law. Presently, only New York City's Department of Sanitation will remove bicycles from public property after the bicycle meets various criteria of being unusable. In a discussion with a police officer about these matters, a lifelong resident was told, "Someone in City Hall likes bikes!" Vehicular traffic, including bicycles, and pedestrian safety are presently part of Mayor de Blasio's zero tolerance policy.

The parallel cultures at work here display different "definitions of the situation." Long-term working-class residents are mobile by walking, using public transportation, and cars. They are less likely to use bicycles as a form of transport. Long-term working-class residents have historically stored bicycles, including those belonging to children, inside their homes, apartments, or some other place in their own living space. They are a cared-for commodity, not to be ruined by weather. Long-term resident home owners are not happy to have bicycles, which do not belong to anyone in their building, parked on their property. As one person said, "If someone trips over it, you're responsible. You'll be sued!" Home owners perceive these acts as a violation of existing practices and social norms. The following account illustrates the conflict between long-term resident home owners and gentrifiers over bicycles.

A resident home owner explained:

A few times there have been bicycles chained to the pole in front of our house. They're sometimes there for days. The first time, we thought it was being parked for the winter! My neighbors told me to clip the chain and throw the bike away, but I wasn't comfortable doing that. So I called the Community Relations Officer at the precinct who I knew, and asked if I could get rid of the bike. He told me not to touch it. He took my address and put me on a list at the precinct to have it removed. The police will

confiscate them. Another time, there were two bikes left. My wife put a
note on one saying that if they weren't removed, we will have the police
take them. A couple of days later, my neighbor told me that late at night
a car pulled up, two people got out and unlocked the bikes. One read the
note and started cursing like crazy. They put the bikes in the trunk of the
car and drove away.

Policy regarding the enforcement of bicycles has changed through the years
in New York City to one that is pro-bicycle. Bicycle lanes have been placed
throughout city streets. Parking and bicycle storage, to a large extent, however,
has been missing from the policies, as well as enforcement of vehicular traffic
laws. These collisions of parallel play and ultimately clashing cultures are created in part by incomplete urban policy. Ordinary residents attempt to preserve
their way of life, while gentrifiers seek to change those ways or the local culture
to suit their own lifestyle.

The following exchange occurred between a resident home owner and another resident who is a member of a local synagogue. The synagogue was located
across the street from where the home owner lived. The congregant said, "I was
thinking about putting up a sign saying people can lock bikes on the synagogue
gate." To which the home owner replied, "That's good because I don't want them
in front of my house!"

The member of the synagogue is a gentrifier who joined the congregation
upon moving to Greenpoint. His position on bicycle parking differs from that
of long-term home owners since his views are similar to those like him. Besides,
the synagogue is not his home, so his decision does not directly affect him.

Noise

Greenpoint is usually a relatively quiet place, but it is also part of "the city that
never sleeps." Thus, on occasion, there is street noise: people shouting, loud parties and music, car horns and alarms blaring, fireworks, bottles smashing on the
ground, and the sirens of emergency vehicles. For the most part, these events are
treated as background noise. Sometimes, residents will respond to noise to see if
anything extraordinary is happening. The focus of this analysis is not on these
extremely loud street noises, but on noise associated with everyday life, such as
people talking, spending time outdoors, babies crying, noises that are generally
perceived as commonplace. With the mixing of gentrifiers and working-class
people, their parallel play involves different perceptions and levels of tolerance
for the clamor of everyday life associated with each parallel culture. The following interactions illustrate that noises originating in private space or public
space affect each other. These exchanges were conveyed to me as I participated
in neighboring.

One example concerns a young working-class woman who grew up in
Greenpoint and resides in her childhood home with her husband and young

children. Her next-door neighbors are new gentrifiers. She shared the following interaction:

> When [my son] was a baby, he went through a period of night terrors and screamed all night. My neighbors left a nasty note saying that his scream-ing disturbed their sleep and maybe we should move his room away from [the common wall near] their house.

In Greenpoint most houses are attached on both sides. People meet and talk to each other as they move in and out of their homes. This is a component of quotidian mobility. Noise is often heard from a neighbors' private space as well as from public, and quasi-public/semiprivate spaces.

In Greenpoint, car parking is done curbside. Driveways and garages are few. Car owners must also attend to street-cleaning regulations, which dictate no parking during certain days and hours. Given these parameters, cars are often parked blocks away from one's home. In order to avoid a fine, residents are seen racing to their cars to move them because of parking rules. Another exchange occurred between a working-class resident and a new gentrifier. This was re-garding the blaring sound of a car alarm.

> My husband leaves for work early and he accidentally set off his car alarm. A neighbor came out yelling, "What are you crazy!" My husband thought he was yelling, [because our neighbor was] thinking that someone was breaking into our car. So my husband yelled, "It's fine." But he continued to scream, "Are you crazy—we're trying to sleep!"

Street noises like car alarms disturb everyone. They are part of the sound track of city life. In this instance, the car sounding the alarm belonged to someone living nearby. It is not uncommon for alarms to resonate for hours because the owner lives blocks away and is unaware of its shrill. The interesting part of the interaction is that it was initially thought by the working-class resident that the neighbor's yelling was about protecting his property, an act of friendship and community cooperation, and not a matter of noise control.

Another woman who grew up in Greenpoint and now has adult children who were also raised in Greenpoint had the following comments about her new neighborhood:

> It's disconcerting that I know few people on my block. We now have a loft in a building on our corner [formerly industrial space]. People were having roof parties, walking up and down the block late at night. It's very transient. There's no investment in the community. Our friends [who are resident home owners] rent to two people, and then there are three or more living in the apartment. They were going onto the roof even after they were told that it was off-limits. People like the high rents they can get,

but it comes with a price. Another friend rented her upstairs apartment to
a couple who were drug dealers. The cops came and arrested them!

This view describes aspects of gentrification that are sometimes missed. For the resident home owner who can rent an apartment in their house, the higher rents that can be collected in a gentrifying neighborhood is a positive outcome. A major investment finally pays off. However, as suggested, it comes with a price. This respondent is grieving over the loss of community, no longer knowing neighbors, and seeing friends lose control over the goings-on in their homes. Because the respondent is mobile on foot, she notices the loss of her "home territory" (Lofland 1985). This is similar to Lyn Lofland's analysis of her friend's experience residing in the place in which they were raised: "She can see, and recognizes that she must cope with the fact, that what was once an environment of personally known others, is becoming, however limited the degree, a world of unknown others . . . the world of strangers has penetrated" (179). Everyday life in Greenpoint has been disrupted by increasing gentrification. In Greenpoint, parallel cultures maintain worlds of strangers.

Neighborhood Children

As parents spend time interacting around children's activities, information and opinions about local institutions are discussed.

Schooling

Parallel cultures also exist in Greenpoint regarding the schooling of children. This aspect of everyday life and the interaction between gentrifiers and long-term residents documents the strategies used by gentry families to gain admission of their children to public schools outside the neighborhood. This behavior is in contrast to working-class residents whose children attend local schools. Gentry families overwhelmingly reject local schools, both their physical and social space; thus, they reject a neighborhood institution. The rejection of social/physical space by gentry families creates a dynamic whereby social relations between gentrifiers and working-class residents are segregated and stratified.

Although a few of the local elementary schools are highly rated based on citywide and state test scores, and others are academically average, gentrifiers are critical of them. The local schools are negatively judged because of their traditional approach, including "teaching to the tests."

In Greenpoint, the gentry prefer public education over private education. Catholic schools are not an option because, as a group, gentrifiers are more secular than their working-class neighbors who support the local religious institutions. Furthermore, tuition in private, nonreligious elementary schools in New York City can cost upward of twenty thousand dollars annually.

A major strategy developed by the gentry in Greenpoint to address their displeasure with local schools is enrolling their children in talented and gifted programs and alternative education programs in public schools primarily in Manhattan and, to a lesser extent, other parts of the city. They have learned to "work the system" to their advantage. Groups of small children and parents crowd subway platforms headed for Manhattan. Car pools of parents and numerous children attending the same school leave various blocks every morning from Greenpoint and return in the afternoon in possibly a different car or minivan driven by a different parent.

One of the first generations of children from Greenpoint attending elementary school in Manhattan has advanced to middle school and high school. They are attending some of the "best" (Hemphill 1999) public middle schools and high schools in New York City. It seems that because the children attended elementary school in a Manhattan school district, they were given priority for applying to middle schools in the same district. Thus, one finds that gentry families are quite clever in their approach to schooling their children. In this case, they were "tracking" their children to highly rated schools with their initial kindergarten selection.

For the most part, working-class families choose between both local Catholic and local public schools for their children. These families decide to school their children locally.

There are parallel cultures at work here regarding children's mobility. Gentry families expect their children by middle school age to move outside the neighborhood and around the city through the use of public transportation. Instead, the working class places value on the maintenance of community through their children's local mobility based on footwork.

Recreation

Neighborhood children also engage in parallel play forming parallel cultures. The investigation of everyday life continues by analyzing children's patterns of recreation. Children's activities are examined as a reflection of social class and their parents' beliefs and values. Presently in Greenpoint, one observes both informal play among school-age children "on the street," as well as adult-organized, supervised, and structured recreation in the form of playdates, team sports, and birthday celebrations in "party places." Implicit in a discussion of children's play is the intention of parents who direct that play (either by design, routine, or tradition). In the end, this discussion is about differing parental ideals regarding their children.

The concept of "ordinary" is used here to express that which is typical and has come to be the neighborhood tradition created by a local culture. Greenpoint's ordinary kids are from working-class and poor families, some of whom are relatively recent immigrants. Most of the American-born children are from families with numerous generations living in the community. They experience generational continuity, inheriting a legacy of community in Greenpoint as their "home."

Children old enough to be outside on their own roam the streets, visiting local establishments like parks, the library, and pizzerias, using the neighborhood as their playground. They ride bicycles, skateboards, and scooters, play basketball, stickball, handball, and more sophisticated versions of games like tag and hide-and-seek. Some observers think that these children, who wander the local streets, have nothing to do, but while they are doing "nothing," they engage in verbal exchanges, decision making, problem solving, and endless negotiation. They create and participate in the community.

To an unwitting onlooker, children wandering the streets, changing locales and activities, appear to be unsupervised. For ordinary kids in Greenpoint, that is seldom the case. There are multiple social networks operating in which adults, sweeping sidewalks, hanging or gazing out of windows, or simply passing by, keep an eye on the children. As one resident said, "I know that [my son's friend] climbs the fences into the abandoned factories. My son knows he better not go there. I tell him, 'We're watching.'" Interestingly, in this family, both parents work full-time. So the idea of "we're watching" is actually a reference to an assortment of local family, friends, and neighbors.

Residents will also utilize their relationships when warranted. Children are sometimes confronted directly or their parents are contacted when an incident occurs. One resident explained:

> We were out for a walk and noticed these kids sitting in my wife's car. It was parked near the factory. My brother happened to be approaching us. I signaled to him and we ran toward the car. They saw us coming and got out and started running, but I recognized one of the kids. I went to his house and spoke to his father. They paid us for the broken window.

Ordinary children in Greenpoint have the freedom to explore the neighborhood terrain, while subject to the scrutiny of adults. With the emergence and widespread use of cell phones, there is more ongoing contact with parents. One mother said, "We have him [her son] call in."

Ordinary children in Greenpoint are given the same allowances as their parents were given growing up in the neighborhood. They are following the established tradition. One mother remarked, "Groups of us would go camping for days. You want your kids to have experiences in life." Like ordinary children in Greenpoint, the children of gentry families are also seen strolling the streets of Greenpoint, visiting the video store, the library, riding skateboards, and playing kickball. However, groups of local children participate in parallel play. Gentry children play with other gentry children, and ordinary children play with peers like them. This is similar to Hall's (see Chapter 7 of this volume) finding on her walk in Northcote, Melbourne, in which she notices that people spend time with others like themselves. On the streets, in the parks, and engaged in more formal arrangements like a local swim club, to a large extent, the children are not integrated with each other in the community. In fact, one gentry mother commented about the children of her working-class neighbors, "They are boys in need of supervision!"

The children of gentry families also participate in organized sports, but they have not joined a community-sponsored baseball league or basketball team. Instead, their parents have formed the Greenpoint/Williamsburg Youth Soccer League. From September to December, a multitude of children play their weekly game. For the most part, these are the children of gentrifiers. One mother expressed, "It's nice after six years; the kids are off in different middle schools but get to see each other in soccer." In terms of both play and organized sports, and schooling, gentry children are segregated from their ordinary neighbors. The lives of gentry children take them outside of the neighborhood.

The parallel cultures of gentry children reflect that of their parents in Greenpoint. They are participants of their own community, with people like themselves.

Housing

Among Greenpoint residents, while walking around, it is common to hear and participate in conversations regarding housing. The topic will cover a wide range of inquiries from who has new tenants, who is renovating and/or selling, to the condition of houses and apartments, the price of market rents, what house sold, and for what price. In the course of these conversations, the dissimilar interests of working-class residents and new gentrifiers emerge. One illustration is a conversation between a lifelong resident home owner and a gentry resident home owner who live on the same street. They were discussing a house that was being sold with an asking price of $1.4 million. The gentry home owner remarked, "I can't believe it's only $1.4 million." The lifelong resident responded, "I can't believe the price either!" The interest of the gentry homeowner is for booming real estate prices, giving her investment more monetary value. The comment by the lifelong resident was a statement that she could not believe a house in Greenpoint would ever cost that much money.

Another area of difference focused on housing is with regard to aesthetics. The local practice has been to maintain houses in practical ways using materials that are effective and cost efficient but not always aesthetically pleasing. The gentry are more interested in aesthetics and support the idea of historic preservation through restoration to original façade. The following interaction highlights this point:

Strolling through local streets, a couple stopped to examine and admire the wood shingle of a newly restored home in the historic district. The owner noticed them and came out. They talked for a while about the renovation and the owner remarked, "You don't live in the historic district, so that's good." To which the response was, "Why is that good?"

This exchange presents a number of things. It indicates support by gentrifiers for the aesthetics achieved through historic preservation and restoration. There is also an acknowledgment that there is more social status and economic value in places designated "historic." It is the preferred place of residence for the gentry. For the resident home owner, living outside the historic district gives one more options regarding renovation and its cost. In historic districts, rules designated by the NYC Landmarks Commission limit one's choice of building materials and color of the building's exterior, and stipulate an approved architectural plan and permits. Approved restoration is a relatively costly endeavor. Once again, the different standpoints regarding housing costs, location, and appearance, ascertained "on the ground" by moving around, are brought to light and provide an additional layer to the meaning of gentrification in everyday life. The respective parallel cultures also include varying material values and attendant social status.

Another layer to a discussion of housing in Greenpoint focuses on affordability. Affordable housing emerged as the primary issue of the working-class community as the Greenpoint waterfront was being rezoned from industrial to residential use. Gentrifiers expressed a need for open space, parks, and aesthetics. As one resident expressed, "Aesthetic concerns are a luxury of affluence." The culture of walking allowed for successful mobilization. The working-class community organized through the tradition of the local Catholic Churches.

The issue of affordable housing took on "a life of its own" and became the major concern of rezoning and redevelopment for the working class. Ultimately, city government was inundated by community voices giving priority to affordable housing, with the churches and local politicians supporting and working toward this end. Open space, parks, and the height and bulk of new towers were and remain subjects of concern of the gentry. In the end, affordable housing became part of the redevelopment plan.

Conclusions

This analysis raises a number of issues regarding quotidian mobility and public space. The notion of mobility was investigated on a couple of levels. A culture of walking exists in this neighborhood that promotes informal social relations and the development of community. For the most part and at present, the community operates as parallel cultures in which working-class and gentry residents partake in parallel play forming third places with others like themselves. Quotidian mobility, as is evident in this chapter, functions differently for working-class and gentry residents. For working-class residents, movement is more locally focused than for their newer neighbors. They remain committed to maintaining community and accomplish this by schooling their children locally, supporting local institutions, and maintaining social relationships from child-hood. In addition, for many working-class residents, the fact that generations of their families and the families of friends continue to reside in Greenpoint clearly suggests their dedication to local sustainability. Building and maintaining com-munity are part of the working-class experience. In contrast, geographical mo-bility is part of the gentry's social script, precisely indicating how this group arrives in Greenpoint. Their social class position and identity creates greater physical movement from a younger age, which includes boarding at college, studying abroad, and living independently as a young adult. In addition, school-ing children outside the neighborhood indicates a commitment to something other than participating in a community with their working-class neighbors. These groups in Greenpoint individually form different "life worlds."

Mobility was also employed in this chapter as a research methodology and approach to data collection. As de Certeau has noted, in looking down on a place from a height far above, social relations appear orderly. One must, however, be "on the ground" moving next to and involved with those of interest. One finds that being up close, living with others, requires negotiation. That is why, as Krase suggests, we must be close enough to see everyday life, and by being a part of it one is able to notice change in the making. This is the case for both residents and scholars alike.

Finally, this chapter elucidates that public space has diverse meaning for the gentry and working class. Their parallel cultures view and use physical space in different ways. Sidewalks are an example and provide some insight. Residential sidewalks are viewed and used as public space by gentrifiers in which dogs are walked, bicycles are parked, and independent films are recorded. To the resi-dent home owner, residential sidewalks are quasi-private spaces. In fact some may view sidewalks as private property, an extension of their private homes. As quasi-private or private spaces, home owners are responsible for maintaining them so that they are passable and walkable, free of obstructions and hazards, such as snow, ice, and debris. The everyday life of gentrifiers contradicts the working-class view of sustainability. In the final analysis, this chapter suggests the value of mobility as an approach to sociological research as the dynamics uncovered in this chapter are further explored.

REFERENCES

Anderson, Elijah. 2004. "The Cosmopolitan Canopy." *Annals of the American Academy of Political and Social Science* 595:14–31.
de Certeau, Michel. 1984. *The Practice of Everyday Life*. Berkeley: University of California Press.
Engels, Friedrich. [1845] 1987. *The Condition of the Working Class in England*. London: Penguin.
Goffman, Erving. 1959. *The Presentation of Self in Everyday Life*. Edinburgh: University of Edinburgh Social Sciences Research Centre.
Greenline. 2001a. March. Loft Regulations Urged.

———. 2001b. March. Skyrocketing Rents.

Hemphill, Clara. 1999. *Public Middle Schools: New York's Best*. New York: Soho Press.

Kornblum, William. 1974. *Blue Collar Community*. Chicago: University of Chicago Press.

Krase, Jerome. 2012. *Seeing Cities Change: Local Culture and Class*. Farnham, UK: Ashgate.

Liebow, Elliot. 1967. *Tally's Corner*. Boston: Little, Brown.

Lofland, Lyn H. 1985. *A World of Strangers: Order and Action in Urban Public Space*. Prospect Heights, IL: Waveland.

Mason, Lorna, Ed Morlock, and Christina Pisano. 2012. "Mapping a Changing Brooklyn, Mapping a Changing World: Gentrification and Immigration, 2000–2008." Pp. 7–50 in *The World in Brooklyn: Gentrification, Immigration, and Ethnic Politics in a Global City*, edited by Judith N. DeSena and Timothy Shortell. Lanham, MD: Lexington Books.

Mooney, Jake. 2009. "Polish Is Still Spoken, but Industry Is History." *New York Times*, 31 May.

Oldenburg, Ray. 1989. *The Great Good Place: Cafes, Coffee Shops, Community Centers, Beauty Parlors, General Stores, Bars, Hangouts and How They Get You through the Day*. New York: Paragon House.

Park, Robert E. 1925. *The City: Suggestions for the Study of Human Nature in the Urban Environment*. Chicago: University of Chicago Press.

Parten, Mildred. 1932. "Social Participation among Pre-School Children." *Journal of Abnormal and Social Psychology* 27(3):243–269.

Scott, Rebecca. 2003. *Inclusionary Zoning: A Proposal for North Brooklyn and New York City*. Unpublished report.

Smith, Dorothy E. 1987. *The Everyday World as Problematic: A Feminist Sociology*. Boston: Northeastern University Press.

Susser, Ida. 1982. *Norman Street*. New York: Oxford University Press.

U.S. Bureau of the Census. 2010. *Census of Population and Housing*. Retrieved September 18, 2012. http://factfinder.census.gov.

Whyte, William Foote. 1955. *Street Corner Society: The Structure of an Italian Slum*. Chicago: University of Chicago Press.

9

From Shipping to Shopping

Providence's Capital Center, Nervous Landscapes, and a
Phenomenological Analysis of Walkability

KRISTEN A. WILLIAMS

We've gone from being a blue-collar city to a white-collar city and a
visitor destination.

—Mayor Vincent "Buddy" Cianci, *USA Today*, December 31, 1996

D rawing inspiration from the class dimensions of urban economic renewal referenced in the above-quoted statement by former Providence
mayor Vincent "Buddy" Cianci, this chapter evaluates the interplay
between public histories and contemporary urban economies in Providence,
Rhode Island. Specifically, I examine the politics of creating a "walkable city"
as a tool of state-sponsored historically themed urban economic redevelopment.
At the center of my examination is Capital Center, a seventy-seven-acre parcel of
land located in Providence's downtown core. This parcel, created between 1970
and 1994 by moving train tracks and excavating rivers, was explicitly designed
to serve as a "tourist bubble" combining retail and business opportunities with
walkable civic space. Intended to attract visitors and residents alike to the city's
downtown core, the parcel reunites the sections of a historic city that had been
divided by train tracks and overland road construction during its principal eras
of industrialization. Without question the single most notable element of Capital Center has been the excavation, relocation, and combination of three major
rivers into one urban water park and the subsequent creation of three focal attractions: Waterplace Park, the Riverwalk, and the Providence Place Mall.

Long buried under acres of concrete parking lots, the Moshassuck, Woonasquatucket, and Providence Rivers were excavated and rerouted as part of what
became known officially as the Capital Center Plan. Formerly conduits of domestic and international trade, these rivers now guide residents and tourists
alike from disparate surrounding neighborhoods to the new "downcity" center via a pair of "riverwalks" that stretch nearly seven thousand feet and come
together to form the ultimate showpiece of twenty-first-century downtown
Providence: an urban water park known as "Waterplace" unveiled in 1994 that

features an amphitheater for outdoor entertainments and a 240-foot diameter basin commemorating the Great Salt Cove that once marked the city center.[1] The parcel also backs against the Providence Place Mall, which opened in 1999 and features upscale retail shopping as well as a movie theater and several full-scale restaurants; the Providence train station (to the east); and the State House (to the north).

Given the scope and scale of the alteration to Providence's built environment that the creation of Capital Center entailed, it is hardly surprising that this effort at urban revitalization received widespread acclaim and has come to be recognized as the jewel in Providence's renaissance crown by both local boosters and national associations. Indeed, the Rhode Island Department of Transportation and architect William D. Warner received an award in 1994 from the Waterfront Center in recognition of the River Relocation Project that helped establish Capital Center. The D.C.-based national nonprofit stated that the project constituted "nothing short of the wholesale remaking of the Rhode Island state capital."[2] Following this early recognition, the city also won the 2003 Rudy Bruner Silver Award for Urban Excellence "in recognition of the city's resurgence and its success in the complex process of urban placemaking" (Leazes and Motte 2004:xix).

During the two decades that have passed since its initial unveiling in 1994, however, much of Capital Center's open civic space has disappeared beneath a high-rise luxury housing complex, the new national headquarters of a leading gaming technology and services company, and a Ruth's Chris Steak House. Accordingly, I examine the dominant tourism and public history narratives made available to visitors and residents alike, and question whether this downtown redevelopment has been as overwhelmingly successful at creating walkable civic space in Providence as its boosters would suggest and, if so, what the limitations of that achievement might be. While I am interested in adding my voice to the chorus of urban studies scholars whose recent critiques complicate the decidedly pro-tourism, pro-business rhetoric of urban renaissance, my work here moves beyond accounting for the material inequalities occasioned, exacerbated, or simply ignored by urban renaissance planning. While I do make use of traditional approaches to public history, analyzing some of the origins and goals of dominant historical tourism narratives and efforts at city-branding, I combine this analysis with the theoretical tools of cultural anthropology, cultural landscape studies, and performance studies to suggest that even the current theoretical and practical emphasis on downtown walkability might fall short of its goals of creating increasingly democratized (that is, equally accessible) public space. Crafting a specifically interdisciplinary theoretical paradigm, I bring together scholarly analyses of walkability by city planners like Jeff Speck, the power of public memory, and the notion of a "usable past" so famously explored by David

---

[1] "Doves, Politicians Open Waterplace Park" (1994).
[2] "River Relocation Wins Washington Group's Praise" (1994).

Rosenzweig and David Thelan, and the idea of the sorts of "nervous landscapes" that result from recreating downtown city centers as "contact zones" in which a variety of populations meet and interact, not always peaceably (Byrne 2003; Rosenzweig and Thelan 2000; Speck 2012). This theoretical paradigm, in its reliance on the observation of material bodies in real space and time, necessarily constitutes a phenomenological approach to the study of both official and vernacular/quotidian uses of walkable urban space.

Accordingly, my methodology complements my theoretical approach, and relies on my own firsthand experience as a native and longtime resident of Providence, Rhode Island. An auto-ethnographic research method yielded site-specific documentation in the form of written observations as well as a large collection of photographs of Capital Center at different times of day, seasons, and even across the span of several years. Additional interviews with locals and tourism officials allowed me to gain insight into both official/intended and unofficial/quotidian uses of public space. My work in the Providence City Archives provided insight to the history of the parcels of land in question, the populations that have used it, and the events it has come to memorialize. Finally, textual analysis of proposed and implemented city plans, mayoral addresses, and reports from nongovernmental organizations provided important contextual information to my study.

My commitment to phenomenological theories and methods, both of which account for material experiences of reality, has uniquely enabled me to address the cultural politics of urban redevelopment strategies that rely on the creation of walkable urban landscapes intended to function both spectacularly, as tourist-friendly monuments to certain aspects of Providence's past(s) and in the daily lives of residents. By accounting for both official and vernacular uses of urban public space, I am able to consider how Providence's Capital Center and its repurposed urban waterfront enable walkability in efforts to serve present commercial interests and encourage tourism. How does a more walkable downtown serve not only residents but also visitors by explicitly connecting everyday activities such as eating and running errands with Providence's past life as a locus of colonial and industrial era trade? As part of my answer to this question, I evaluate the uses intended for Capital Center by the policy elites and organizations that created it. But this analysis occasions a second question about the unintended uses to which this location is/can be put through quotidian, rather than spectacular walkability. Accordingly, I observe and provide an example of some vernacular uses of Capital Center. Finally, I conclude my analysis by considering the cultural politics of walking in contemporary downtown Providence, recently labeled "a walker's paradise" by Walkscore (2012). While downtown walkability has been defined by planners and academics alike as a core element to the economic, cultural, and environmental revitalization and sustainability of midsize and large urban areas, I argue here that achieving such walkability within the downtown core has little impact on the health of the city (and its residents) and will do little to encourage civic engagement, unless that downtown core is effectively reconnected to the rest of the city, not just its most desirable and tourist-friendly areas. Accordingly, the question I pose in my conclusion is the following: Does the city of Providence currently promote neighborhood walkability and advocate the development of its public transit system as a means of supporting extant businesses and residents or is the goal to displace and then replace this population with representatives of the much-lauded "creative class" of educated young professionals identified by Richard Florida (2004, 2007)?

Given the emphasis placed on walkability and the reurbanization of down-town city centers by contemporary city planners and urban theorists alike, my goal here is twofold. First, I want to apply and advocate for a phenomenological approach to the definition of cultural landscapes and urban studies more generally—an approach that explicitly accounts for human behavior (performance) in public space. Second, with this emphasis on the performance of the human body in space, I want to introduce a discussion about the limits of walkability as a trope of economic and cultural sustainability. While I concur that the degree of walkability of a downtown core correlates directly to environmental sustainability, I argue that it is not necessarily a reliable predictor of economic or cultural sustainability unless it is accompanied by other complementary strategies.

Ramble, Stroll, or Stride?: The Walkable City as a Performative Cultural Landscape

According to geographer Richard Schein, a cultural landscape is less a specific physical *site* than a "a geographically specific exercise that requires interrogating the role of landscape in social and cultural reproduction, as well as understanding the landscape within wide social and cultural contexts" (1997:660). Such geographical specificity need not entail the identification and documentation of one singular point on a map or given terrain. Instead, a cultural landscape may be cognitive, and often it will exist in a number of manifestations—in people's memories, emotions, thoughts, bodies, and practices, as well as in locations that can be charted via traditional means. Such is the case, I argue here, with the Capital Center parcel that relies explicitly on the performance of both natural and built environmental elements such as walkways, rivers, water basins, public art projects, and live site-specific performances to create a new sort of civic center featuring a dynamic interplay between contemporary place and memory, and between citizen-consumers and the laborers who have made their leisure possible in both the past and present.

Indeed, performance theorist Richard Schechner makes clear that spaces, not just people, are performative—they collaborate with bodies (and vice versa) to produce site-specific performances. For Schechner, then, space is fluid, an agent in its re-creation through use and practice. To enable a given human performance (any action in space and time), Schechner (1994:20) concludes, space must be organized, but not necessarily controlled. He suggests that people need to know how a space works before they can use, apply, or harness the power of that space and argues that any given space has properties and energies that should be respected and understood apart from the performance that will occur within it (31).

My methodological approach to analyzing the urban cultural landscape of Capital Center thus works within the theoretical parameters outlined above and, like many other inquiries into site-specific performance, draws on French philosopher Michel de Certeau's (1984) idea that there are (at least) two ways to tell "spatial stories," or narratives of places as they are practiced by humans and other agents.[3] First, he suggests, there is the "touring narrative," which accounts for the experience of space by humans: an experience that involves the material realities and skewed perceptions of the present as well as memories generated by both mind and body as the specific site is experienced. However, there also exists the "mapping narrative," the perhaps more familiar approach that explains a given urban geography in terms of relational location and/or latitudinal and longitudinal coordinates.

A touring narrative of Capital Center in downtown Providence might go something like this:

Start at Kennedy Plaza, where the buses are lined up belching exhaust, where working-class teenagers argue violently about custody of their young children alongside local college students from Brown University and the Rhode Island School of Design connected to iPhones and programming apps on their smartphones. The post office will be at your back. Remember when the river went underneath it. Walk along the plaza to city hall. Think back to the 1980s, when you could get a quick hamburger or hot dog at Haven Brothers, the mobile diner that used to be parked outside, offering a respite from winter nights for a mixed bag of locals: city officials in suits ducking out for a quick bite during or after work; working stiffs in thermal shirts, fiberfill vests, and steel-toed boots; young punks from suburbia in garish plaids and safety-pinned jackets, tattoos and piercings barely visible under mismatched layers of winter gear. Haven Brothers was a fixture for years and aptly named. A haven for locals. Take a right. The Biltmore Hotel, opened in 1922 as Providence's only luxury accommodations, will be on your left, across from the Fleet Bank ice-skating rink. Keep walking straight, past the new Westin Hotel on your right and the Convention Center on your

[3] De Certeau also provides helpful definitions of "space" and "place" that differ from those advanced by other scholars of cultural landscapes. According to de Certeau, "A space exists when one takes into consideration the vectors of direction, velocities, and time variables. Thus space is composed of mobile elements" (1984:117). He goes on to argue that while place "is the order (of whatever kind) in accord with which elements are distributed in relationships of coexistence," space "is a practiced place" whether that place be a written or other type of text (117).

left. If you can afford it, stop in at the new Ruth's Chris Steak House in the bottom of the GTECH World Headquarters and have a drink before wandering back out onto the network of pedestrian pathways collectively referred to by local tourism professionals as Riverwalk. This tree-lined concrete walkway can take you north to the historic State House, east to colonial era College Hill, or west to the Providence Place Mall, opened in 1999 and now home to retailers ranging from Macy's to Tiffany's.

This type of touring narrative takes the traveler on a journey that, even if undertaken alone, nevertheless traces a path someone else has trod before. This narrative is *experiential* (based on past experience and predictive of present experience) and *performative* (insofar as it is based on the notion of committing an action), but it is also *directional* and makes explicit reference to bodily engagement and physical activities including walking and looking (de Certeau 1984:119). This strategy of telling place not only relates how to get somewhere but also what one can expect to see and experience on the way.

The second type of narrative associated with de Certeau's "spatial stories" is the "mapping narrative," which describes the cityscape according to proximity and relational place: A police officer could tell a weary tourist, "Waterplace Park is across the street from the Providence Place Mall. You can't miss it." As this example makes clear, mapping narratives rely on the fact that a given site can be documented and represented by specific latitudinal and longitudinal coordinates—that the site, in this case Waterplace Park, can be pointed to on a map: X marks the spot. You are here.

The reason these types of narratives matter is because they demonstrate how vernacular spaces can be practiced, documented, and told by the people who use them. Cities are not constituted by independent sites that coldly determine (or are determined by) the activities taking place in their environs. Instead, they are dynamic locations, always in the process of coming into being through the practices of agents in the space (Speck 2012). It is this reliance on practice found in de Certeau's work that so clearly points to one of the most problematic aspects of interpreting urban cultural landscapes: It is difficult to figure out where they are, and even more difficult to determine how to "tell" those sites, or communicate their cultural significance to those who might be unfamiliar with them. As John Chase, Margaret Crawford, and John Kaliski's 1999 edited collection *Everyday Urbanism* makes clear, one person's parking lot might be another person's place of business. An alley can be a homeplace, and the curbs of an affluent neighborhood on trash day can be a shopping center. Only an analysis of Capital Center as a constantly evolving cultural landscape can therefore reveal the myriad ways in which this urban water park functions as both a physical site (with both official and vernacular uses) and as a symbol of the dynamic interplay of memory, history, and the power of usable pasts constructed in the present for the shaping of the future.

Water Routes for Work and Play: Waterplace Park as Site, Symbol, and Success Story

One of the primary goals in creating Capital Center was to establish land for commercial development, and the opening of Providence Place Mall in 1999 certainly accomplished that. However, some the earliest official uses of the newly created Capital Center promoted the cultural resources of Providence and reintroduced the new parcel to visitors and residents alike through the recreational attractions associated with Waterplace Park and the self-guided Riverwalk tour of pedestrian walkways that connect Providence's downtown core with the rest of its neighborhoods.[4]

Riverwalk

Though the tourism division of the Rhode Island Historical Society offers "Riverwalk" tours on spring and summer evenings before scheduled Waterfires are lit, most visitors and residents experience Providence's network of pedestrian pathways independently, as they make their way to and from local restaurants, government buildings, and architectural attractions, or as they run the most rudimentary errands. While such informal walks along the Moshassuck, Woonasquatucket, and Providence Rivers are easily undertaken in these piecemeal forms, it is no easy task to take a more formal and comprehensive self-guided tour that will offer a complete narrative of downtown Providence's evolution with a clear beginning, middle, and end. There exists no authoritative map outlining the best approach to traveling the scenic walkways that line Providence's three rivers, and locals working outside the tourist industry do not seem to recognize the term *Riverwalk* in relation to their city. Indeed, though Waterplace Park and its constitutive series of concrete walkways were completed by 1994, when I returned to the city more than a decade later in 2008 and again in 2011 and 2014, specifically hoping to take a tour traditionally made available to visitors, even Rhode Island Historical Society library personnel were not exactly sure what I meant when I said I wanted to tour the "Riverwalk," suggesting a disconnect between the traditional academic and research functions of the society and their more recently established attempts at local heritage tourism. Though this term is used in the *Providence Journal* and by real estate developers to refer to the interconnected series of walkways wending their collective way along the Providence rivers as they pass through the city's downtown, it is clearly part of the tourism lingo rather than the local vernacular.

By 1996, however, the *Providence Journal* reported the permanent placement of twenty-one fiberglass panels that would deliver the story of Providence's

[4] For the use of the term *Riverwalk* by the Rhode Island Historical Society, see the tourism section of their website: http://www.rihs.org/events_walking_tours.html. In 1995, the *Providence Journal* reported the creation of a heritage trail through Providence that still has not materialized. See Imbrie (1995). Finally, for the *Providence Journal*'s official use of the term *Riverwalk*, see DuJardin (1996).

cultural, architectural, and civic development. According to *Providence Journal* reporter Richard C. DuJardin, by 1996 Waterplace Park had become "more than a place to contemplate the city's waterways." Instead, DuJardin argues, the park and its series of connected walkways are also a genuine element of historic tourism. DuJardin (1996) argues, "[The park] has also become a place to learn more about the remarkable transformation of Providence from a small farming village to a city that regularly sent scores of trading ships on voyages around the globe—a city that by the end of the 19th century could also boast of being a major industrial center, with 1,200 mills and manufacturing plants that sent their finished goods throughout the nation."

If a tourable "Riverwalk" exists in Providence, then, it is largely as result of these strategically placed panels, designed by architect William D. Warner from materials including maps and historic images furnished by the Rhode Island Historical Society. According to Albert Klyberg, president of the society in 1996 when the panels were constructed and posted, the placards have effectively become "an outdoor exhibit for [the Rhode Island Historical Society]. They are extraordinarily well done, and the placement is good." Walking along the rivers and reading the panels, Klyberg asserted in a 1996 interview, is "almost like coming to one of our lectures" (DuJardin 1996).

The particular benefit of the panels, of course, is that they enable visitors and residents alike to take a self-guided tour of any part of the Riverwalk at any time, and to do so at their own pace, or to simply happen upon these informative panels in their everyday travels to and from work or social events. The panels are easy to read and include clear illustrations of the evolution of the city's water routes since the first Anglo settlers arrived in 1636, as well as demonstrate the inextricable connection between those water routes and the development of cultural and civic life in Providence.

Providence Place Mall

Perhaps the single greatest symbol of the Renaissance redevelopment of Capital Center has been the one that was intended to be the new parcel's greatest financial asset: the Providence Place Mall. Indeed, at the heart of the economic renewal projects of Providence and similar postindustrial waterfront cities are the retail and entertainment complexes known as "festival marketplaces," a term first coined by real estate developer James Rouse to reference the pleasure pavilions created by quasi-public corporations along derelict urban waterfronts. In his 2001 article on the redesign of Manhattan's South Street Seaport, John Metzger defines the festival marketplace as a phenomenon largely characteristic of the 1970s and 1980s. Metzger notes the ways in which the festival marketplace both adheres to and diverges from the traditional design of suburban shopping malls. He articulates the characteristics of such retail palaces as follows: "Festival marketplaces were distinguished from other shopping centres by the absence of 'anchor' department stores, their unique locational advantages (such as urban waterfronts) and the distinct and colorful shopping environments, comprised of a critical mass of food vendors and restaurants, a creative mix of tenants, attractions for tourists and special events" (2001:26).

Described by former mayor of Atlanta Andrew Young as "public interest capitalism," festival marketplaces were considered valuable potential boons to run-down city centers lacking a strong retail presence. In his 1997 genealogy of urban retail, Kent Robertson notes that these marketplaces "represent an approach to downtown redevelopment that attempts to take advantage of historical buildings" and other elements not found in the suburbs (390). Not surprisingly, then, these marketplaces have traditionally been the centerpieces of downtown redevelopment plans that attempt to emphasize walkability and revitalize the warehouse districts and expansive brownfields bordering the historic ports of eighteenth- and nineteenth-century cities. These festival marketplaces are expressly intended, then, to offer cultural landscapes replete with waterfront views, outdoor amphitheaters, and "river/lake walks."

Making use of dilapidated port areas, urban waterfront redesigns anchored by festival marketplaces effectively transform spectral landscapes of maritime trade and industry from sites of dereliction, absence, and loss to cosmopolitan spectacles of postmodern consumption. Once the site of trade, shipbuilding, and other forms of industry (including twentieth-century steel production, paper pulping, and textile milling), the waterfronts of an increasing number of eighteenth- and nineteenth-century cities, Providence included, now exist primarily as commodities to be consumed by both local and regional tourists, a function wholly in line with the rest of the cultural landscape H. V. Savitch has referred to as "postindustrial." Citing Savitch's 1988 text, Richard Marshall articulates the characteristics of the postindustrial city and, specifically, the potential meanings that can be extrapolated from an analysis of these cities' respective waterfront areas. He states:

> The post-industrial city deals with processing and services rather than manufacturing, intellectual capacity rather than muscle power, and dispersed office environments rather than concentrated factories. These changes manifest themselves into the building of a new physical environment constructed specifically to meet the needs of the twenty-first century. Examining the redevelopment of the urban waterfront tells us a lot about what we as a culture believe those needs to be. (2001:8)

Besides crafting a concise definition of "postindustrial," Marshall's phraseology also offers some valuable insight to the politics of urban waterfront renewal, noting a shift from the "muscle power" that has traditionally characterized factory work to the "intellectual capacity" required for jobs in the financial and service sectors of the contemporary city. Clearly, then, one of the tensions in urban waterfront renewal is the conversion of sites of labor (populated primarily by a blue-collar and largely ethnic working class) to locations Thorstein Veblen

([1899] 2001) famously referred to as "sites of conspicuous leisure," or spaces occupied and used primarily by elites for recreational purposes and to demonstrate or perform class status within the public sphere. While some might argue, and, indeed, have argued, that these new waterfronts have rescued postindustrial sites from the oblivion of dereliction and transformed them into the types of democratized gathering spaces imagined by philosophers from Jean-Jacques Rousseau to Jürgen Habermas, I argue that the central role played by the festival marketplace in these waterfront projects is actually resulting in what social geographer Denis Byrne (2003) has referred to as "nervous landscapes" fraught with cultural tension.

Walking the Spectacular City Center: Nervous Landscapes and Urban Economic Renewal

According to Byrne, who coins this phrase in reference to the extant racial tensions between aboriginal and settler populations in New South Wales, Australia, "nervous landscapes" result not from the success of identity-based policies of containment and practices of segregation (such as apartheid), but from their failure (2003:188). The anxieties produced within such landscapes are especially heightened, he argues, when "the separating space reduces to zero—when [different types of] bodies actually touch" (170). Accordingly, I draw on Byrne's work to support three general conclusions regarding the urban waterfront redesign of Capital Center and its supposed success. First, despite some scholars' claims, the redevelopment of urban port areas through spectacular commerce has not stripped such areas of authentic historical significance or meaning, but it has resulted in some potentially negative effects that relate to my second and third conclusions, which have to do with the specious nature of the claims made by tourism boosters and policy elites regarding the democratization of public space in Providence and the supposedly equal opportunity for all bodies to actively access and use the newly created Capital Center parcel as it currently exists. I will address each of these conclusions below in turn.

First, I do not believe that urban port areas have necessarily been "cheapened" or robbed of any authentic historical significance by the encroachment of spectacular commerce. Indeed, both North American aboriginal and European settler populations grew up around waterways specifically for their resources and/or their commercial potential, and they were often considered socially sordid locations even by elites in the eighteenth and nineteenth centuries. Therefore it is neither the commercial focus nor the spectacularity of these waterfront redesigns that establish these sites as "nervous landscapes" in my view. Instead, it is the ways that these sites rely on tropes of walkability (an idea that promises public access) and recursive events (such as Waterfire, a lighting of Providence rivers that is free to attend) to establish a guise of democratization—the idea that all populations enjoy equal access to Capital Center. This official approach renders invisible the spatialized power dynamics of Waterplace Park, the River-walk, and the Providence Place Mall as encompassed in what is in fact a "tourist bubble." While ethnic, immigrant, and working-class populations dominated eighteenth- and nineteenth-century Providence's commercial waterfronts, lei-sured elites, particularly affluent Anglo women, were largely absent from such locations of industry and commerce. Yet a leisured elite class is exactly the one the new Capital Center was engineered to attract.

My second general conclusion is that while redesigned waterfronts with shopping malls such as Providence Place do not necessarily displace the work-ing class (after all, all bodies are able to walk in the public areas of Capital Center), they do render both labor and the laboring body invisible within the performative spectacle of commerce-as-neoliberal-leisure (Frieden and Sagalyn 1989; Teaford 1990). Within the festival marketplace, the "festival" atmosphere relies on consigning both work and the working body to peripheral occupational locations, including underground or internal loading docks, parking garages, food courts, and custodial closets. The building of luxury condominiums and/or apartment complexes with waterfront views functions similarly, and both ventures come dangerously close to abrogating the very public space that was originally created by establishing these urban parks, leaving little physical space in the newly created Capital Center parcel for activities such as picnicking, sun-bathing, kite launching, and, even, perhaps, gathering for public demonstrations or protests. In short, spectacular consumption and its privileging of leisure has not only changed the quality and function of public space in Providence but has also significantly reduced its quantity.

Finally, the identities of the bodies using the Capital Center parcel for work and play contribute substantially to the production of "nervous landscapes." While racialized and class-specific uses of space are certainly productive of such landscapes within these urban waterfront redesigns, so too does gender produce anxiety. As is noted by a number of feminist and labor historians alike, deindustrialization has had a significant impact on the gender politics of urban built environments. While feminist historians, including Mary Ryan (1992), Gail Bederman (1995), and Sarah Deutsch (2000), have documented well the late nineteenth-century rise in the social acceptability of women laboring in urban environments outside the home (with specific populations of women engaged in specific types of work, of course), urban studies scholar Lynn Appleton (1995) notes that as of the mid-1990s the majority of America's female-headed families were living in cities. Additionally, the shift from an industrial to a service and tourism economy has rendered the city "feminized" (largely considered devoid of the kinds of itinerantly "masculine" muscle power so symbolic of industrial labor). This critique seems especially appropriate to Providence, Rhode Island, a location whose major contemporary industries are no longer fishing, trade, or even textiles manufacturing but the female-dominated industries of health care and tourism. Indeed, rather than exporting materials to the world, Providence, like many of the United States' most historical ports, now serves as the locus for retailing goods manufactured elsewhere, often by nonwhite, non-Western female bodies. Finally, the very retail establishments marketing such products (such as the Providence Place Mall) rely on an infrastructure supported by local populations marginalized by ethnicity, immigration status, gender, class, and other identitarian categories.

It is not a new idea to understand urban environments, set apart from the traditional rugged American mythologies attendant to farming and/or "working the land" as cosmopolitan sites of leisure, tourism, and other enterprises that have traditionally been considered "nonproductive," effete, and feminized. But I am suggesting that this idea needs some revision in the wake of new scholarship that suggests the dynamic interplay of urban space, waterways, work, global capitalism, and conceptions of American citizenship. The ways in which Americans identify and define work and its power to shape local, regional, and national identities are shifting; particularly, I would argue, in rural and urban areas where entire populations are experiencing or anticipating the devolution of their professions or industries—and, by extension, the possibility of their own irrelevance within an increasingly expanding global economy in which local cultural landscapes are often operated and influenced by off-site organizational forces.

Owned and operated by just such an off-site real estate giant named General Growth Properties, which completed a merger with the Rouse Company in 2004, the Providence Place Mall illustrates the type of national and global politics of urban American retail establishments (see http://www.ggp.com/company). Opened in 1999 by the Chicago-based company after an excruciatingly long and contentious planning period (the mall was first proposed in 1985 and has had a number of developers associated with various phases of the project), this mall, which cost nearly five hundred million dollars to build, constituted the single most expensive quasi-public project of Capital Center (by comparison, Waterplace Park cost only $169 million) (Leazes and Motte 2004:73). It also sparked significant controversy given the proximity of retail hubs and malls in Warwick, located just ten miles south of Providence; North Attleboro, Massachusetts; and even in downtown Providence itself, which features the historic Providence Arcade, the oldest indoor shopping mall in the United States. According to Leazes and Motte, the Providence Place Mall was able to overcome complaints of superfluity by functioning as a kind of postmodern community center:

> Providence Place is very much designed to be a center of community activity. The mall has 1.35 million square feet of retail space occupied by 150 retail stores and anchored by Lord and Taylor, Filene's, and Nordstrom. About 2,500 people work in Providence Place. A seven-hundred-seat food court, with a variety of fast-food venues that feature American and ethnic cuisines, is located in a third-level "wintergarden," a high-ceilinged, glassed area that links the "Cityside" of the mall (the south) to its "Stateside" (the north) and provides a spectacular view of sunsets to the west and of Capital Center to the east. Above

> this area are a sixteen-screen stadium-seating Hoyts cinema complex
> and an IMAX theater. There are also several full-service restaurants,
> ranging from the Napa Valley Grille to Joe's American Bar and Grill.
> Dave and Buster's supplies arcade fun and food. . . . The mall is linked
> physically by a skybridge walkway to the Westin Hotel/Rhode Island
> Convention Center complex. The Friedrich St. Florian–designed sky-
> bridge is the symbolic link between the old and new retail centers of
> the city. (147)

Despite the multiple services associated with the mall, including the Providence
Skills Center, a nonprofit corporation "dedicated to improving the lifestyles of
individuals from a variety of backgrounds" that offers GED classes and pharmacy technician and customer service training, Providence Place is recognized
by locals as an upscale shopping center.

Conclusion: Walking in the Spectral City: The Practice of Place in the "Nervous Landscape" of the Historic City

The only way to measure the success of Providence's urban renaissance, geographers Francis Leazes and Mark Motte argued in 2004, is to see whether or
not people are using the new parcels of land in the ways for which they were intended, and both scholars believe that people are. Besides everyday usage of the
Riverwalk, the Providence Place Mall, and the recursive staging of Waterfire,
events such as the Gravity and Xtreme games, both high-profile, cutting-edge,
and youth-oriented events, have also been hosted at the park in recent years.
According to Leazes and Motte, "The river relocation and Waterplace have created a special, authentic sense of place. Since their unveiling, the rivers and their
allied beautification projects have become vital to much of the new economic
activity in the central city" (2004:139–140).

While the influence of local preservationists and the economic impetus
to re-create Providence as a tourist attraction certainly had an impact on the
plans commissioned by and submitted to the city of Providence, public officials
and business leaders were also clear regarding their goal to create parcels of
land that could be developed into commercial office space and other revenue-
enhancing private projects. Though the creation of Capital Center improved
access to and reunited certain areas of the city, contemporary development of
the land (particularly the placement and design of the Providence Place Mall,
the new GTECH office tower, and the luxury condominium high-rise) has arguably negated some of the Capital Center Commission's other goals, including
the creation of open public space and increased access to all surrounding areas
of the city. The Providence Place Mall and Interstate 95 restrict access between
Providence's downtown and its once highly industrialized west side, as well as
further marginalizing lower-income neighborhoods located on the outskirts of

the city, including South Providence, Olneyville, Elmwood, and Silver Lake, all areas featuring high percentages of recent immigrants and black Americans.

If the downtown revitalization strategy has appeared overwhelmingly successful in attracting new businesses and revitalizing the physical terrain of downtown Providence, critics of the Providence renaissance argue that only already-privileged local and statewide populations are able to access or make use of Capital Center as "civic space," reigniting the types of conflicts over equal access to leisure areas that have plagued downtown Providence since the late nineteenth century, when the cove lands that would later become Capital Center were sodden marshes whose future sparked heated debates between elites and the city's working-class populations.[5]

Accounting for the "nervous landscapes" produced by the overlapping strata of labor and leisure in Providence's Capital Center since the opening of the mall in 1999 also calls attention to extant frictions between representational and nonrepresentational philosophical approaches to cultural landscape studies. While a number of scholars work with a type of representational theory that, according to geographer Nigel Thrift, relies on a view of the world as if the scholar is not "slap bang in the middle of it, co-constructing it with numerous human and non-human others," Thrift (1999:296–297) instead aligns himself with phenomenological scholars and advocates abandoning traditional approaches which take the view that space is "built" by the mere overlay of the discursive onto the physical.

Since this type of theory would divide culture and nature, as well as neglect the performative role a human body plays in shaping the environment it uses, Thrift dismisses it and instead prefers a "dwelling perspective" in which nature and culture must be understood as mutually constitutive and developed through the performance of some kind of activity, be it intentional or not, observed or not. This perspective aligns well with de Certeau's notion of a site-specific "touring narrative" as well as other approaches recently championed by scholars of walkability who are necessarily interested in the interplay between human bodies and the natural as well as built environments. Accordingly, my analysis here interprets the cultural landscape of Capital Center as a series of performances achieved in and through specific natural and human-made spaces and activities, their surrounding structures, and their attendant spatial and social politics. The official narratives accompanying this cultural landscape provides a nostalgic sense that Providence's maritime and industrial pasts are alive and well, linked symbolically to the city's postindustrial present

[5] The role of railroads and rivers to issues such as city planning and public health was addressed by a number of Providence's mayors over the years in public speeches. In 1887, Mayor Gilbert Robbins's main concern was creating a centrally located terminus, and by 1889 Henry Barker advocated the consolidation of four railroad companies into two. The final sale of the cove lands occurred in 1894. Not until 1902 did Mayor Daniel Granger turn his attention toward making Providence beautiful and healthy again, advocating the planting of trees and repurchasing tracts of lands exclusively for recreation use (information from the Providence City Archives collection).

through carefully curated public spaces and architectural choices. At the same time, however, Providence's new downtown core represents to visitors and residents alike a commitment to the contemporary neoliberal cultural values of late capitalism, serving as proof that the historical, walkable city is not so much a dynamic, living entity fashioned and refashioned through vernacular use as it is a tool to be wielded strategically by specific forces at specific times to produce desired types of economic renewal.

Downtown Providence's successes, while they may not prove sustainable in the end, have for the moment provided the cultural and financial momentum enabling the recent political administrations of Providence, under the leadership of first Mayor David Cicilline and then Mayor Angel Tavares, to turn its attention toward implementing a new comprehensive plan for Providence that moves beyond the "tourist bubble" of downtown Providence to address the needs of the city's urban residents. Entitled "Providence 2020," the new plan picks up where "Providence 2000" and "Providence Tomorrow" left off and focuses explicitly on neighborhood rejuvenation via the city's new renaissance era resources and urban cosmopolitan brand. With an emphasis on increased public transit (including the proposed addition of a streetcar line) and walkability within individual neighborhoods throughout the city, the newest city plans may well expand accessibility to Capital Center (and encourage increased pedestrian traffic into the contiguous neighborhoods) and restore what cultural geographer David Harvey (2013), in homage to Henri Lefebvre, refers to as the "right to the city"—not only to tourists but also to longtime residents.

REFERENCES

Appleton, Lynn. 1995. "The Gender Regimes of American Cities." Pp. 44–59 in *Gender in Urban Research*, edited by Judith A. Garber and Robyne S. Turner. London: Sage.
Barker, Henry. 1889. "Mayoral Address." Providence City Archives.
Bederman, Gail. 1995. *Manliness and Civilization: A Cultural History of Gender and Race in the United States, 1880–1917.* Chicago: University of Chicago Press.
Byrne, Denis. 2003. "Nervous Landscapes: Race and Space in Australia," *Journal of Social Archaeology* 3(2):169–193.
Chase, John, Margaret Crawford, and John Kaliski. 1999. *Everyday Urbanism.* New York: Monacelli.
de Certeau, Michel. 1984. *The Practice of Everyday Life.* Berkeley: University of California Press.
Deutsch, Sarah. 2000. *Women and the City: Gender, Space, and Power in Boston, 1870–1940.* Oxford: Oxford University Press.
"Doves, Politicians Open Waterplace Park." 1994. *Providence Journal*, 13 July.
DuJardin, Richard C. 1996. "Riverwalk Retraces City's Steps." *Providence Journal*, 3 October.
Duncan, Dustin, T. Jared Aldstadt, John Whalen, Steven J. Melly, and Steven L. Gortmaker. 2011. "Validation of Walkscore for Estimating Neighborhood Walkability: An Analysis of Four MUS Metropolitan Areas." *International Journal of Environmental Research and Public Health* 8:4160–4179.

Florida, Richard. 2004. *The Rise of the Creative Class: And How It's Transforming Work, Leisure, Community and Everyday Life.* New York: Basic Books.

———. 2007. *Flight of the Creative Class: The New Global Competition for Talent.* New York: Harper Business.

Frieden, Bernard J. and Lynne B. Sagalyn. 1989. *Downtown, Inc.: How America Rebuilds Cities.* Cambridge, MA: MIT Press.

Granger, Daniel. 1902. "Mayoral Address." Providence City Archives.

Harvey, David. 2013. *Rebel Cities: From the Right to the City to the Urban Revolution.* New York: Verso.

Imbrie, Katherine. 1995. "A Providence Promenade Heritage Trail Is a Civilized Stroll through the City, Past and Present." *Providence Journal*, 31 March.

Leazes, Francis and Mark Motte. 2004. *Providence: The Renaissance City.* Boston: Northeastern University Press.

Marshall, Richard, ed. 2001. *Waterfronts in Post-Industrial Cities.* London: Spon.

Metzger, John. 2001. "The Failed Promise of a Festival Marketplace: South Street Seaport in Lower Manhattan." *Planning Perspectives* 16:25–47.

"River Relocation Wins Washington Group's Praise." 1994. *Providence Journal*, 26 October.

Robbins, Gilbert. 1887. "Mayoral Address." Providence City Archives.

Robertson, Kent. 1997. "Downtown Retail Revitalization: A Review of American Development Strategies." *Planning Perspectives* 12:383–401.

Rosenzweig, Roy and David Thelan. 2000. *The Presence of the Past: Popular Uses of History in American Life.* New York: Columbia University Press.

Ryan, Mary. 1992. *Women in Public, between Banners and Ballots: 1825–1880.* Baltimore: Johns Hopkins University Press.

Saltzman, Jonathan. 1996. "*USA Today* Recognizes Providence's Renewal." *Providence Journal*, 31 December.

Savitch, H. V. 1988. *Post Industrial Cities: Politics and Planning in New York, Paris and London.* Princeton, NJ: Princeton University Press.

Schechner, Richard. 1994. *Environmental Theater: An Expanded New Edition Including "Six Axioms for Environmental Theater."* New York: Applause.

Schein, Richard. 1997. "The Place of Landscape: A Conceptual Framework for Interpreting an American Scene." *Annals of the Association of American Geographers* 87(4): 660–680.

Speck, Jeff. 2012. *Walkability: How Downtown Can Save America, One Step at a Time.* New York: Farrar, Straus and Giroux.

Teaford, Jon C. 1990. *The Rough Road to Renaissance: Urban Revitalization in America 1940–1985.* Baltimore: Johns Hopkins University Press.

Thrift, Nigel. 1999. "Steps to an Ecology of Place." Pp. 296–297 in *Human Geography Today*, edited by Doreen Massey, John Allen, and Phil Sarre. Cambridge: Polity.

Veblen, Thorstein. 2001. *The Theory of the Leisure Class: Modern Library Paperback Edition.* New York: Modern Library.

Walkscore. 2014. "Living in Providence." Retrieved July 3, 2014. http://www.walkscore.com/RI/Providence.

IV

Politics and Power

That urban space, like social space, is shaped by and reflects power manifest as inequality is hardly a controversial claim in contemporary urban studies. In this regard, urban space is one more context for social processes and social forces in general, and, as such, is an area of fundamental concern to sociology. But if the investigation of the connection between power and urban space is not surprising as a topic, research on everyday urban spaces reveals much of the ubiquitous ordinary operation of power and the most visible forms of social inequality. Public space, by its very nature, is widely known to urban dwellers. In these spaces, power is often unnoticed but never invisible.

In this part, contributors elaborate on the connections between everyday and exceptional forms of mobility, mainly kinds of walking, and politics. The built environment often reflects power through differential access. Some spaces are exclusive; these are generally private or semiprivate spaces but include some kinds of public space, especially where consumption is involved. As urban dwellers readily know, some public spaces are more public than others.

Power is relational; it describes the connection between individuals and groups. For this reason, the field of analysis is often social space. When we refer to relations between social classes, for example, we are talking about social space. But we could also analyze power in geographic space. As Pierre Bourdieu (1990) suggests, the inequalities of social space are also embedded in geographic space. Bourdieu (1990:126) claims that there is a "tendency toward spatial segregation," that those with similar positions in social space tend also to be proximate in geographic space.

Michel Foucault (1977) notes also how the configuration of space leads to power relations. It is perhaps easier to see power as a restraining force in urban space—signs such as "do not enter" or barriers meant to control the mobility of people in particular spaces. But Foucault reminds us that power is generative, too, and the arrangements of disciplinary power are spatial and temporal. Grids and queues, and schedules, are a ubiquitous part of urban life. Extending this observation, we can ask whether and how the configuration of urban spaces produces certain kinds of urban subjects, and further, how resisting spatial practices can be a challenge to power relations.

Henri Lefebvre (2013)—one of the most significant theorists of urban life and urban space—recognized the same relationship between the organization of space and time and the exercise of power. His analysis of the rhythms of modern life reveals the everyday operation of power (and resistance to it). What Foucault called "disciplinary power" Lefebvre called "dressage," the use of spatial and temporal cycles to produce a trained subject. Lefebvre also understood that disrupting everyday cycles is a form of creativity, of resistance.

As discussed in Chapter 1, Jean-François Augoyard (2007) proposed to study quotidian mobility as a kind of rhetoric. The strategies that he identified in his ethnography of a public housing site in Grenoble often involved the subversion of official uses of space—the taking of shortcuts, for example. He describes one telling instance of an architectural detail, a round opening in the wall of one of the buildings of the complex, designed to enhance the light and visual field, that was being used by people to cut from one corridor to another even though the opening was clearly not intended to be a passage.

Municipal authorities have long been concerned with the mobility of urban dwellers, especially those lower in the class hierarchy. Mobility, particularly at night, was seen as decadent and perhaps criminal (Schlör 1998).[1] Much has been written about Baron Haussmann's remaking of Paris, but it is of interest to note how much of the redesign (the making of modern Paris) had to do with mobility—the movement of goods and people, and of course, the movement of police/military forces to exert control over potentially unruly communities (Harvey 2006).

Economic and social power is reflected in the built environment, especially in commercial spaces. Benjamin Shepard and Gregory Smithsimon (2011:1411) show that the design of urban plazas in New York—"unwelcoming, harsh environments"—were intentionally antisocial. The presence of ordinary urban dwellers had to be actively repelled by the design of the space, to preserve the space as a monument to economic power and to reinforce the separation of social groups. In this regard, space is not simply a metaphor for the operation of power, but is in fact its field of operation.

Guy Debord (1957, 1958, 1961) and his Situationist colleagues were especially concerned with the way that urban planning and architecture were trans-

---

[1] As Schlör (1998) notes, much early urban ethnography was concerned with the everyday mobility of the urban poor, especially with regard to crime and prostitution. Urban walking has a long history of being the object of study as well as a primary method.

forming the urban environment to suit the needs of mass consumerism. The dominant uses of space and time in the consumer capitalist city produced patterns of daily life that domesticated the untamed energy of the city. Capitalism requires that consumers be docile bodies. Space and time had to be routinized and monitored to accomplish this. The capitalist city is full of uniform public spaces, where everyone looks and acts alike but thinks of himself or herself as an individual. The elite spaces of the capitalist class are an exception, but they are not really public spaces because they are hidden from the mass consumer.

Debord proposed a radical repurposing of space and time as a remedy to the regime of the Spectacle. The Situationists sought to provoke "situations," the dynamic use of space and time in unproductive activities to create an emergent sense of community. If routinized space/time could domesticate the minds of urban dwellers, then "situations" could free them. The lesson for contemporary urban ethnography is to attend to the ways that everyday practices in ordinary space and time push people toward submission or toward resistance.

As urban politics concerns, in large measure, racial, ethnic, and class inequalities, these chapters consider walking as a form of resistance to power and to the institutions that represent the interests of the powerful. As discussed in the introduction to Part III, Elijah Anderson's (2011) "cosmopolitan canopies" concept is especially useful to see how ordinary spatial practices enact power relations. Dominant groups, Anderson notes, are more likely to be able to upset the sense of shared space; this is a form of spatial privilege.

Amber N. Wiley examines the complexity of the meaning of "walkability" in the context of urban planning and the geography of place in Chapter 10. She draws on auto-ethnographic research in New Orleans and brings the dimensions of race and class into the examination of mobility in public spaces. She contrasts everyday walking ("purposeful") and the spectacular, based on the city's history of processional collective activity. Urban planning, and especially infrastructure support, in conjunction with economic development make New Orleans a city of distinct spaces along a racial and class divide. The tourist space of the French Quarter and the Central Business District are walkable because they are designed that way to service powerful constituencies. Vernacular spaces, the places where poor and working-class African American residents live, present significant mobility obstacles. The history of processional public performances demonstrates an assertion of power (a tactic, in Michel de Certeau's sense) that could be the basis for reform in urban design.

In Chapter 11, Evrick Brown investigates the meaning of a neighborhood protest march in East Flatbush, Brooklyn, in order to elaborate on the place-based social construction of urban spaces. This neighborhood is a mixed African American and black Caribbean community, and the political and social competition between the two groups is the context for community building. Brown uses a walking method ("footwork") to bring the research close to the residents' view on the streets and his walking-as-research mirrors the walking-as-practice of these urban dwellers. In vernacular neighborhoods like this,

sidewalk sociability is an essential element of the construction of the neighborhood as place. This is contrasted with the more spectacular mode of collective
activity represented by the protest walk, where the collective action—even if
spontaneous—is oriented toward claims making. (In the instance Brown describes, the protest against police brutality was a claim for justice, as he notes
one protestor commenting, "They'll think twice about shootin' one of us again.")
Both of these forms of mobility, everyday and exceptional, generate the social
bonds that make a specific place into a neighborhood.

The research reported by Paul R. Watts, in Chapter 12, connects walking as
an embodied mobility and the material landscape of Washington, D.C. Watts
studied thirty protests in the U.S. capital. The use of walking as a collective
practice in a city where political power is both symbolically and institutionally
located recreates (and continues) the tradition of public assembly and political
dissent. Protest marches combine walking and public assembly; the physical
presence of the march—the mass of marchers (however large) and the way that
their collective mobility disrupts everyday routines (in the case of large marches,
by blocking or rerouting traffic and in the case of smaller ones, by altering the
visual, spatial field of the streetscape)—is combined with the built environment
to not only represent power from below, but also to enact it.

As with the research reported by Wiley and Brown, Watts shows how walking is transformed by its deployment as protest but as embodied mobility retains
the same properties—slowness, pausability, and so forth—that generate a specific kind of sociability. These bonds create community but also create (or promote) movements. Social movements have broad repertoires in contemporary
societies, of course, but mass collective action in public space is as powerful as
any of them. As Watts puts it, reflecting on his own experience in the marches
he studied, "As an individual, being on the street made me feel small, yet I also
felt empowered because I was part of large, unified group."

Brian B. Knudsen, Terry Nichols Clark, and Daniel Silver, in Chapter 13,
use comparative data from the United States, Canada, and France to explore
how walking enhances urban dwellers' creative engagement with their communities. They test quantitative models of the multidimensional relationship
between walking (and walkability), social movement organizations, and arts
establishments. Among the hypotheses they propose concerns the interaction:
"Walking in locales with more arts activity will have more impact on the incidence of social movement organizations." They find substantial support for
this in all three countries. (The multiplicative term, walking × arts index, has a
larger effect than the walking term alone.)

Wiley, Brown, and Watts all use walking as a form of auto-ethnography
of urban spaces. This reflexive posture gives us a glimpse of the rich narrative
detail that urban dwellers can produce. Knudsen and his colleagues use demographic and geographic data to test hypotheses about the effects of walking on
social movement organizations. This is a nice contrast of the relative advantages
of idiographic and nomothetic approaches to urban life and everyday mobility.

REFERENCES

Anderson, Elijah. 2011. *The Cosmopolitan Canopy: Race and Civility in Everyday Life.* New York: Norton.

Augoyard, Jean-François. 2007. *Step by Step: Everyday Walks in a French Urban Housing Project.* Minneapolis: University of Minnesota Press.

Bourdieu, Pierre. 1990. *In Other Words: Essays towards a Reflexive Sociology.* Stanford, CA: Stanford University Press.

Debord, Guy. 1957. *Report on the Construction of Situations.* Translated by Ken Knabb. Retrieved August 5, 2014. http://www.bopsecrets.org/SI/report.htm.

———. 1958. *Theses on Cultural Revolution.* Translated by Ken Knabb. *Internationale Situationniste* 1. Retrieved August 5, 2014. http://www.bopsecrets.org/SI/1.cultural-revolution.htm.

———. 1961. *Perspectives for Conscious Change in Everyday Life.* Translated by Ken Knabb. *Internationale Situationniste* 6. Retrieved August 5, 2014. http://www.bopsecrets.org/SI/6.everyday.htm.

Foucault, Michel. 1977. *Discipline and Punish: The Birth of the Prison.* Translated by Alan Sheridan. New York: Vintage.

Harvey, David. 2006. *Paris, Capital of Modernity.* New York: Routledge.

Lefebvre, Henri. 2013. *Rhythmanalysis: Space, Time and Everyday Life.* Translated by Stuart Elden and Gerald Moore. London: Bloomsbury.

Schlör, Joachim. 1998. *Nights in the Big City.* London: Reaktion Books.

Shepard, Benjamin and Gregory Smithsimon. 2011. *The Beach beneath the Streets: Contesting New York City's Public Spaces.* Albany: State University of New York Press.

10

Geography, Planning, and Performing Mobility in New Orleans

AMBER N. WILEY

> From the perspective of mobilities, cities and environments are not
> static, simple objects with singular identities, but are understood
> equivocally and lived and actualized by competing actors with
> unreconciled interests.
>
> —Phil Steinberg and Rob Shields, *What Is a City?*
> *Rethinking the Urban after Hurricane Katrina*

> Infrastructure is a mirror that reflects our civic values, cultural identity,
> and collective hopes for a better future.
>
> —William R. Morrish, "After the Storm:
> Rebuilding Cities upon Reflexive Infrastructure"

"Do you think New Orleans is walkable?"
I asked this simple question with pointed intent. For most people
I polled the term *walkable* was urbanist jargon that might require
further explanation. Rarely, however, did any of my respondents ask for further
clarification. Instead, by and large, the answer I was given was a simple yes. I
asked this of New Orleans residents, some of whom had lived their whole lives
in the city; some were newcomers like myself. They spanned various racial and
ethnic groups, age ranges, and income brackets. I asked this of people who no
longer lived in New Orleans—those who had attended college in the city, those
who visited for a conference or a weekend reunion with old friends, or those who
attended one of the famous music festivals.[1] While the answer was frequently in
the affirmative, my respondents usually followed with qualification: "Yes, but

---

[1] I spoke to people who had attended Tulane University, Loyola University, and Xavier University;
who had attended Jazz Fest and Essence Fest; who were season ticket holders to New Orleans Saints
games at the Superdome; who attended public middle and high schools; who held a variety of positions from social worker to university professor; and so forth. The sample was not random, as these
were all associates from various stages in my life.

only certain neighborhoods, at certain times of the day, depending on where you need to go, as long as you don't need public transportation, if it's not too hot outside." This would often lead me to ask the question again. The second answer with reconsiderations was always less positive and more complicated: "Actually, New Orleans walkability is defined by districts." "I would call it a 'nodal' walkability."

This line of questioning helped me draw some useful conclusions. The first is that many New Orleanians and tourists generally feel the city is walkable—their first instinct was to answer in the affirmative. The second is that with a line of further questioning on the practicality of *purposeful* walking in the city, as opposed to walking for leisure, there was a clear implication of the obstacles and factors that would alter their attitude toward the quality of walkability in the city. My intent was less focused on seeing how the city measured up in the latest urban trend and more interested in exploring various dichotomies in the lived experience of *mobility* in the city. As a three-year resident, but still a relative outsider and newcomer, I stood firmly within the camp of "no." New Orleans was not walkable. I lived in Washington, D.C., for five years without an automobile and navigated the city almost seamlessly on foot with the assistance of public transportation. I could not imagine living in New Orleans and moving with as much ease without an automobile.

Despite images of densely packed tourists in the French Quarter walking the streets, New Orleans is not a pedestrian-friendly city. Sidewalks are discontinuous, dangerous, and riddled with obstacles such as tree roots and broken segments that keep joggers at bay. The most dedicated runners prefer to share the neutral ground with streetcars and inhale exhaust from automobiles traveling down St. Charles Avenue, or go to designated green spaces such as Audubon Park situated in the Uptown neighborhood or City Park in Mid-City for a bucolic running experience.[2]

Conversely, and somewhat ironically, New Orleanians *inhabit* the street at a rate far greater than their counterparts in many other North American cities. What is more, not only is everyday life dependent on the automobile or a bicycle; the public infrastructure in the city only exacerbates the problem. The paradox here is that the lack of pedestrian and public-transit-oriented infrastructure in the city does not negatively affect cultural custom. The dysfunction actually feeds cultural customs of resistance. While dangerous sidewalks and infrequent streetcars and buses do not solve problems of mobility for a whole segment of the population that cannot afford cars, New Orleanians are empowered by their musical customs and relationship to the street. From countless festivals, second lines, funeral processions, and parades, New Orleanians reclaim the vehicular thoroughfare and render it a place of occupation, celebration, and community. As Michel de Certeau argued in *The Practice of Everyday Life*, "Space is a prac-

---

[2] *Neutral ground* is the New Orleans term for median. For detailed analysis of the use and health benefits of City Park, see Renne and Bennett (2010).

ticed place" (1984:117). New Orleanians have practiced the space of the street on foot for more than two centuries. Furthermore, these cultural practices, musically infused pedestrian processions in New Orleans, reveal spatially determined sites of hierarchical power, places of struggle, claims to territory, visibility and mobility (or lack thereof), and a sense of place.

This chapter examines the multidimensionality of mobility in New Orleans. Mobility is assessed by the overall geography of place, intimacy of scale, racialized spaces, physical barriers brought about through planning and infrastructure, and, finally, through the tradition of parade culture. Walking is considered in two different frameworks—purposeful and processional. The way that mobility differs in these contexts brings to the fore inequity in city planning, services, and disparate cultural practices of procession that are indigenous to the city.

New Orleans reveals important points about the power of walking in the city, how it is supported by infrastructure, how it implicates spaces of neglect or failure in the city, and how it creates community. In New Orleans infrastructural privilege is centered on tourism: the French Quarter, the Central Business District, and key arteries related to the tourist-centric image of the city (Shannon 2012).[3] The practice of walking in New Orleans—official (permit-required group processions) and unofficial (purposeful)—reaffirms the political power of walking. As scholar Catherine Michna noted, blues and jazz performances in New Orleans "permeate the city's sidewalks, neutral grounds, and interstate underpasses, a continuous and dynamic mass incarnation of blues- and jazz-based radical democratic epistemologies" (2011:4). New Orleans processionals' focus on places of memory creates an expansive and important narrative of the city that is overlooked but has the potential to push urban policy *if* preexisting walking routes were considered blueprints for infrastructure.

This chapter engages these discussions and situates them within larger issues related to geography, urbanism, infrastructure, cultural practice, and memory. More importantly, it pushes this analysis in the direction of policy formation and urban design initiatives. The act of occupying the street is one of cultural and political resistance. The ultimate goal is to situate the conversation of mobility in New Orleans not only within processional traditions that have deep spiritual and political spatialized meaning but also in conversations by urbanists and architects about walkability, infrastructure, and how these factors relate to public space and the unique geography of the city.

Unique Geographies: Racialized Spaces or Spatialized Race

New Orleans resisted the twentieth-century trend of exponential annexation and growth because of extremely restricted geographies. While nineteenth-century

---

[3] Shannon's article concludes with the expectation that roadwork would be complete before the Super Bowl in February 2013. These tourist-centric concerns are generally at the center of planning deadlines. See also Moises (2013).

expansion from the French Quarter to the American Sector, adjacent faubourgs such as Tremé and Marigny, and independent towns such as Carrolton was possible in New Orleans, the spatial organization of New Orleans is reflective of a geography finitely restricted by the presence of major bodies of water—the Mississippi River, Lake Pontchartrain, and swamps.

When annexation became the norm for American cities in the mid to late twentieth century, New Orleans did not expand at a comparable rate or scale to other major urban centers. Cities like Atlanta, New York, Los Angeles, and Phoenix grew as New Orleans kept its tight boundaries. This factor is significant for the relative walkability (or perception of walkability) of New Orleans. New York is the most walkable large city in the United States despite significant annexation in the twentieth century. This is a result of its unique geography, as well—the top twenty walkable neighborhoods in New York are all located on the island of Manhattan (see http://www.walkscore.com/NY/New_York). Thus, the majority of the walkable neighborhoods are part of a restricted and dense urban fabric.

Urban scholars, ethnomusicologists, and geographers perceive New Orleans as an atypical regional hub that is ambiguously situated between the United States and the Caribbean (Lipsitz 2011). These perceptions inform policy decisions related to the city and push urbanists and other serious scholars of the city to view it as anomalous. As urban historian Carl Abbott noted:

> Postmodern theory directs attention to people and societies that are poised, pushed, and pulled between competing influences. . . . "Centers" are often fixed and unchanging, but edges are where dominant ideas may be weakest and where regional cultures can coexist and interact. Edges are places of conflict, change, and creativity, churning local expectations about culture and behavior, forcing the repeated renegotiation of a dominant local identity. (1999:16)

This observation certainly holds true for New Orleans, and is one of the most significant contributing factors to the marginalization of the city's urban poor. The practice of walking in the city reinscribes this tension in the urban fabric.

The geography of New Orleans, particularly the circuitous route of the Mississippi, dictated the direction and irregularity of streets; therefore, it is one of the least legible and "imageable" cities in the country. Kevin Lynch theorized on the imageability of a city: "Environmental images are the result of a two-way process between the observer and his environment. The environment suggests distinctions and relations, and the observer—with great adaptability and in the light of his own purposes—selects, organizes, and endows with meaning what he sees" (1960:6). This reciprocal relationship is primarily dependent on organization of the environment and its interpretation and personalization by its inhabitants. The Mississippi becomes the dominating factor in understanding how residents orient themselves within the city proper. As the geography of the

Mississippi meanders, so does the understanding of the landscape of New Orleans, and residents no longer reference cardinal directions—instead points are riverside, lakeside, Uptown, and Downtown—infinitely confusing to a visitor but extremely intimate and personal to the New Orleanian. Imageability is not solely about personal identification with place and wayfinding. As architectural theorist Delia Duong Ba Wendel contended, "Space is not merely a context defining the limits of injustice. Space is proleptic, in that its 'imageability' is pivotal to the process of imagining and providing 'just' spaces" (2009:346). Ba Wendel used the theoretical propositions of imageability as being *central* to creating and defining equitable spaces. This can be understood through the alternative narratives of geography in New Orleans with terms such as *backatown* that denote secondary spaces of habitation for the city's African American population.

The complexities of race are an omnipresent factor of everyday life in New Orleans. It is inextricably tied with class, as well as policy-making decisions that dictate the quality of life for residents in the city. Cultural practices are spatialized and articulate how urban and social policies perpetuate the disenfranchisement and marginalization of a significant portion of the city's poor, urban, black population.[4] Historians Arnold Hirsch and Joseph Logsdon (1994:198) illuminated how infrastructure building in New Orleans, particularly the emergence of pump and levee systems, rendered many previously uninhabitable backswamp and lakefront land occupiable. Black neighborhoods expanded into less desirable lands that were "the first to flood and the last to be pumped dry" (1994:199).[5] This was true for Uptown black enclaves, as "modern technology accelerated the growth of that black concentration and the process of racial segregation" (199).

In New Orleans these practices of infrastructural inequity are also exemplified by the construction of the I-10 overpass through the Fifth, Sixth, and Seventh wards and the historic Faubourg Tremé neighborhood, as well as the long-unrealized plans for a civic center on the site of Congo Square that is now the location of Louis Armstrong Park (Crutcher 2001; Sakakeeny 2010). Hirsch and Logsdon argued, "The city's social history was both paralleled and influenced by its physical development. If the city's geography had once forced New Orleanians into intimate association, physical changes in modern [twentieth-century] New Orleans facilitated the drive of white supremacists toward racial segregation and polarization" (1994:197–198).

The palpability of racial tension in New Orleans was laid bare in 2006 by the infamous and hotly contested remarks by then mayor Ray Nagin in the aftermath of Hurricane Katrina. Nagin claimed that he would work to restore New Orleans to its "Chocolate City" roots, putting voice to fears of gentrification

---

[4] For further scholarship on using spatial production theory to understand racial relationships, see Neely and Samura (2011).

[5] For a contemporary view of the long-standing effects of this geographical segregation, see Asomaning-Asare (2008) and Ehrenfeucht and Nelson (2011).

after the displacement caused by the disaster. Afro-diasporic scholar Christopher Dunn used this moment to illustrate how this political proclamation "raised the question of the 'race of place,'" which he argued was a subtext for all political issues facing the city. Dunn then queried, "How does race figure into the fragmented and contested 'imagined community' of New Orleans?" (2007:847). The processional occupation of the street delineates the answer to this question in no unclear terms. As musicologist Matt Sakakeeny noted when describing ring shout festivities of slaves in Congo Square and the history of second lines: "with the freedom of relatively unrestricted movement, musical voices resounded in spaces where political voices had been silenced" (2011:313).

Because of the significant black and Creole population, New Orleans is a center of cultural production even as those populations were systematically disenfranchised through law and disinvestment. This disenfranchisement led to tension that lingers to the present day, and disinvestment in the infrastructure of mobility is still stark. It is important to note, however, that race and socioeconomic status are often conflated in New Orleans. Issues of mobility are situated most squarely along socioeconomic lines, though the racial component has a very real and complex relationship with class.

Infrastructure, Tourism, and "Mobility Privilege"

Urban designer William Morrish, writing on post-Katrina New Orleans, noted in 2008, "A disaster's swift currents not only alter the familiar topological contours of the distressed community; they also reveal major gaps in civic practices and social justice, surprising changes in local culture and ecologies, and a swarm of unsettling questions about the viability of the entire civil infrastructure network" (993). The devastation of Hurricane Katrina illuminated many of the inadequacies of New Orleans's infrastructure. Before a disaster of that magnitude, the attitude toward such issues was rather nonchalant. As Dunn noted in 2007:

> It was common to see bumper stickers blithely celebrating the city's dysfunction and underdevelopment with the slogan, "New Orleans: Third World and Proud." Today I see fewer of these bumper stickers, which seemed especially popular among college students and others who didn't have to worry much about the scandalous inadequacy of the public school system and other basic services that primarily affected working-class black communities. (851)

The problem with the infrastructure in the city is reflective of decades-long neglect, misappropriation of monies, and the infamous corruption in local city politics. Morrish (2008:995) noted that "infrastructure failure is now a daily fact of life in New Orleans," while economist John Bratland (2010:35) characterized the situation as a "systematic failure" of maintenance in the city. The 2004 City Planning Commission report clearly articulated the shortcomings of mobility in the city, but editors Phil Steinberg and Rob Shields noted in *What Is a City? Rethinking the Urban after Hurricane Katrina* that the commission was "uncritical in addressing those problems" (2008:107). Instead, the report celebrated and focused on the successes of mobility in tourist-centric areas of the city. Before Katrina, city officials and New Orleanians' open acknowledgment of infrastructural failure was considered just another quirk of this "border" city negotiating its identity as American with major Caribbean, African, and European influences.

Steinberg and Shields introduced two concepts of mobility that are useful in this chapter's discussion. First, they noted, "An *ideology of mobility* permeates public policy at every level of the U.S. federalist system" (2008:99). We can understand this ideology of mobility as a system of beliefs that move toward an abstraction of thought that becomes divorced from everyday material concerns and the idiosyncrasies of place. This belief system, based on the priorities and concerns of lawmakers who are beholden to the tourism industry, created what Steinberg and Shields called an "uneven distribution of mobility privilege" (2008:109). They explain: "'Mobility privilege' operates both culturally and materially through changes in the built environment. Operating in much the same way as does 'white privilege,' 'masculine privilege,' or 'heterosexist privilege,' the privilege of particular forms of mobility contributes to a wide variety of class and policy practices that continue particular forms of dominance" (101). Mobility privilege is evident in the prioritizing of highway construction that decimated neighborhoods in New Orleans. Steinberg and Shields (109) argue that even after Katrina many of the initiatives to rebuild the city, including the Bring New Orleans Back Commission of 2006, focused on transportation but did not address the inequity in mobility.

One of New Orleans's most celebrated attributes, the streetcar, is central to this discussion on mobility. Once a robust system that supported various areas of the city, the decline of the streetcar occurred contemporaneously with the advent of integration in the city and large-scale white flight to the suburbs (Giusti 2009).[6] By the late 1960s and 1970s there were fewer lines serving the city, accompanied by infrequent and increasingly unreliable service. The most famous streetcar line in New Orleans, which runs down St. Charles Avenue, has become more of a tourist attraction than a reliable means of transportation for New Orleans residents.

In March 2013 the New Orleans Regional Transit Authority (RTA) released the RTA Social Equity and Environmental Justice Policy in accordance with the Title VI of the Civil Rights Act of 1964. The first two goals of policy are to:

- Ensure that transportation service is available and accessible for every person, regardless of their race, color, or national origin.
- Identify and limit negative impacts on human health and the environmental—including social and economic effects of major service

[6] See also Post (2006) and Mizell-Nelson (2001).

changes on minority and low-income population (New Orleans Regional Transit Authority 2013:3).

These points acknowledge the shortcomings of the RTA and an attempt to address mounting public criticism in post-Katrina New Orleans. The policy aims to rectify adverse effects in air, noise, and water pollution, displacement of persons and businesses, isolation or exclusion, employment effects, community cohesion, and separation from community (New Orleans Regional Transit Authority 2013:11).

One of the greatest challenges to pedestrians in New Orleans besides inadequate modes of public transportation is the surface of streets and sidewalks. This adds another dimension to the issues of personal cognition and an embodied experience of the street. This dimension is of a more straightforward tactile and physical nature than legibility or imageability. The grand live oaks that provide a generous canopy against the sun in the summertime are the neighborhood monuments of streets uptown and in the Garden District. They also disrupt the sidewalks with uneven profiles because of the growth and expansion of their strong roots. Pedestrians often prefer to walk *in* the street, as it is less treacherous than the sidewalk (this says nothing of the danger of being a pedestrian fatality to automobile traffic). The street surface, however, is riddled with potholes as a result of subsidence. These problems are widespread and not concentrated in any particular neighborhood (Editorial Board 2010; see also http://livingwithwater.com/projects/gnowms/issues/subsidence-issues/).

If sidewalks are important components of urban infrastructure, as planning scholars Renia Ehrenfeucht and Anastasia Loukaitou-Sideris argued in "Planning Urban Sidewalks: Infrastructure, Daily Life and Destinations," then their function in the daily life of New Orleanians should not be as treacherous as their current state. Purposeful, need-based walking (in the absence of automobile ownership) in New Orleans is highly complicated. Pedestrianism should be supported by clear waymaking signals such as signage and geographical legibility, a safe road and sidewalk infrastructure, and also by a robust public transportation system (Todes 2012; U.S. Department of Transportation Federal Highway Administration 1992). Sidewalks should act as energizing spaces. Urban scholar Joseph Heathcott theorized for an "Infrastructure 2.0" that abandoned long-held notions of automobile-centered mobility for a transportation system that:

> Optimizes the flexibility of human mobility across a nested series of scales. Sidewalks constitute the first layer of mass transit and should be treated as such in investment decisions. Creating a *human-powered transit infrastructure* cannot be restricted to the practice of painting bicycle paths and crossing lanes on top of the automobile's domain; instead, where possible we should invest in methods to separate our transit modes by their relative speed and mode of power. . . . The aim should be to make our cities temples of transit, graded from the intimate point

of shoe leather or wheelchair on pavement to the mass experience of the bus and train. (2010:55, emphasis added)

Heathcott argued for a flexible, complex, and fluid view of transportation that not only separated various modes of mobility on the basis of speed and power but also reconceptualized how these modes interacted with each other. This is a long way from the type of infrastructure planning going on in the United States. The possibilities of this idea are bountiful, however, especially when examining a city such as New Orleans in which mobility is both challenged and subverted through recreational celebration.

There are a number of neighborhoods within the bounds of the New Orleans city limits that, by virtue of their historical heterogeneity of industrial, manufacturing, and residential use, do support a more walkable environment. These neighborhoods are the French Quarter, the Warehouse District, the Irish Channel, the Lower Garden District, Bywater, Marigny, and the Seventh Ward (including historic Tremé). These spaces, comprising the original French and American settlements in the area, are compact and self-contained. These areas provide for all quotidian needs of their residents—spaces that support recreation, worship, markets, commerce, and community.

Jane Jacobs, in her polemic *The Death and Life of Great American Cities*, discussed the need for density to support cultural vitality and diversity in cities ([1961] 1992:200–221). She argued for economic diversity as well as diversity of functions and uses—residences, offices, corner stores, parks—in close proximity to one another. This is what the most walkable neighborhoods offer to their residents, and what continues to make them attractive in today's real estate market. Political scientist Billy Fields argued that density is relevant for a sustainable urbanism in post-Katrina New Orleans: "An important component of achieving climate change reduction goals at the urban level is to encourage quality, walkable environments linked by transit. . . . This 'walkable urbanism' approach to managing the urban landscape holds promise because it is both an effective tool in reducing greenhouse gas emissions from the transportation sector as well as an increasingly marketable real estate product" (2009:326).[7]

The New Orleans Convention and Visitors Bureau (NOCVB) emphasized the city's walkability on its website by proclaiming that "One of New Orleans' best assets is its walkability. The city is conveniently compact and easy to navigate. On foot, visitors can slow down, stroll, take in the remarkable architecture, browse eclectic shops and stop along the way at one of the city's many eateries or bars" (http://www.neworleanscvb.com/visit/maps/walkable/). This observation

---

[7] Fields's research also discussed the highly contentious disconnect between planners and African American New Orleanians who considered a conceptual green space map by Bring New Orleans Back an affront to their communities. For further discussion on the relationship between neighborhood scale, the built environment, and walkability/pedestrianism, see Archer (2005) and Wood, Frank, and Giles-Corti (2010).

is neither facetious nor misleading if taken within the context of the neighbor-hoods that the website highlighted. The boundaries of "Walkable New Orleans," as depicted by the NOCVB, do not extend beyond the confines of the aforementioned neighborhoods. This limited view of the city and its pedestrian naviga-bility denies the issues that truly affect the city as a whole, outside the narrow view of the tourism industry. This narrow view, complacent in promoting the tourism industry's nostalgia in the face of today's reality, is part and parcel of some the deepest-rooted issues that afflict the city.

The walkability of the French Quarter is historic since it was the earliest settlement of New Orleans. However, because of its current use as a tourist at-traction, the significant percentage of absentee landlords renting out units, and the lack of affordability for potential homeowners, the walkability of the French Quarter is one of privilege (see http://www.city-data.com/poverty/poverty-New -Orleans-Louisiana.html). As Steinberg and Shields noted:

> While central New Orleans—in particular the downtown and French Quarter districts—has been the beneficiary of investment over the past several decades as the city promoted itself as a cultural and tourist destination, there have been few economic benefits for the city's lower-income communities. A mobility infrastructure linking lower-income residents in need of jobs to places of employment has, likewise, not be forthcoming. (2008:103)

French Quarter residents are largely middle-aged, white, male, and 97.7 percent childless. A third of French Quarter residents reported that they walked to work in 2010, while slightly more than 5 percent of Orleans Parish residents reported the same (see http://www.gnocdc.org/NeighborhoodData/1/FrenchQuarter/).

New Orleans's total walk score, including the whole bounds of Orleans Parish, has an average of fifty-six and is considered "somewhat walkable" (see http://www.walkscore.com/LA/New_Orleans). The most populous neighbor-hood designation, with 31,159 residents, Edgelake/Little Woods in New Or-leans East is one of the least walkable neighborhoods in the city with a score of twenty-six (see http://www.walkscore.com/LA/New_Orleans/Little_Woods). Conversely, the neighborhood that scored the highest on the walkability index, the French Quarter, is home to 3,691 residents. Walk scores are calculated with various factors in mind, including how close a particular address is to everyday amenities, as well as population density, block lengths, and so on (Walk Score, "Walk Score Methodology," https://www.walkscore.com/methodology.shtml). Two major factors should be considered when looking at these neighborhoods and their walkability. The first is that the French Quarter is the oldest portion of the city, built well before the advent of the automobile, and it has a dense urban fabric reflective of its historical position. Edgelake/Little Woods, on the other hand, was developed on an automobile-centric suburban scale and expanded between 1968 and 1985, in a semirural portion of Orleans Parish, outside the original boundaries of the city of New Orleans (City of New Orleans 2006:3; Souther 2008). This majority black neighborhood is a middle-income area where automobile ownership is high, as opposed to numerous neighborhoods that are not walkable, like Central City and the Lower Ninth Ward, which are majority African American neighborhoods where one-third of the population does not have access to an automobile (see http://www.gnocdc.org/NeighborhoodData/2/ CentralCity/index.html and http://www.gnocdc.org/NeighborhoodData/8/ LowerNinthWard/index.html).

Mobility privilege is manifest in various ways in these two scenarios. It exists in the French Quarter by virtue of the urban fabric, walkability, and access to a car. The French Quarter is also comprised mainly of middle-aged (presumably able-bodied) males. In Edgelake mobility privilege is present, too, though walkability is low. This is a result of automobile accessibility to residents in the neighborhood. Though walkability varied in these two examples, mobility for either population—automobile-centric Edgelake or walkable French Quarter—is relatively high. This is reflective of the socioeconomic status of Edgelake neighborhood residents, who could afford one or more automobiles per household, and that of French Quarter residents who could afford the high rents and mortgage payments in the neighborhood. Here the connection between mobility privilege and socioeconomic status is clear, though the nature of mobility in this case is different.

The Walking Practitioner: Marching, Music, Mobility

Walking is multifaceted as an everyday practice—it is an active force, a means to get from one point to another. It is also a ritual that charts personal preference and individual choice, influences of the built environment, places of comfort and familiarity, and places of avoidance. In his seminal essay "Walking in the City," de Certeau characterizes walkers as the text writers of the city, creating its stories but unable to access the collective knowledge that they produce: "The ordinary practitioners of the city live 'down below,' below the thresholds at which visibility begins. They walk—an elementary form of this experience of the city; they are walkers, Wandersmänner, whose bodies follow the thicks and thins of an urban 'text' they write without being able to read it" (1984:93).

Walking is an act of cultural production in New Orleans. This chapter uses the lens of walkers as practitioners to push past our cursory knowledge of how people interact with their built environment and create a narrative of place. In New Orleans walkers are practitioners of an ephemeral yet timeless folklore. In this case it is ultimately critical to abandon notions of the walker as *flâneur* and voyeur for a productive theory of how walkers mark and produce space, and how we can learn from, build on, and adapt to this production.

In New Orleans walking takes on a strong association with performativity that highlights the production of ethnic identity as well as claims to urban space within the contested landscape of the city. As geographer Helen Regis has noted:

"Promoting spectacle, performance, and historic preservation are increasingly seen as reasonable paths to economic development for urban areas. Inevitably, these concerns produce an environment ripe for highly politicized struggles over space and the ownership of the cultural capital of the city" (2001:753). Processions are lived and observed and produce interplay between the everyday/quotidian aspects of life and the significant/surreal that complicates accepted understanding of the oppositional qualities of the ordinary and extraordinary. In New Orleans processions are both ordinary and extraordinary, and represent different forms of agency. This is a pointedly different way of looking at the practice of walking in the city and issues of walkability. This idea moves past "walkable" as an attractive quality of a neighborhood and mobility as a means of oppression or characteristic of privilege to walking as an active force that highlights various disparities, recreates narratives, and pushes people to reconsider the urban landscape and their relationship to it. In a city like New Orleans, the struggles over urban space and the ownership of cultural capital have become increasingly intense.

This chapter is situated within a much larger discourse between ethnomusicologists, anthropologists, social historians, urbanists, and scholars of the African diaspora who have examined the racialized landscape of New Orleans and the long-standing history of cultural continuity, fusion, and expression in the city. Critical examinations of African American processional musical traditions in New Orleans include Rachel Bruenlin and Regis's (2006) examination of the post-Katrina Ninth Ward landscape and second-lining, and Regis's (2001) work on the politics of public memory in jazz funeral processions. Sakakeeny's (2002, 2008, 2010, 2011) thorough research on Mardi Gras Indian processions, brass band culture, and music as a "circulatory system" in New Orleans shows a clear relationship between localized musical performativity, political empowerment, and the built environment. Joel Dinerstein (2009:616) developed a theory on "aesthetic racism," a form of ignorance about the origins and long history of black cultural expression in a discussion on the meaning of second-line processions in the post-Katrina city. The interdisciplinary foundational work of these scholars is evoked throughout this analysis.

The parading culture in New Orleans is manifold and includes second lines, Mardi Gras Indians, and jazz funerals. These traditions are born out of a distinct Afro-Caribbean history that was transported through the Black Atlantic slave trade and Middle Passage. Art historian Robert Farris Thompson and other scholars of the African diaspora have written extensively about Black Atlantic visual, musical, and religious connections from Africa to North and South America, and how these connections continue to resonate in contemporary time (Bolke Turner 1999; Lipsitz 2011; Spitzer 2003; Thompson 1983). As Michael P. Smith noted, "Though many generations removed from its African origins, and despite the Middle Passage and oppression of slavery, this culture continues to instill a deep-seated African ethnic pride in the black working-class community and serves to strengthen individual spirits *against the ill effects of modern urban-*

ization and racism" (1994:60, emphasis added). The traditions are historical and global. They are also urbanistic and responsive to racial and cultural hegemonies in the city. These factors aid in understanding the discursive relationship between urban planning and cultural practices.

The second-line, jazz funeral, and Mardi Gras Indian tribe processionals are manifestations of New Orleans residents walking as practitioners. While these three walking traditions have often been conflated in cultural portrayals of New Orleans from the outside, they are each distinct and have different rituals and participants, although overlap is certainly possible in all three circles. As Smith noted, "Nearly all traditional musicians in New Orleans begin their music education in the street at the second-line parades, join in the Indian gang practices, and eventually jam with a number of brass bands in the neighborhood music clubs before becoming professionals" (1994:65). To be sure, many of New Orleans's cultural practitioners play numerous roles within the community such as musician, Mardi Gras Indian, storyteller, cook, and so forth.

Second lines are parades thrown by social aid and pleasure clubs in New Orleans on Sundays throughout the year. Clubs members dress in distinct and flamboyant color-coordinated outfits, select a queen for the year's event, and pay brass bands to perform. They then parade through the city, stopping at local bars, houses, and other institutions and sites considered significant to the club members. There is also an important socioeconomic revelation about the geography of the second lines. As Jason Neville and Geoff Coats noted in "Urban Design and Civil Society in New Orleans: Challenges, Opportunities, and Strategies in the Post-Flood Design Moment":

> The Social Aid and Pleasure Clubs and their street celebrations demonstrate the intersection of specific history and the built environment. It is no coincidence that these appropriations of public space occur primarily in the older core neighborhoods that were built at a more human scale rather than the city's suburbs. It is often noted that while many New Orleanians moved from the old neighborhoods to the post-War suburbs of New Orleans East—and then on to gated communities if finances allowed—the parading traditions tended to remain in "the old neighborhood" where the urban fabric was more conducive to these public gatherings. (2009:313)

This point is central to the argument about mobility, human scale, the built environment, and the positive attributes of the older fabric of New Orleans. Given that these same places are seen as conducive to the parade culture in the city, why do so many portions of the older city rate as average or even below average in the walkability aspects? It is a confounding concept, but one that is much clearer when put into the discussion of various modes of mobility, privilege, infrastructure, public transportation, territory, urban poverty, and racialized spaces in the city.

Cultural historian Dinerstein has characterized the second line as "a rolling block party, a cultural institution, a community event that carnivalizes
and colonizes the public sphere, a weekly celebration of neighborhood or clan,
a walkabout for urbanites" (2009:618). Of the participants, geographer Regis
noted, "Second liners are a massive and heterogeneous group of individuals drawn from all walks of life. The distinctive interaction between the club
members, musicians, and second liners produces a dynamic participatory event
in which there is no distinction between audience and performer" (2001:755).
Smith described the size and magnitude of second lines as "parades [that] would
stretch over a distance of ten to twenty city blocks, with five to ten thousand
second-liners in attendance, coursing a ten to twelve-mile route through the
black neighborhoods of the city" (1994:67). These three descriptions highlight
the social and cultural elements of the second line and the community-building
aspects, as well as the distinct place-based aspects.

Jazz funerals are soulful cultural practices that combine the mourning process with musical expression and celebration. Similar to second lines, families of
the deceased hire brass bands to accompany the procession that might include
places of significance for the deceased—home, church, favorite bar, homes of
friends. The combination of public mourning and celebration is a show of layered histories and memories in tandem with exuberant displays of resilience
against negative and harsh realities of everyday life in New Orleans. As Regis
noted upon attending the funeral of a young man who had died a violent death
in the city, "His [jazz] funeral also reveals how a traditional idiom is actively
reinvented and re-deployed by people who are fighting to repair their communities and to take back their streets" (2001:762). This is both a literal and physical
act of reclamation, one that is often viewed as symbolic. The act of reclamation
has the power to push policy if viewed through the lens of cultural practices
informing and revealing hierarchies of racialized space in the city.

Mardi Gras Indian processions are rooted in a tradition of resistance, one
that originated in the swamps of the Louisiana bayou. The story of the origin of
Mardi Gras Indians is a distinct fusion of folklore and fact. It focuses on the relationship between runaway slaves and Native Americans who were indigenous
to Louisiana before the abolition of slavery (Lipsitz 1988; Roach 1992; Sakakeeny 2002; Smith 1994; Wehmeyer 2010). The continued antagonism between
Mardi Gras Indians and law enforcement carries on a tradition of resistance
that is territorial and reflective of racial tension in the city. The antagonism
also reflects the constant confrontations between the cultural practices of the
city (such as live music and processions) and authoritative policing and control
of public space. Smith characterized the autonomy of Mardi Gras Indians as
one of their key points of agency: "The largely underclass black Indian gangs
remain outlaws. They remain tribal and anonymous, perform their own music,
and march through the city on the back streets, where they come and go as they
please" (1994:48).

Countless authors have discussed the territorial aspects of parading in New Orleans. Walking practitioners react and push back against the built environment physically, sonically, and through the routes they map along their paths. They draw the lines of contested spaces, challenge authority, and make the streets communal spaces of memory, mourning, and celebration (Gaffikin, McEldowney, and Sterrett 2010; Neville and Coats 2009; O'Reilly and Crutcher 2006; Raimondi 2012; Regis 1999; Sakakeeny 2008). The everyday nature of these traditions often leads to the assumption that New Orleans neighborhoods are walkable, but clearly this only applies to a specific section of the city. This chapter has addressed those assumptions, and asked what are the real impediments to mobility. These impediments are often obfuscated by the intense pedestrian celebrations in which New Orleanians occupy the street. Why should we think of a connection between walking celebrations, infrastructure, and mobility?

I attended my first second line on Easter Sunday in 2012. It was tradition for the Original Pigeon Town Steppers, a New Orleans social aid and pleasure club, to second line on that day every year. The second line began in Uptown New Orleans at Big Man's Lounge on Louisiana Avenue. The Pigeon Town Steppers had hired Stooges Brass Band to play for them as they came out the establishment to present themselves to the public, and to continue playing along their route for the rest of the procession. Since I lived in the Uptown neighborhood, I walked a few blocks to the Big Man's Lounge where the second line would start. I was dressed in all white. It was April. By the time I reached my destination I was perspiring severely. The crowd gathered for the festivities was racially diverse, and young toddlers as well as senior citizens waited anxiously for the music and dancing to begin.

Once the procession commenced, accompanied by a float to hold the queen and her court, people walked, skipped, and danced down the center of the street to the next location, the Fox II Lounge. Since we second liners were able to occupy the street (a permit had been acquired by the club beforehand), we danced carelessly (though in the extreme heat and sun) to the next location—down Louisiana Avenue, down South Claiborne Avenue, down Toledano. By the time we reached the second location, I knew I would not last and turned back. I was not alone, groups of two or three second liners of similar mind-set had also started the journey back. The parade would last four hours, and transverse across Uptown New Orleans, dropping off and picking up people as it moved through the city streets.

It was an arduous process, moving along the sidewalks of New Orleans back to my apartment. The art of second lining includes strategy—often people pair up with friends, drive two cars, drop one off at the destination spot, get in the other car together, then head to the point of origin. That way they can park at the beginning and have a ride back when they are through. The lack of a useful public transport system mandates that such tactical planning be at the heart of second lining, as well, since most second lines do not end at the same point from whence they began.

How do these various points on mobility inform the understanding of the city? Residents individualize their personal geographies in New Orleans. These geographies are oriented by and reflect their relationship to their foundational center of power—the Mississippi. Moving past this initial orienting device, walker practitioners begin to develop a narrative that is ordinary and extraordinary, quotidian and unique. This kind of contrast in everyday life is possible in New Orleans—a city on the periphery of regional geographies and a melding of cultural identities.

The street in the parading culture of New Orleans is a place of instruction, continuity, tradition, invention, and inclusion (Appleyard 1980). Its symbolic resonances are clear on the local and national levels. This symbolism, however, needs to be engaged and addressed in a manner that is also *instructive* for planners and city officials, not as a tradition that must be contained but one that must inform an understanding of mobility privilege of the city. Various geographers, historians, and musicologists have studied the cultural memory and site-specific meaning embedded in second lines, jazz funerals, and Mardi Gras processions. These investigations should not remain only in the realm of folklorists and scholars interested in the history of place and music; they should also be foundational blueprints for people who are involved in creation and manipulation of space in the city—planners, architects, and politicians. As scholar Michna noted, "Through various place-making, discursive, and artistic tactics, the possessors of subaltern geographic and historic knowledges produce spatial modes of resistance, memorialize counter-histories in public spaces, and theorize counter-hegemonic spatial possibilities" (2011:3–4).

These counterhistories and counterhegemonic spatial possibilities should be considered as inseparable prerequisites to conceptualizing the future at any particular "design moment" (Wagner and Frisch 2009). Journalist Jordan Flaherty contended that the people of New Orleans are "historically overexploited and underserved by [the] government and politicians, fighting for community control of both the decisions and finances behind the reconstruction of [their] city" (2008:30). This is certainly true, but the remarkable aspect of this reality is that they are neither complacent nor silent about the situation. Agency is developed through the everyday parading culture, the retelling of history, and the interrogation of the built environment through embodied procession and occupation of streets, sidewalks, and buildings. But is this enough? Shouldn't these processions and histories move forward our understanding of design, urbanism, infrastructure, and institutionalized inequity?[8]

In their article "Putting the Ninth Ward on the Map: Race, Place, and Transformation in Desire, New Orleans," Regis and Bruenlin used the theoretical framework of Abdou Maliq Simone, who made the argument that *people* form

---

[8] For further discussion on similar theoretical concepts, see Zewde (2010).

the infrastructure of a city. Bruenlin and Regis show how residents of the De-sire projects created community before and after the devastation of Hurricane Katrina. With the formation of a second-line club, "The Nine Times," in 1998, Bruenlin and Regis noted, "We can see that second-line organizations' public performances claim a space in public discourse for alternative notions of value, land, and dwelling together in place in the restructuring city" (2006:753).

Planners need to take head of these alternative value systems and cultural practices that are intimately tied to specific geographies. People should directly inform how infrastructure works. People and their parading patterns are cen-tral to understanding the inequity in mobility that is present in the city of New Orleans. There are countless other factors that also contribute to the poor main-tenance of infrastructure and the issue of widespread poverty in New Orleans. These cannot be addressed with a simple query on the walkability of a city or people's notions of how to navigate the city without the assistance of a car, how-ever, there is a lesson to be learned from the connection between the proces-sional walking practices as a form of resistance to the challenges of everyday walking. These are key themes that are brought to the fore when utilizing a rather simple query—"Is New Orleans walkable?"—to address larger, more com-plex manifestations of urban design, racial segregation, and cultural practices of resistance.

Morrish stated, "Infrastructure that derives its form, function, and opera-tion from a synthesis of natural and *cultural processes* represents a more sustain-able set of systems and services with the potential of backup resources to absorb the impact of natural or human-made disasters" (2008:1009). This statement implies that planners should not only observe the work of nature on an area to understand how to design for the future but also be cognizant of *the work of culture*, as well. Historical cultural practices are enlightening and relevant to anthropologists, geographers, and musicologists, but should also be instructive to those members of society whose job it is to shape the future of the urban built environment.

REFERENCES

Abbott, Carl. 1999. *Political Terrain: Washington, D.C., from Tidewater Town to Global Metropolis*. Chapel Hill: University of North Carolina Press.
Appleyard, Donald. 1980. "Livable Streets: Protected Neighborhoods?" *Annals of the American Academy of Political and Social Science* 451:106–117.
Archer, John. 2005. "Social Theory of Space: Architecture and the Production of Self, Culture, and Society." *Journal of the Society of Architectural Historians* 64(4): 430–433.
Asomaning-Asare, Samuel K. 2008. "Environmental Health Hazards: Spatial Analysis of New Orleans after Katrina." Master's thesis, Department of Geography, Binghamton University–State University of New York.
Ba Wendel, Delia Duong. 2009. "Imageability and Justice in Contemporary New Or-leans." *Journal of Urban Design* 14(3):345–375.

Bolke Turner, Christina. 1999. "A Comparison of Black Street Parades in New Orleans and Gremio Fiestas in Yucatan." *Caribbean Quarterly* 45(4):80–98.

Bratland, John. 2010. "Capital Concepts as Insights into the Maintenance and Neglect of Infrastructure." *Independent Review* 15(1):35–51.

Bruenlin, Rachel and Helen A. Regis. 2006. "Putting the Ninth Ward on the Map: Race, Place, and Transformation in Desire, New Orleans." *American Anthropologist* 108(4):744–764.

City of New Orleans. 2006. "Edgelake/Little Woods Neighborhood Planning District 9 Rebuilding Plan." New Orleans Plan Database. Retrieved November 10, 2012. http://www.nolaplans.com/plans/Lambert%20Intermediate/District_9_Plan_FINAL%20PLAN%20REPORT%20Edgelake-%20Little%20Woods%2010-12-06.pdf.

Crutcher, Michael Eugene. 2001. "Protecting 'Place' in African-American Neighborhoods: Urban Public Space, Privatization, and Protest in Louis Armstrong Park and the Tremé, New Orleans." Ph.D. dissertation, Department of Geography and Anthropology, Louisiana State University, Baton Rouge.

de Certeau, Michel. 1984. *The Practice of Everyday Life*. Berkeley: University of California Press.

Dinerstein, Joel. 2009. "Second Lining Post-Katrina: Learning Community from the Prince of Wales Social Aid and Pleasure Club." *American Quarterly* 61(3):615–637.

Dunn, Christopher. 2007. "Black Rome and the Chocolate City: The Race of Place." *Callaloo* 30(3):847–861.

Editorial Board. 2010. "Potholes, Leaky Sewers, Crumbling Bridges: New Orleans Infrastructure Study Analyzes 'The Price of Civilization.'" *Times-Picayune*, 14 August. Retrieved April 10, 2013. http://www.nola.com/opinions/index.ssf/2010/08/potholes_leaky_sewers_crumblin.html.

Ehrenfeucht, Renia and Anastasia Loukaitou-Sideris. 2010. "Planning Urban Sidewalks: Infrastructure, Daily Life and Destinations." *Journal of Urban Design* 15(4):459–471.

Ehrenfeucht, Renia and Marla Nelson. 2011. "Planning, Population Loss and Equity in New Orleans after Hurricane Katrina." *Planning, Practice, and Research* 26(2):129–146.

Fields, Billy. 2009. "From Green Dots to Greenways: Planning in the Age of Climate Change in Post-Katrina New Orleans." *Journal of Urban Design* 14(3):325–344.

Flaherty, Jordan. 2008. "New Orleans' Culture of Resistance." Pp. 30–56 in *What Is a City? Rethinking the Urban after Hurricane Katrina*, edited by Phil Steinberg and Rob Shields. Athens: University of Georgia Press.

Gaffikin, Frank, Malachy McEldowney, and Ken Sterrett. 2010. "Creating Shared Public Space in the Contested City: The Role of Urban Design." *Journal of Urban Design* 15(4):493–513.

Giusti, Autumn C. 2009. "Commentary: New Orleans Streetcar Expansion Should Be True to City Roots." *New Orleans CityBusiness*, 14 December.

Heathcott, Joseph. 2010. "Infrastructure 2.0: A Stimulus Package for All of Us." *National Civic Review* 99(2):54–58.

Hirsch, Arnold and Joseph Logsdon, eds. 1994. *Creole New Orleans: Race and Americanization*. Baton Rouge: Louisiana State University Press.

Jacobs, Jane. [1961] 1992. *The Death and Life of Great American Cities*. New York: Vintage.

Lipsitz, George. 1998. "Mardi Gras Indians: Carnival and Counter-Narrative in Black New Orleans." *Cultural Critique* 10:99–121.

———. 2011. "New Orleans in the World and the World in New Orleans." *Black Music Research Journal* 31(2):261–290.

Lynch, Kevin. 1960. *The Image of the City*. Cambridge, MA: MIT Press.

Michna, Catherine. 2011. "Hearing the Hurricane Coming: Storytelling, Second-Line Knowledges, and the Struggle for Democracy in New Orleans." Ph.D. dissertation, Department of English, Boston College, Boston.

Mizell-Nelson, Michael. 2001. "Challenging and Reinforcing White Control of Public Space: Race Relations on New Orleans Streetcars, 1861–1965." Ph.D. dissertation, Department of History, Tulane University, New Orleans.

Moises, Christian. 2013. "New Orleans Puts Emphasis on Lower 9th Ward Streets." *New Orleans CityBusiness*, 1 February.

Morrish, William R. 2008. "After the Storm: Rebuilding Cities upon Reflexive Infrastructure." *Social Research* 75(3):993–1014.

Neely, Brooke and Michelle Samura. 2011. "Social Geographies of Race: Connecting Race and Space." *Ethnic and Racial Studies* 34(11):1933–1952.

Neville, Jason and Geoff Coats. 2009. "Urban Design and Civil Society in New Orleans: Challenges, Opportunities and Strategies in the Post-Flood Design Moment." *Journal of Urban Design* 14(3):309–324.

New Orleans Regional Transit Authority. 2013. "Title VI and Environmental Justice Policy Manual." New Orleans Regional Transit Authority website. Retrieved April 10, 2013. http://www.norta.com/_meta/files/BusinessCenter/RTA-TitleVI -PolicyManual03-13.pdf.

O'Reilly, Kathleen and Michael E. Crutcher. 2006. "Parallel Politics: The Spatial Power of New Orleans' Labor Day Parades." *Social and Cultural Geography* 7(2):245–265.

Post, Robert C. 2006. "The Machine in the Garden District." *Technology and Culture* 47(1):91–94.

Raimondi, Julie Michelle. 2012. "Space, Place, and Music in New Orleans." Ph.D. dissertation, Department of Ethnomusicology, University of California, Los Angeles.

Regis, Helen A. 1999. "Second Lines, Minstrelsy, and the Contested Landscapes of New Orleans Afro-Creole Festivals." *Cultural Anthropology* 14(4):472–504.

———. 2001. "Blackness and the Politics of Memory in the New Orleans Second Line." *American Ethnologist* 28(4):752–777.

Renne, John Luciano and Peter Bennett. 2010. "Giving Parks Back to People: A Transportation Study of New Orleans City Park with Implications for Improving Public Health." *Local Environment* 15(9–10):879–890.

Roach, Joseph. 1992. "Mardi Gras Indians and Others: Genealogies of American Performance." *Theatre Journal* 44(4):461–483.

Sakakeeny, Matt. 2002. "Indian Rulers: Mardi Gras Indians and New Orleans Funk." *Jazz Archivist* 16:9–24.

———. 2008. "Instruments of Power: New Orleans Brass Bands and the Politics of Performance." Ph.D. dissertation, Department of Ethnomusicology, Columbia University, New York.

———. 2010. "'Under the Bridge': An Orientation to Soundscapes in New Orleans." *Ethnomusicology* 54(1):1–27.

———. 2011. "New Orleans Music as a Circulatory System." *Black Music Research Journal* 31(2)291–315.

Shannon, Robin. 2012. "DDD Gets State Money to Spruce Up New Orleans Sidewalks." *New Orleans CityBusiness*, 26 November.

Smith, Michael P. 1994. "Behind the Lines: The Black Mardi Gras Indians and the New Orleans Second Line." *Black Music Research Journal* 14(1):43–73.

Souther, J. Mark. 2008. "Suburban Swamp: The Rise and Fall of Planned New-Town Communities in New Orleans East." *Planning Perspectives* 23:197–219.

Spitzer, Nicholas R. 2003. "Monde Créole: The Cultural World of French Louisiana Creoles and the Creolization of World Cultures." *Journal of American Folklore* 116(459):57–72.

Steinberg, Phil and Rob Shields, eds. 2008. *What Is a City? Rethinking the Urban after Hurricane Katrina.* Athens: University of Georgia Press.

Thompson, Robert Farris. 1983. *Flash of the Spirit: African and Afro-American Art and Philosophy.* New York: Random House.

Todes, Alison. 2012. "New Directions in Spatial Planning? Linking Strategic Spatial Planning and Infrastructure Development." *Journal of Planning Education and Research* 32(4):400–414.

U.S. Department of Transportation Federal Highway Administration. 1992. "National Bicycle and Walking Study FHWA Case Study No. 9: Linking Bicycle/Pedestrian Facilities with Transit." U.S. Department of Transportation Federal Highway Administration Safety website. Retrieved April 11, 2013. http://safety.fhwa.dot.gov/ped_bike/docs/case9.pdf.

Wagner, Jacob A. and Michael Frisch. 2009. "Introduction: New Orleans and the Design Moment." *Journal of Urban Design* 14(3):237–255.

Wehmeyer, Stephen C. 2010. "Feathered Footsteps: Mythologizing and Ritualizing Black Indian Processions in New Orleans." *Social Identities* 6(4):427–445.

Wood, Lisa, Lawrence D. Frank, and Billie Giles-Corti. 2010. "Sense of Community and Its Relationship with Walking and Neighborhood Design." *Social Science and Medicine* 70:1381–1390.

Zewde, Sara. 2010. "Theory, Place, and Opportunity: Black Urbanism as a Design Strategy for the Potential Removal of the Claiborne Expressway in New Orleans." Master's thesis, Department of Urban Studies and Planning, Massachusetts Institute of Technology, Cambridge, MA.

11

Mobility Method and the Ethnic Community

Walking and Community Activism

EVRICK BROWN

In this chapter I draw from past and current research exploring the cultural and political landscape of a mixed African American and black Caribbean community in Brooklyn, New York, to investigate the deeper meaning of a neighborhood protest march. A focus here is on the utilization of "footwork" or walking and its related sidewalk activity not only as a methodological tool but its implication as a means of comprehending residents' construction and perception of an urban environment. It was the reflexive process borne out of a methodological necessity to access data that highlighted the potency of a neighborhood walk that conveyed the relevancy of a contextual embodied experience (Crawford 1996; Rose 1990).

Walking is already an embedded practice; however, in the urban literature there is a growing understanding that the complexity of the city lends itself to multiple interpretations and subjective realities that this form of quotidian mobility provides. In essence, it is not a top-down or aerial view of the city that becomes relevant here but a command perception as described by Michel de Certeau (1984). This everyday use of the city creates a multilayered dynamic reality via pedestrian activity. Such views of the city have their origins in classical studies of city life that note that urban dwellers often "live" in symbolic interpretations of their physical environment (Stone 1954; Wohl and Strauss 1958). The seeming collage of inanimate objects such as rivers, parks, buildings, and other "anchors" of a community collectively contribute to a symbolic interpretation of, and fondness for, an area. Understandably the strength of such an experience is conveyed most adequately through the process of walking as the effective form of mobility. As suggested by previous research, the relationship between a slow-paced pedestrian environment, semiotics, and its methodological implications empowering researcher rapport with the community through the shared use of space is worthy of study (Demerath and Levinger 2003). Unlike spaces designed for automobile use that are severely restricted and controlled, the pedestrian environment allows for more relaxed routines. Sidewalks contain no controlled obligatory rules of use or pace; pedestrians can suddenly stop and interact even within the transitional or "place between places." Loren Demerath and David Levinger (2003) argue that one of the beneficial characteristics of walking in a slow-paced environment is the full sensorial exposure they discuss and categorize as the breadth of experience, identity expression, pausability, and collaborative creativity. Each of the four properties allows immersion into a community, thus encouraging an in-depth understanding of its nuanced micro-social phenomena through an embedded slack-paced process that allows a purposeful drift. Mobilization of a Situationist concept of the *dérive* applied to the study of a community conveys a full authentic range of the urban vernacular landscape from the vantage of the community residents which includes exclusivity and invitations of city space in the form of "go" and "no-go" or "between" spaces (Jenks and Neves 2000). The deployment of this concept contributes to the subjective sensuous experience extending to a perception of the city as a lived parochial social reality teeming with an interpretive understanding of the environs imbued with the robustness of the senses-scape of resident routine activity. When submerged in a community, it becomes almost inevitable that the researcher begins to absorb the ambient properties of a social environment, its physical and cultural ebbs and flows (Lefebvre 2004).

There is an understood correlation between the visual and social as the former reveals the physically constructed dynamic nature of social meanings and the ways in which urban space is the product of ethnic and class transformations (Krase and Shortell 2011). The strength of images elicits a behavioral response that includes those signifiers of ritualized identity (expressive), routine activity (phatic), and those that can be considered ethnic turf markers (conative) to "the other" or community outsiders (Jakobson 1972). Thus, stores with painted images of palm trees evoke an affinity to a place that stirs intimate feelings of a home carpeted with green fields and stout palm and coconut trees, with oceans teeming with king fish and snapper—all relevant familial images to those from the Caribbean region but may have little meaning to nonresidents. Grasping the underlying meaning of those signifiers is tantamount to understanding not only the routinized activity of residents but its reified symbolic meaning.

My early forays learning the ins and outs of community politics in the East Flatbush community yielded few interviews and referrals. In fact, when investigating such a contested terrain, recommendations for further interviews proved a compromising challenge (Brown 2012). Interviews provided a limited guide to understanding this ethnic-based community. Reflexivity, as part of this immersion research method, was necessary to assess which research instruments were effective and contribute to a change in tactics (Pillow 2003). Lengthy interviews in someone's home or front porch forcing recall lost salience. The respondent was removed from the social environment and away from the web of multiple conversations, expressions, and gestures that fuel the embedded experience. Essentially removing them from the stimulants which reinforce their sense of belonging to place and identity (Vannini 2007). Thus, for an authentic semiotic experience, immersion was a necessity. Being present in the everyday life of the community, reflecting on its social order, and acquiring socially situated knowledge that emerges and resonates from the ambience represent an invaluable tool that can trump interviews and reveal lived authenticity. To grasp the indigenous meaning of the community it was necessary to be continuously present listening and absorbing the signs, actions and processes of co-creation of areal identity.

Classical urban studies revealed a duality of city life. City dwellers "live" in their interpretations of their communities while physically dwelling in them (Park and Burgess [1925] 1967; Stone 1954). Robert E. Park and Ernest W. Burgess ([1925] 1967:1) referred to the city as not simply a collection of buildings or people but a "state of mind, a body of customs and traditions, and of the organized attitudes and sentiments" of its denizens representing a process and product of meaning imputed on place.

An ethnographic approach to investigating the routinized behaviors within an ethnic community necessitates walking as an embedded excursion (Butcher and Nutch 1999). This is a reflexive process that empowers the researcher to gain knowledge about the networks, micro systems of power, and nuances of a community's structure detailing the normative and mobile rhythms of a community (Lefebvre 2004). Walking is not only a means to survey and access a research site for data in the form of interviews but an experiential occupation of the environs to better understand the subjective nature of the community under study.

Symbolic Identity and the Quotidian Mobility Method

Although Sharon Zukin (1995) described the conventional cultural perception and symbolic presentation of an area as generally a mass-marketing tool for economic gain either for gentrification or tourism, it need not be limited to upwardly mobile segments of a city. Elaine B. Sharp (2013) provides a quantitative empirical study in support of a thesis describing the development of a postindustrial city that caters to upwardly mobile residents and tourists while ensuring their safety through policing with an emphasis on order. This is done for the purposes of increasing the symbolic, hence, economic value of an area that acknowledges its presence prior to the boost. There is this symbolic identification with an area that has its indigenous organic roots. Although it has been cornered by the discourse on gentrification, it is present in all communities and cultivated by area residents. Pierre Bourdieu (1989) argued that habitus, a component of cultural capital that influences perception and synthesizes meaning, consists of "mental structures" used for interpreting and presenting dispositions to the social world with reinforcing "linked social agents." The presence of compatriots reifies communal identity along with the confluence of social and cultural capital in ethnic-based communities further influencing a distinct perception of urban life based on the lived experience.

Social capital has often been understood as a resource contributing to a generalized trust of others leading to increased civic engagement (Putnam 2000). It has been clarified to include bridging and bonding as subcategories to differentiate alternative types. *Bridging* refers to the weak ties that extend social resources outside a close-knit group in the form of business- and job-related connections supporting interethnic tolerance, branched social networks, multiculturalism, diversity, and overall civil society. *Bonding* appears as a polar opposite, denoting intragroup ties that not only strengthen and maintain close-knit communal relations but foster social isolation and mistrust of outside groups or " others," as well (Oxendine 2012). The primary bonds are possible as those who inhabit a common area share a collective identity reinforced by common embodied dispositions or social presentations (Bourdieu 1989). Residents share not only a common daily routine but a similar way in which they experience it. Therefore, those who ride the city buses and dollar cars and use the sidewalks feel and portray themselves as belonging by having and displaying a tacit knowledge of the neighborhood and their fellow neighbors.

This stresses the importance of a researcher's immersion when engaging in ethnographic inquiry to discern, among the variety of micro-social processes, a viable means of access for his or her topic. For example, in his urban anthropological study of Community District Four in Queens, New York, Roger Sanjek (1998) employed an ethnographic practice of observing and essentially became a fixture in the neighborhood by attending formal and informal community events and planning board meetings to understand localized political mobilization in an urban environment. Jonathan Rieder's (1985) study of the southeastern portion of Brooklyn (Canarsie) involved similar research tactics with sparse interviews in comparison. For a period of time Elijah Anderson (1990) was involved with a local organization working for the improvement of public school education that eventually yielded a potent understanding of the social-psychological interplay of street-level interaction. The results of his ethnographic work yielded informative accounts and explicit descriptions of neighborhoods in Philadelphia while explaining the norms which guided the fragile and strained interactions of pedestrians (Anderson 1990, 1999). Although the researchers conducted formal interviews, a significant bulk of their data stemmed from recorded observations while they were present within the field. Knowledge gained by Sudhir Venkatesh (2002), a researcher of Asian Indian descent, provided contextually pertinent information during his study of a predominantly African American income housing project in Chicago and helped him gain access as an academic "hustler." Greg Scott (2004) employed this understanding as he studied the relationship of gang members prior to and after incarceration in Chicago. His purposeful "Ethnographic Immersion" involved a revelation of past deviant activity to informants that increased his level of access as his intensity of confidentiality with respondents increased (Scott 2004:114). Finally, Margarethe Kusenbach (2003) utilized a similar strategy pinpointing the activity of what she called the "go-along" in which she accompanied individual informants in their "natural" settings while they were going about their daily routines. "Go-alongs" unveiled perceptions of her informants' social and physical environment and offered insights into the "texture" of spatial practices by revealing the various degrees and types of engagement.

In summary, research that highlighted the symbolic and sociocultural aspects of communal life revealed properties that distinguished certain semiotics of place under the guise of what Lyn Lofland (1998) identified as realms. She defined the latter as space imbued with social meaning and significance that varies according to usage. Space characterized by a continuous presence of strangers or "others" is noted as the public realm. In such spaces, people are gauged based on manner of dress, body language, and other mainly nonverbal cues that are expeditiously condensed and categorized for quick assessment. Even in the presence of multiple strangers, there is the common norm of "civil inattention," consisting of social rules that govern interaction based on an informal consensus of recognized social distance or personal space (Goffman 1963). These rules are often adhered to and respected with few folkway violations (for example, a crowded subway or other thoroughfare during rush hour). Most often, however, individuals seek and create their own private space or, in the case of groups, parochial realms that represent carved social niches. Often such locales are defined as situational and temporary as a group that claims a niche does so for a specific event or culturally specific ceremony as when a family decides to occupy a portion of a public park for a picnic. In this manner, as claimed social space for semiprivate use, communities, particularly ethnic communities, can represent forms of relatively non-situational and stable parochial realms. The claim for turf is understood to be taken by those who share bonding social capital. Thus community and neighborhood members may not only claim a similar ancestry but engage in historically significant shared cultural practices such as a carnival or parade that reinforce aspects of the parochial realm through territory or turf (Jacobs 1961). Permeating boundaries hardened by territorial claims may confound the process of researcher access to data—residents must assess the investigator as foe or not. Once those boundaries are crossed and access gained, there is an understanding of the process of meaning imputed on space and delineations of who, as members of the community, is qualified to participate and what happens when those norms are violated.

The point here is that community residents are active collaborative authors of their subcultures stoked by a need to defend their daily routines. Thus, the classical areal-based understanding of urban communities is relevant as this chapter focuses on a specific ethnic-based community in Brooklyn. Such neighborhoods are often characterized by a preponderance of the bonding social capital. I argue that bonding social capital underwrites a symbolic representation of New York City by East Flatbush residents through collaborative embodied dispositions that presented itself during a wildcat protest. Essentially, the dynamic semiotic interplay or construction of social meaning in the ethnic community of East Flatbush, labeled as Caribbean New York by Phillip Kasinitz (1992), solidifies a tightly knit areal identity transcending its objective physical surroundings. As de Certeau (1984) suggested, communities can be the spatial synecdoche of a city, a neighborhood may be a portion of a borough within a larger metropolis, but the representation of New York City that residents sense and portray is based not only on their immediate surroundings but the co-perception of others, as well. Residents of the largely Caribbean community of East Flatbush Brooklyn claim the neighborhood not only as a depiction of life in the Caribbean with their spatial appropriation of it as they see fit but as their representation of New York City as well. When this lived, spatial portrayal of the city is challenged by outside forces, citizens made attempts to reclaim it through protests in defiant ways to claim a parochial right to experience and realize their perception of New York City.

The pace, culture of the residents, rhythm of the social landscape, and spatially infused social meaning of the East Flatbush community through the routine social practices of its citizens was absorbed (Monahan and Fisher 2010). Prior to relating the protest experience, a brief walking tour of East Flatbush from one busy intersection to another by a widely used commercial street involving automobile and foot traffic seems appropriate.

Profile of East Flatbush

The overall casual scene of the neighborhood strikes a stark contrast to the fast-paced borough of post-911 Manhattan representing the epicenter of public space regulation—residents control and set the pace, not representatives of authority (for example, police). Certain properties seem to permeate throughout the borough as even in this Brooklyn neighborhood there are those pedestrians who seem to be in a constant rush. They are not the rule in this residential neighborhood, however, which can be considered a resolute dependable sanctuary, a welcomed respite for those who earn their living in another part of the metropolitan area of New York.

Brooklyn is one of the apparent entry points for the black Caribbean population, with a reported 51.3 percent of black people living within the borough declaring West Indian ancestry. The political and administrative subdivision with the highest Afro-Caribbean population is officially designated as Community Board District 17 with the majority of its black residents claiming a West Indian Ancestry (63.9 percent, according to the 2011 American Community Survey) in a community that is predominantly African American (88.4 percent non-Hispanic black people). This one square mile area sitting in the south central portion of the borough just south of Crown Heights, the location of the well-known Caribbean Carnival, contains a group of residents who see this section of East Flatbush as their own version of the Caribbean in New York City. If one is not confronted by the blaring music coming from speakers flanking the entryway to storefronts, then it is the various island flags or bundles of tall stalks of sugarcane being sold by vendors. One of the streets with the heaviest foot and automobile traffic is a shopping strip known as Church Avenue that bisects the district. As one walks west from the East Eighteenth train station near the western border of East Flatbush there is a slew of vehicle and pedestrian traffic. Continuing on this eastern path, Church Avenue bisects Flatbush avenue, an intersecting commercial shopping strip followed by the Nostrand Avenue train station filling the sidewalks with more commuters who either transfer to the B41 and B35 city busses or, take a "dollar car" (an informal taxi) while the remainder walk.

At this busy intersection of Nostrand Avenue and Church (a public transportation hub) there is a pharmacy franchise, a fast-food restaurant, and two corner grocery stores next to entrances to the number 2 and 3 trains. On the southeast corner, an elevator to the train station was recently added, creating another obstacle to maneuver among the throng of pedestrians, customers shopping at a nearby fruit stand, and commuters waiting for the B35 to take them farther into East Flatbush. After a few feet of traveling through the gauntlet, the crowd wanes slightly, but there is still a mass of pedestrians zigzagging in and out of the health food stores selling a proprietary blend of home remedies, bakeries, restaurants, and convenient stores that flank Church Avenue while avoiding honking "dollar cars"—unless they are seeking them—that compete with the Metropolitan Transportation Authority for passengers. Once past Brooklyn Avenue, while continuing to head east, the stores become more dispersed and the crowd of pedestrian traffic wanes with the exception of nests of shoppers hovering by a large fruit stand and clothing store. This continues until approaching Schenectady Avenue, three blocks west of Utica Avenue, another major intersection, and the crowd becomes noticeably thicker along with the stores, which include more nail salons, beauty supply stores selling human hair and other sundries, along with hair salons, barbershops, and a local supermarket chain. The pace is far slower than it is one mile west at Nostrand, and some pedestrians even loiter outside fast-food restaurants and convenient stores, chatting with each other or enjoying the ambience of the neighborhood. When crossing the busy intersection at Utica, one can detect the heavy activity of the crowd. On the southeastern corner there is a van attached to a flatbed truck stacked with speakers adorned with banners informing passersby of a local religious institution while blaring religious music with a distinctive Caribbean beat. In front of this display are people selling gospel music, books, and other religious paraphernalia, attracting the attention of some pedestrians who begin to jive or "get caught up in the spirit" of the music with its heavy bass. Meanwhile, the hustle and throng of pedestrians continue as the presentation coalesces with the collection of various tonalities from car horns of "dollar cars" or vans and music booming from other vehicles.

Still heading east, in contrast to the mass of people who spill out of and mill about the Nostrand Avenue subway station exit one mile west, the pace seems to slacken even more, which is partially explained by the displays of fruit stands jutting out on the sidewalks, forcing pedestrian movement to a crawl. There are more street displays, which warrants a relaxed pace as the presence and aroma of jerk chicken cooked over split metal barrels converted to makeshift grills is made known. During the weekdays, most often during the spring and summer months, one can find most residents strolling the sidewalks with their bags of groceries dangling loosely at their sides, swaying to the cadence of their walk while their owners scan other pedestrians for a familiar face or listen for a familiar sound—often an accent. Many find time to loiter and chat with friends, associates, or acquaintances they see daily. There is little need for an excuse to strike up a conversation in such a familiar environment as there are plentiful cues, including the display of consumer goods on the sidewalk that seems to spill out of some of the densely packed stores.

The routinized actions set the comparative backdrop for what is to follow. The sights, sounds, and changing pace of the pedestrians in certain areas become what is known as the common rhythm of the community. The mutual adaptation of the pace and relaxed acceptance of the signs, sounds, and smells that incorporate the synesthetic experience refer to the synchronicity of the senses (Low 2012). Particulates of the social ambience may be unseen but sensed as components that coalesce to the familiar in a city ruled by unseen economic forces and commercial interests. A neighboring borough like Manhattan, with its daunting artificial canyons, foreign faces, smells, and rushed awkward paces, becomes more tolerable as residents can retreat to the familiarity of a community where their influence through the co-imputation of meaning heightens their feelings of self-efficacy (Karp, Stone, and Yoels 1991).

Residents are likely to convene at the various social anchors in the community—pausible places where they can stop and dawdle with neighbors or even familiar strangers such as the "Coconut Man" street vendor selling corn and jerk chicken roasting in a grill at a makeshift sidewalk food stand. Or they can find others convening at the southeast corner of Church and Utica Avenues and listen to the boisterous gospel music from the mobile display described earlier or just watch the crowd. For those continuing their walks to their various destinations there are the multitude of Korean-owned vegetable stands, most of them open twenty-four hours, that represent places to not only shop but socialize, as well, along with the Caribbean street vendors selling various items. These represent resistance to a quickened pace as one is likely to come across a neighbor or other acquaintance. Even within the local commercial stores a customer might strike up a conversation with a merchant or worker at a frequently patronized establishment. The familiarity among the people and the area gives one a sense of command to justify the familiar. One has control navigating the sidewalks and walkways and even a bit of pausibility in the streets as drivers (particularly those operating the "dollar car" jitney cabs) will remain a few seconds longer at a green light or slow to a crawl to catch a few words with a friend—unadvisable but done. It is an environment that fosters a collaborate sense of camaraderie with one major exception.

One other presence that becomes most apparent after crossing Utica Avenue is the police standing as sentries on the corners and strolling the streets with blank looks on their faces. A few talk to each other or maybe a curious resident with a general query. As one approaches a Chinese American food store on the southwest corner of East Fifty-Fifth Street, a shrine to sixteen-year-old Kimani Gray, a former resident of East Flatbush and Canarsie, is a reminder to residents of why the police are there.

Kimani Gray and the East Flatbush Protest

On March 9, 2013, Kimani Gray was leaving a social event at East Fifty-Second Street and Church Avenue when he was shot seven times and killed by police. What often sows the seeds of uncertainty in such cases was also present here: Witnesses state the police shot an unarmed black male, while officers at the scene state that he was armed. The local televised news presented the image of a revolver on the ground as confirmation of police accounts. A Twitter protest on March 11 (#Brooklynprotest) initially took place as a rally outside the Sixty-Seventh Precinct in the western portion of the district near Nostrand, but it quickly turned into a riot as some reportedly sixty youths left the vigil and vandalized a local drug store and fruit stand/grocer. By March 12 a brief video showing the young people entering the Rite Aid and attacking a customer was posted on YouTube. It was also believed, and the impression was given through the media, that the protest was mainly youth oriented, and the presence of encouraging older adults was suppressed. What follows is a first-person account. While on my way home, heading east on Church Avenue, I ended up in the middle of an ad hoc march. I provide a description wherein I, as the researcher, "attuned" myself to the practices and experiences of the protestors through the sensory sociality of walking (Pink 2008).

On March 12, I exited the train station at Nostrand Avenue and decided to catch the B35 bus that was heading east. The bus made it only a few blocks beyond the stop as traffic was no longer moving. There was a sudden appearance of flashing emergency lights from police vans that were at the four corners of the nearest intersection. A few protestors stepped out of a corner bodega on the north side of Church Avenue between East Thirty-Second and East Thirty-Third Streets followed by more coming from the side streets. The crowd proceeded to step off the sidewalks and into the road and started banging on vehicles, alarming the passengers inside. Since the bus was no longer moving, the driver allowed willing passengers to exit, and I took the opportunity to do so. I was immediately greeted by a swarm of protestors heading in the opposite direction (west) toward the local police precinct. Others were standing on the portion of the sidewalk not covered by police, talking among themselves and giving approving glances to those in the march. Being curious, I followed the members of the crowd while eyeing the police, who flanked protesters at a distance. I noticed that in the group of people, who at first appeared to be in their late teens to early twenties, some were exclaiming, "Look—the police are scared. They're doin' nothin' but watchin' us." Others stated, "We outnumber them" and "They'll think twice about shootin' one of us again." These words and the absence of police barricades to cordon off the mobile protest vitalized the group as more proceeded to defiantly step into the streets, heading toward the local precinct where a large group was already present. By this time, I noticed the crowd contained more than the youths depicted in the news. There was an obviously older group relating tales of family members who had suffered from some form of police harassment or brutality. This caused a few to shout obscenities at the weary-eyed officers. A few motorists appeared to be in shock, while others honked their horns in approval as I noticed more protestors coming from the east accompanied by police helicopters buzzing overhead. The latter's presence as a form of crowd control and monitoring has become uncomfortably common in East Flatbush. However, from the crowd's perspective, the upgraded presence of the police was a testament to their strength and effectiveness. Their declaration of their identity through the fluidity of oscillating between the sidewalks and street challenged the police's efforts at maintaining order. As this continued, the officers, patrol cars, and vans did not attempt to limit the motion or guide the movement of the protestors. I went back to the sidewalk and watched the westward flow of protestors, who were merrily hopping on and off the sidewalk. The B35 bus and vehicle traffic managed to crawl to the next wide avenue and turn south off Church, and the continued foot traffic that controlled the streets was less impeded. I walked eastward, following the flashing blue, red, and white lights of the police vans at every intersection on the way to Utica Avenue about a half mile east. The crowd noticeably thinned by the East Forties but quickly picked up with a mix of regular pedestrian traffic as the automobiles once again had control. By the time I crossed Utica Avenue, there was a spattering of protestors heading west toward the precinct but even more heading toward the shrine at East Fifty-Fifth Street for Kimani Gray.

A crowd began to mill and grow at the southwest corner where the shrine was set up with tall religious votive candles, including images of Kimani in various poses with family members on the east wall of a building that houses a Chinese American fast-food restaurant. This group of protestors contained a mix of individuals of various ages peppered with a younger crowd that was attracted to the growing commotion. Since there was no flow of protestors, their movements were limited; they saturated the sidewalk and spilled into the streets, creating a narrow passage for vehicle traffic. Near the shrine, however, there was a police presence as they set up metal barricades in preparation for Geraud Gray, Kimani's father, who wanted to speak to the local press. As the crowd grew, so did the agitation. Kimani Gray's sister, Mahnefah, attempted to cross the street and the barricades, and she was detained and placed in a police car, which caused the crowd to shout, "That's the daughter!" and hurl bottles and bricks at police. The police responded by forming a wall of officers to corral and contain the protestors, a process known as kettling, leading to some arrests. The subsequent days of the protest included various skirmishes between the police and protesters until the demonstrations eventually simmered to silence. Reporters from local and internet news agencies paced east and west on Church from Utica Avenue to the memorial at East Fifty-Fifth Street, scouring for interviews. Most reporters found pedestrians unwilling to talk, as if there was a code of silence, and resorted to store workers or business owners to question if and how their businesses were affected. Any attempts at a backstory or gathering information on Kimani Gray or his family were met with guarded stares and response of ignorance—there was little desire to speak to outsiders. Indeed, the presence of reporters, the increased police presence (particularly the buzzing helicopters and the fleet of scooter patrols lined up at the curbs), and the organizational activists from other neighborhoods seemed like an invasion. Each group was competing to occupy a portion of space for its own definition and interpretation of what East Flatbush and the Kimani Gray shooting represented while corralling the residents vying for their attention, most of the latter undoubtedly waiting somewhat impatiently for the "outsiders" to leave. Not surprisingly it was the more investigative reporters who ate at the local restaurants, were embedded with the protesters, and observed and listened to conversations who acquired decent interviews and yielded entrenched information (Pinto and Devereaux 2013).

The largest of the conflicts took form when the police tried to control the crowd's options for motility (Kaufmann 2002). Vincent Kaufmann identified three layers of motility as: (1) access to the range of mobile possibilities, including spatial population distribution; (2) competence, which relates to skills and abilities, including the physical ability to transfer an entity (for example, a group of protestors) from one place to another, given constraints, with acquired skills related to rules and regulations of movement (licenses, permits, terrain codes, organizational skills, and planning); and (3) appropriation, which refers to how agents interpret and act on perceived or real access and skills depending on needs, plans, aspirations, strategies, motives, values, and habits. Thus, restricting the movement of the crowd represented more than containing the protest; it was a challenge to a motility-based cultural practice involving the free-flowing movement of participants empowered to stop and control automobile flow by a division of a local authority, the police. Members of the crowd expected to move on and off the sidewalk freely in a similar action to the carnival as a presentation and declaration of their Caribbean ancestry to mark and define the properties of the neighborhood; however, the greater police presence challenged that presentation of community identity and contributed to the clash between the police and protestors.

Discussion and Conclusion

The protest provided a glimpse of the everyday life and a cultural practice of this ethnic community. I argued that bonding social capital (the strong neighborhood ties) underscored the behavior of the protestors. In this case it was partially in the form of shared embodied dispositions that co-constructed meaning. Everyday residents see those with a similar ethnic background implementing their daily routines in their distinct but shared way. This variegation of cultural practices include the shared clothing, accents, and hairstyles (for example, dreadlocks) to street preachers and vendors selling roasted breadfruit. Church Avenue serves as a major commercial strip where this communal ethnic identity is often displayed, shared, defined, and redefined as a powerful cultural anchor rivaled perhaps by the West Indian Day Carnival on Eastern Parkway. The Carnival event takes place once a year on a roadway that otherwise contains heavy motor vehicle traffic, and Church Avenue, although characterized by heavy vehicle use, contains more automobile controls in the form of traffic lights, shorter blocks, and slower-moving traffic, supporting a greater laxness of pedestrian controls. During any given day, a pedestrian may walk on the shoulder of Church Avenue between parked cars and mobile traffic, something that is less likely to occur without great risk to health on the wide boulevard of Eastern Parkway.

Bonding appeared in the form of neighborhood community support for the tactics of involving motility control used by the indigenous protestors; undoubtedly, it was present before it. As stated earlier, the community represents a respite where residents construct their own place-based meaning with its theme focused on informal arrangements and relaxed perception of the social and physical environment. It is a location where its regulars can unwind from the rest of the city consisting of strangers with varied cultural practices and guarded expectations. However, the protest temporarily disrupted the lazy tempo of this Brooklyn community. The typical residents were unable to lounge on corners or near local bars with open containers, in the accustomed manner, without attracting police, reporters, or activists from elsewhere. Organized groups like FAITH (Fathers Alive In The Hood) and anti–stop and frisk activist Jose LaSalle—both from outside East Flatbush—attempted to use the emotional momentum to rally support for their causes and control the ebb and flow of the protest (Pinto and Devereaux 2013). The informal and expressive nature of the community did not permit the typical control of any leadership. Indeed, throughout the remaining days of protest it appeared as if no one person or group was in charge. Locations of a rally or a destination of a protest was announced, but there was very little control of the crowd, aside from police corralling and some kettling, once they were under way. In a community accustomed to a relaxed, free, unrestricted flow of foot traffic with an ethnic-based familiarity, resistance to a formal structure, and some community support for the police, seeing no blatant consistent leader was not surprising. Two City Council members received media coverage, but neither were far-reaching in their control of the crowds of protestors, certainly not those who flooded the sidewalks and streets without a permit. Unsurprisingly, those vying for leadership positions struggled to maintain their hold at the vanguard. They were competing with not only each other; they were competing with a community culture.

There is also the continued police presence throughout East Flatbush. Citing the past incidents of gang violence and being leery of groups of idling teenagers, residents had requested sustained police coverage in the area for several years prior to the Kimani Gray incident. Thus, although there were some who were uneasy about officers patrolling the sidewalks, there were others who were not and welcomed them. The police may have prohibited certain escalation of the protest and been looked on with suspicion at first, but they were eventually treated as mobile security fixtures, similar to surveillance cameras. They represent an uneasy but familiar scene in East Flatbush as sentries intertwined with the reality of the residents' lives as necessary equipment on the main commercial strip. The limited police presence is tolerated and seen as safeguarding but not preventing the continuous co-creation of an authentic community. Officers on patrol and street corners are known to enforce criminal laws and, to a lesser but increasing extent, quality-of-life violations.

Most residents from the Caribbean are comfortable with operating a commercial business out of their own homes with little fear of being reported—they are accustomed to the informal nature of seemingly formal transactions. In New York City commercial property is not permitted to operate in a residential zone unless there is a special variance involving the New York City Department of Buildings, a formal centralized authority. Similar official rules that designate the sidewalk for pedestrian activity and streets for automobile use require permits for street protests. In contrast, informal rules are embedded in the daily transactions of the community, such as allowing a familiar customer to "purchase" items on credit, and a laid-back view of certain quality-of-life violations with little to no complaints about loud neighbors or no one reporting individuals dumping private garbage in public bins—acquiring a permit is a customary non sequitur.

The Kimani Gray protest provided a glimpse of the East Flatbush community culture if not only to the residents themselves, then to New Yorkers and the world as an image of a black male youth being subdued and handcuffed on the trunk of a police car circulated among news websites. Undoubtedly the prevailing view was of some generic black neighborhood in disarray protesting a common story throughout black history—racial injustice. In essence, it was a story that fell victim to stereotypes—it was seen, categorized, and faded to the past, and the community continued.

In April, a month after the Kimani Gray protest, I was walking home on Church Avenue when I saw a man standing in the middle of the street, blocking traffic. He stood in front of one car and then jumped on its hood and rolled off to the driver's side and opened the door to assault the driver. As he attempted to pull the driver out, two officers approached, and he proceeded to fight with the officers, who wrestled him to the ground. Then things began to escalate. One dark unmarked police car approached, with its lights flashing, from Utica Avenue and more officers got out, followed by a blue-and-white police car and then a van. The two officers became a swarm of ten or more who pinned the cursing man to the ground. A group of males pulled out their cell phones and filmed while the first two officers subdued the man. As the number of police increased, they told the males filming, who were within ten feet of the scuffle, to get back. The males cursed at the officers, calling them the "N" word—keep in mind that the officers they were directing their verbal insults at were predominantly white and Latino, although the first two officers on the scene were black. The officers shoved those who were filming farther back—sixty feet and more. They proceeded to form a defensive line/perimeter, now wary of all spectators because of the number of males who continued to curse at them. After the police arrested and took the man to the precinct, the remaining "protestors," now a collection of younger and older black males and females, dissipated.

Finally, what is interesting, not necessarily surprising, is that the repertoire of insurgency tactics still reflects the protest used by African Americans in the past even in this predominantly black Caribbean community. There may have been some nuances requiring an interpretive explanation based on knowledge gained through the practice of walking; however, that reality displayed is more than likely trumped by race. The expression of identity through the neighborhood's failure to endorse a certain tactic and organizational structure, as mentioned before, may be missed by outsiders, which is why no predominant group or leadership arose from the momentum. Perhaps viable leadership could have risen, providing those who made attempts understood that a continual presence through a diffusive, relaxed involvement while being absorbed in the daily routines, conversations, and street rhythms of the residents was necessary. An organizational or formal rally might stir the short-term interest of the masses, but the remainder prefer a sustained, casual, familiar presence.

REFERENCES

Anderson, Elijah. 1990. *Streetwise*. Chicago: University of Chicago Press.
——. 1999. *Code of the Street*. New York: Norton.
Bourdieu, Pierre. 1989. "Social Space and Symbolic Power." *Sociological Theory* 71(1):14–25.
Brown, Evrick. 2012. "An Ethnography of Local Politics in a Brooklyn Caribbean Community." Pp. 313–336 in *The World in Brooklyn: Gentrification, Immigration, and Ethnic Politics in a Global City*, edited by Judith DeSena and Timothy Shortell. Lanham, MD: Lexington Books.
Butcher, Dick and Frank Nutch. 1999. "Reflections on Doing Interactive Ethnography." *Discourse of Sociological Practice* 2(1):10–14.
Crawford, Lyall. 1996. "Personal Ethnography." *Communication Monographs* 63(2): 158–170.

de Certeau, Michel. 1984. *The Practice of Everyday Life*. Berkeley: University of California Press.

Demerath, Loren and David Levinger. 2003. "Social Qualities of Being on Foot: A Theoretical Analysis of Pedestrian Activity, Community, and Culture." *City and Community* 2(3):217–237.

Goffman, Erving. 1963. *Behavior in Public Places*. New York: Free Press.

Jacobs, Jane. 1961. *The Death and Life of Great American Cities*. New York: Vintage.

Jakobson, Roman. 1972. "Verbal Communication." *Scientific American* 227(3):72–80.

Jenks, Chris and Tiago Neves. 2000. "A Walk on the Wild Side: Urban Ethnography Meets the Flâneur." *Cultural Values* 4(1):1–17.

Karp, David A., Gregory P. Stone, and William C. Yoels. 1991. *Being Urban: A Sociology of City Life*. 2nd ed. New York: Praeger.

Kasinitz, Phillip. 1992. *Caribbean New York*. Ithaca, NY: Cornell University Press.

Kaufmann, Vincent. 2002. *Re-thinking Mobility: Contemporary Sociology*. Burlington, VT: Ashgate.

Krase, Jerome and Timothy Shortell. 2011. "On the Spatial Semiotics of Vernacular Landscapes in Global Cities." *Visual Communication* 10(3):371–404.

Kusenbach, Margarethe. 2003. "Street Phenomenology: The Go-Along as Ethnographic Research Tool." *Ethnography* 4(3):455–485.

Lefebvre, Henri. 2004. *Rhythmanalysis: Space, Time and Everyday Life*. New York: Continuum.

Lofland, Lyn. H. 1998. *The Public Realm*. New York: Aldine de Gruyter.

Low, Kelvin. 2012. "The Social Life of the Senses." *Sociology Compass* 6(3):272–282.

Monahan, Torin and Jill A. Fisher. 2010. "Benefits of 'Observer Effects': Lessons from the Field." *Qualitative Research* 10(3):357–376.

Oxendine, Alina R. 2012. "City Seclusion and Social Exclusion: How and Why Economic Disparities Harm Social Capital." Pp. 9–30 in *Urban Social Capital: Civil Society and Civil Life*, edited by Joseph D. Lewandowski and Gregory Streich. Burlington, VT: Ashgate.

Park, Robert E. and Ernest W. Burgess, eds. [1925] 1967. *The City: Suggestions for Investigation of Human Behavior in the Urban Environment*. Chicago: University of Chicago Press.

Pillow, W. 2003. "Confession, Catharsis, or Cure? Rethinking the Uses of Reflexivity as Methodological Power in Qualitative Research." *International Journal of Qualitative Studies* 16(2):175–196.

Pink, Sarah, 2008. "An Urban Tour." *Ethnography* 9(2):175–196.

Pinto, Nick and Ryan Devereaux. 2013. "Everybody Wants a Piece of Kimani Gray." *Village Voice*, 20 March. Retrieved July 6, 2013. http://www.villagevoice.com/2013-03-20/news/kimani-gray-flatbush/.

Putnam, Robert. 2000. *Bowling Alone: The Collapse and Revival of American Community*. New York: Simon and Schuster.

Rieder, Jonathan. 1985. *Canarsie: Jews and Italians of Brooklyn against Liberalism*. Cambridge, MA: Harvard University Press.

Rose, Dan. 1990. *Living the Ethnographic Life*. Newbury Park, CA: Sage.

Sanjek, Roger. 1998. *The Future of Us All: Race and Neighborhood Politics in New York City*. Ithaca, NY: Cornell University Press.

Scott, Greg. 2004. "It's a Sucker's Outfit: How Urban Gangs Enable and Impede the Reintegration of Ex-convicts." *Ethnography* 5(1):107–140.

Sharp, Elaine B. 2013. "Politics, Economics and Urban Policing." *Urban Affairs Review* 20(10):1–26.

Stone, Gregory. 1954. "City Shoppers and Urban Identification: Observations on the Social Psychology of City Life." *American Journal of Sociology* 60(1):36–45.

Vannini, Philip. 2007. "Social Semiotics and Fieldwork methods and Analytics." *Qualitative Inquiry* 13(1):113–140.

Venkatesh, Sudhir. 2002. "Doing the Hustle: Constructing the Ethnographer in the American Ghetto." *Ethnography* 3(1):91–111.

Wohl, Richard and Anslem Strauss. 1958. "Symbolic Representation and the Urban Milieu." *American Journal of Sociology* 63(5):523–532.

Zukin, Sharon. 1995. *The Cultures of Cities.* Oxford: Blackwell.

12

Walking as a Mobile Practice

Landscape and Public Protests in Washington, D.C.

PAUL R. WATTS

In the early 1890s, Jacob Coxey, a stone quarry owner and populist, drafted his "Good Roads Bill," which proposed building a national road network. If funded by the federal government, Coxey reasoned, such a large-scale project could employ thousands during a time of economic recession. Coxey persuaded a Populist legislator to introduce his "Good Roads Bill" to Congress, but the effort failed. California printer and journalist Carl Browne, however, convinced Coxey to organize unemployed men to assemble in Washington and petition Congress in person—a radical idea since activists had traditionally mailed their demands. To garner attention, Coxey's supporters, who observers named "Coxey's Army," walked from Massillon, Ohio, to Washington, D.C. After a monthlong walk, Coxey's Army entered the District of Columbia on May 1, 1894. Upon their arrival, District police cleared spectators from the streets so Coxey's Army could pass, walking in rows to imitate a military parade. When Coxey's Army arrived at the United States Capitol, they were met by hundreds of police officers and thousands of spectators, in what historian Lucy Barber considers to be Washington's first organized public march. Coxey attempted to climb the steps of the United States Capitol and deliver a prepared speech, an attempt that the police thwarted. The police arrested Coxey the following day, and authorities sentenced him to short-term incarceration. In the end, the petition by Coxey's Army failed, yet "they established the precedent for a new type of national public political protest" (Barber 2002:40), one that included walking as a tactic.

This chapter examines walking as an embodied mobile practice within the urban material landscape. Using public protests in Washington as a case study, I argue that walking allows participants to recreate ephemeral and recurring events that spatially engage with the monumental objects of Washington's public spaces, and in doing so maintains a cultural tradition of peaceful assembly and political dissent. My research draws from thirty protests in Washington from May 2005 to October 2006, along with two pilot studies conducted in 2003. During this time, many events in Washington focused on antiwar themes, as the United States was involved in Afghanistan and Iraq in what was referred to as the War on Terror. As a result, protesters and other participants often assembled near and walked past the White House and the United States Capitol—iconic monuments that represented the people and institutions responsible for the wars. I used qualitative-based methods to gather field data, such as taking digital images, writing observational notes, and conversing with participants. I also participated by walking with fellow protesters in an attempt to embody the spirit of protesting. This mobile embodiment was influenced by two theoretical approaches. The first approach, in what geographer Hayden Lorimer (2005, 2008) coined as "more-than-representational," attempts to contextualize the researcher's observations of an event while engaging in its cultural practice. The second approach adopts the reflexive quality of auto-ethnography and reconfigures the researcher-subject framework by positioning the researcher as the primary subject of investigation in order to relate field experiences to broader social meanings (Butz and Besio 2009). Together, these approaches guided my field immersion techniques and resulting subjective interpretations, overlapping with Brown's (Chapter 12 of this volume) use of walking as "footwork."

To complement my empirical findings, I draw on the increasing examination of mobility from the social sciences coupled with theoretical concepts regarding landscape by geographers. From this combined perspective, public protests are more than participants' on-the-ground movement through the city's streets. Rather, the act of walking engages participants with Washington's public spaces and its iconic monuments. Media representations of public protests, however, tend to focus on the spectacle of placards, chants, and other performance-based theatrics, rather than the dynamic fluidity of movement. As a mobile practice, walking is the foundation on which these forms of spectacle take place, for walking facilitates American cultural values of peaceful assembly and public dissent—values that are embodied when protest participants mobilize and temporarily occupy Washington's streets. Moreover, Washington's iconic monuments are not merely a backdrop to frame a protest scene but are inscribed with various meanings by protest participants, and these inscriptions act as a catalyst for political dissent. Although public protests may disrupt Washington's streets and public spaces, their ephemeral and recurring characteristics have made them commonplace. As such, public protests are as much a part of Washington's landscape as its material culture, specifically its iconic monuments.

Public Protests and Mobility in Washington

Public protests in Washington range from large-scale events, in some cases mobilizing more than one hundred thousand participants, to much smaller events attracting fewer than a dozen people. Most events have an overarching theme, but the demands by various protest organizers and other supporting groups differ slightly, as do the political orientations of individual protesters. Protest organizers apply for a parade permit well in advance of an event and negotiate with officials regarding specific times, locations, and routes (Staeheli and Mitchell 2008). During an event, protesters—those people acting in formal opposition to something or someone—engage in varying levels of commitment (Akatiff 1974). Many walk along the established route holding signs, carrying banners, and chanting slogans. A few are willing to trespass and refuse police orders to disperse, which leads to arrests. Arrests are part of the permit process, as protest organizers are required to disclose any planned civil disobedience, intended number of arrestees, and their locations (Metropolitan Police Department 2012). On rare occasions, small groups will commit minor acts of vandalism. Some events will also attract smaller groups of counterprotesters, who are usually stationary and will verbally spar with the passing protesters. Since public protests involve a variety of people, I use *participant* to describe all associated, both directly and indirectly, during an event. *Participant*, therefore, refers to an array of engaged groups or individuals, including protesters, counterprotesters, law enforcement, and the media, among others. This description also includes bystanders. Although bystanders are typically peripheral spectators, they are nonetheless assembling in the same public spaces. Overall, contemporary protests in Washington are safe, highly organized, and legal events protected under the First Amendment to the Constitution of the United States.

Participants embody First Amendment tenets in Washington's public spaces by exercising free speech and peaceful assembly for the redress of grievances. However, access to Washington's public spaces, particularly for political dissent, has been and still is a legal work in progress (Staeheli and Mitchell 2008). At issue is not the restriction of the First Amendment, but where and how its activities take place. Known as "public forum law," various United States Supreme Court and other lower court rulings have established parameters regarding First Amendment activities in public spaces, such as time and location (McCarthy and Mcphail 2006). Beginning with *Hague v. Congress of Industrial Organizations* (CIO) in 1939, the United States Supreme Court ruled in favor of the CIO, upholding access to public spaces but also establishing notions of public order (Mitchell 2003). For public assembly in Washington, political dissent or otherwise, *Hague v. CIO* "established that the streets and parks of cities were a 'public forum' whose use by groups could be regulated but not completely restricted" (Barber 2002:115). In the context of contemporary public protests in the United

States, it is the state's underlying legal system that facilitates participants' mobility, more so than the city's streets.

Public protests require mobility for participants to assemble, participate, and disperse. Mobility is therefore a spatial concept—one that investigates the relationships among actors, processes, and environment. Geographer Tim Cresswell argues that past scholarship has viewed human mobility as a taken-for-granted abstraction of physical movement from points A to B, something that is "contentless, apparently natural, and devoid of meaning, history, and ideology" (2006:3). Quantification of spatial-based data, where social phenomena are analyzed, generalized, and depicted on a map, offers broad-scale accounts, but this methodology does not realize the many on-the-ground and meaningful human experiences, or, namely, that to be mobile people must often negotiate with the facilitators and constrainers of movement (Cresswell 2001). Movement is differentiated in part by fixed-in-place structures, what sociologist John Urry (2007:53) calls "immobile platforms," such as airports (Adey 2006), gas stations (Normark 2006), and train stations (Bissell 2009). Although immobile platforms are stationary, they comprise broader infrastructures that facilitate or regulate mobility (Sheller and Urry 2006). Hence, mobility requires various forms of movement and nonmovement, for "it is precisely because certain subjects and objects are immobilized that others can travel" (Beckmann 2005:84). Furthermore, mobility is multidimensional (see Wiley, Chapter 10 of this volume) and represents an array of interdependent engagements, in what has emerged as a "new mobilities paradigm" (Sheller and Urry 2006). Hannam, Sheller, and Urry (2006:1) explain, "The concept of mobilities encompasses both the large-scale movements of people, objects, capital and information across the world, as well as the more local processes of daily transportation, movement through public space and the travel of material things within everyday life."

Proponents of this new mobilities paradigm strive for a reinvigoration of the social sciences by also examining how underlying political institutions and cultural practices influence, and presuppose, movement (Adey 2010; Urry 2007). In this research, United States Supreme Court decisions and Washington's permit process not only facilitate political dissent but spatially influence where and how protesters express dissent. Protests in Washington take place in the city's public spaces, including the streets, where people are free to participate, yet participation is confined to walking within permitted and predetermined routes.

Regardless of physical constraints, participants' collective sense of power derives from their ability to temporarily disrupt regular uses of the city, which they do in Washington by occupying public spaces, particularly the streets. The use of motorized vehicles is suspended, or at least altered, as the police close streets and reroute traffic. For a typical event, participants assemble at a predetermined staging area, listen to a series of announcements and speeches by organizers and activists, and descend onto the streets. But modern city streets in the United States have been designed for vehicular—not pedestrian—mobility, which is why walking en masse on what is normally a high-traffic Washington thoroughfare is disruptive. For example, during an event I attended on January 18, 2003, participants gathered on the National Mall and, after listening to a number of political speeches, the crowd began to travel east, along Independence Avenue Southwest. The moving crowd was thick, with many less than an arm's length apart. As we walked east, I noticed the United States Capitol grounds to the left. This section was elevated slightly from the street, with its relief supported by a two-foot-high retaining wall. I jumped up on the retaining wall and looked to the west, where I could better view the protest, and saw a slow-moving, dense mass within the six-lane width of Independence Avenue that extended several blocks. Social anthropologist Stef Jansen (2001:50) describes a Serbian protest against the Milošević regime as "one massive human caterpillar that crawled through the Beograd streets." Indeed, a city street confines participants into a linear form and compels mobility where walking serves as a means to collectively take ownership over new territory. Participants also chant, "Whose streets? Our streets!" during events in the United States (Marcuse 2006; Schwartz 2002), including Washington (Noakes, Klocke, and Gillham 2005). As Zajko and Béland (2008:731) explain, this "popular protest rallying cry . . . perhaps best signifies the continued importance of spatial contention within the practice of political protest." Participants engage in this call-and-response chant while walking down the street as an auditory complement to their physical presence. In some cases, participants walking on the streets notice and target those who are less committed. At an event on September 24, 2005, a group of protesters chanted, "Join us for peace, off the sidewalk and on the street" to bystanders flanking the protest route. Several bystanders joined the protesters, and I did after taking a few more pictures. This tactic encourages bystanders to participate and increases the number of people on the street, while chanting invigorates participants' energy. Together, a mass of bodies walking and chanting becomes a powerful tool to demonstrate protesters' solidarity for a political issue and their commitment to occupy a public space.

Washington has several large public spaces that can easily accommodate thousands of people. Its streets, however, are preferable because they provide participants an opportunity to disrupt the city's regular activities. Disruption often draws media attention to an event and thus to organizers' political objectives, which are then broadcast to a larger audience. As a promotional tool, large-scale events, with their potential for greater disruption, have a better chance of attracting mainstream media coverage than do smaller events. Media coverage, however, is not the sole objective of using the streets as a stage for protest. Meridian Hill Park, also referred to as Malcolm X Park, is just more than one mile north of the White House. Ornamented with large, shady trees along its perimeter, the park is at a slightly higher relief than Sixteenth Street Northwest, its western boundary. Saturday, May 20, 2006, was a warm, sunny day, and by my estimation, attracted perhaps three hundred people to an event that assembled in the park. They descended onto Sixteenth Street Northwest, and eventually traveled south where it terminated in Lafayette Square, across

the street from the White House. After several political speeches and announcements, participants grabbed signs and banners and filed down a narrow set of
stairs onto the street. It is at this time when the body of participants transition
from standing to walking—the process of becoming mobile—that protests are
their most exciting. I recall going down the stairs, surrounded by dozens of
other participants, onto the sidewalk and northbound lanes of Sixteenth Street.
We were met by several police officers, who were riding motorcycles and bicycles, ensuring that participants did not cross the double yellow line separating us
from the southbound lanes. Although this was a small event, people were highly
energized by the time most participants were on the street. The protest route
eventually led participants south down Eighteenth Street Northwest, a bustling
two-lane retail strip. The advantage of walking on the streets, as opposed to
other types of public spaces such as parks, is organizers can plan routes that
pass through busy areas. Instead of encouraging people to attend a protest, the
protest comes to you. I could hear car horns as we walked through intersections
and saw a couple of motorists gesture in approval. Customers seated along the
sidewalk eateries turned to watch the passing spectacle, while some protesters
handed flyers to bystanders on the sidewalk. Such a disruption of the regular
neighborhood street scene allowed protesters to engage with bystanders in a
mutually beneficial manner, whereby protesters felt energized by bystanders' attention and bystanders were witness to a playful expression of political dissent.

Not everyone, however, is tolerant of Washington's protests. A Capitol Hill
staffer once told me that, "Nobody in D.C. likes protests." This is because mobile participants temporarily disrupt the regular uses of Washington's streets,
frustrating many bystanders and motorists. To manage an event's disruption,
the police facilitate the movement of protesters and other participants along a
predetermined route. To do this, city workers erect metal barricades before an
event to channel the flow of participants, and law enforcement agencies have a
strong presence of officers to maintain order. Such physical boundaries, coupled
with a police presence, create a stark distinction between where participants
may and may not assemble, what Noakes, Klocke, and Gillham (2005:249) describe as a "partitioning of space." This spatial influence by law enforcement has
been described as a means to physically and psychologically control protesters
(Fernandez 2005) and, for that matter, political dissent (Staeheli and Mitchell
2008). Indeed, the police are active agents in constraining participants' mobility. However, the police also facilitate overall mobility within a protest's predetermined route. Lafayette Square, situated on Pennsylvania Avenue Northwest
across from the White House, is a common assembly area for many events. During an event on August 12, 2006, organizers encouraged participants to walk out
of Lafayette Square and onto Pennsylvania Avenue so the protest could begin.
Law enforcement had erected waist-high metal barricades down the center of
Pennsylvania Avenue, preventing participants from crossing the street and thus
accessing the sidewalk in front of the White House (Figure 12.1, upper left). In
this case, the metal barricades were a means to constrain but resulted in better

Figure 12.1 Protest Marches in Washington, D.C. Upper left: The waist-high metal barricades prevented participants from crossing the street but resulted in better organization that facilitated their movement. Upper right: Participants carry cardboard "coffins" juxtaposed to the United States Capitol. Lower left: A point-of-view image of walking while looking through my camera's viewfinder. Lower right: A small event with participants walking on the sidewalk, revealing the everyday occurrences of protests in Washington. (Images by author)

organization that, within minutes, channeled participants' movement out of Lafayette Square and east along Pennsylvania Avenue. Boundaries compress the open spaces among individual participants, making an event appear unified and well attended. Moreover, the close proximity among participants, in conjunction with their physical movement, produces a collective sense of lasting excitement.

Notions of Landscape and Walking

The police facilitate participants' right to assemble in many of Washington's public spaces. Protesters are attracted to Washington because of the city's concentration of and proximity to political power, which is represented by its iconic landscape in what historian Kirk Savage calls "the monumental core of the nation" (2009:4). Other institutions of power are headquartered in Washington as well, such as the International Monetary Fund, the World Bank, and multiple federal agencies and foreign embassies. Jansen (2001) has shown that protesters tend to gather in and around places with symbolic significance. A protester metaphorically inscribes his or her own political values on at least one monumental object of Washington's landscape—the White House, for instance. This object conflicts with protesters' collective values and becomes a place to gather and express dissent in lieu of having direct access to the individual or group in power.

Objects within a landscape influence where participants assemble. The term *landscape*, however, evokes stasis or something gazed on from a distance. Geographer John Wylie (2007) argues that landscapes produce tensions, one of which is between observation and immersion. The District of Columbia expands across a gently rolling topography and offers several elevated locations from which to view its monumental objects, with the United States Capitol dome and Washington Monument being most prominent. From this distant perspective, and drawing from Wylie (2007), the observer is detached from the landscape and Washington's monumental objects become part of the urban backdrop. Visual representations of the city are often depicted as an assemblage of objects and people, whereas city life is understood through lived experiences. To address this inherent tension means exploring how peoples' experiences are an ongoing contributor to the landscape as much as the assemblage of objects that construct its appearance. Moreover, a cultural practice—the established behaviors that presuppose people's actions—is integral to shaping and is shaped by its related landscape (Cresswell 2003). To be clear, people are not creating a static protest landscape; rather, they participate in ephemeral and recurring events, events based on a spatial relationship that is complementary to, yet petitions against, Washington's monumental objects. In turn, these events reinforce people's notion of Washington's landscape as a public space for peaceful assembly and political dissent as the First Amendment intended.

Scholars note that walking is an essential characteristic during protests (Dragićević-Šešić 1997; Jansen 2001), providing a means to physically engage social movement organizations (see Knudsen, Clark, and Silver, Chapter 13 or this volume). Participants are not wandering spontaneously; instead, they walk as a collective tactic to challenge the dominant uses of an urban environment (Jansen 2001), to temporarily claim control of public space (Erdei 1997), and to sustain their enthusiasm (Spasić and Pavićević 1997). Walking during a protest is therefore done for political reasons, where "one walks to demonstrate one's commitment" (Solnit 2000:216). Early protests in Washington were more paradelike with participants walking past large numbers of spectators: Coxey's Army had an estimated thirty thousand spectators in 1894 and on March 3, 1913, approximately one hundred thousand spectators lined Pennsylvania Avenue to watch the "Women's Suffrage Procession and Pageant" (Barber 2002). Contemporary events in Washington, however, have become more participatory; bystanders are invited to walk with protesters. During an event on May 13, 2006, organizers and event volunteers brought several dozen placards for protesters to carry while walking along the permitted route. This event assembled on the National Mall between the Washington Monument and United States Capitol, surrounded by bystanders enjoying a warm Saturday morning. To encourage additional participation, one organizer announced through his megaphone: "If you don't have a sign, you can borrow one of mine" as protesters were lining up to walk. Several people grabbed a placard; however, I could not determine whether they were bystanders who impulsively decided to join in. Regardless, organizers created an opportunity for participation.

The practice of walking is subject to range of inquiry. This includes placing the human body within the urban environment as a "means through which we experience and feel the world" (Edensor 2000:121). Geographer Paul Adams, for instance, describes the ability to physically sense a hill through one's leg muscles as "a direct imprinting of place on self" (2001:188). Walking can therefore produce sensations that are part of an embedded relationship between human mobility and the landscape. Those participating in an event on September 27, 2006, sought to bring material replications of the distant War on Terror home to Washington. Some walked in tandem, carrying cardboard "coffins" covered with American flags or wrapped in black cloth as a metaphor for death (Figure 12.1, upper right). Symbolically, the "coffins" represented human casualties from the war, and, in this sense, participants walked for those who no longer could. The slow procession of participants carrying "coffins" past the United States Capitol to the event's destination at the Rayburn House Office Building juxtaposed the places where the war was authorized with those who died fighting as a result of that authorization. Anthropologist Tim Ingold (2004) explains that walking upright on two feet distinguishes human evolution from the development of other Hominidae. For many people, walking is seemingly effortless—a taken-for-granted activity that is often characterized as mundane. Yet "walking itself is the intentional act closest to the unwilled rhythms of the body, to breathing and the beating of the heart. It strikes a delicate balance between working and idling, being and doing" (Solnit 2000:5). Perhaps this is why walking remains a powerful form of protest, especially within the antiwar movement: Participants' upright and lively bodies—a vertical existence—is in contrast to the horizontal and stationary bodies of the dead.

Walking represents an array of experiences, from negotiating the city (de Certeau 1984) to strolling around for pleasure (Adams 2001). Sociologist Erving Goffman (1971) argues that urban pedestrians scan their immediate surroundings to avoid colliding with others, a process that creates an ever-changing personal space. In part, walking for many people is a visual activity, requiring the walker to focus not on the self—as in precisely monitoring one's steps on the ground—but instead to pay attention to other people (Ingold 2004). This is what A. Lincoln Ryave and James N. Schenkein (1974:268) refer to as the "navigational problem" as urban walkers make their way through crowded public spaces. Protest participants do not walk in a formal manner as with members of a marching band or soldiers in a military procession. Rather, a collective body of participants has individual rhythms that respond uniquely to the changing dynamics of a protest's flow. Such dynamic variations in public space is what David Bissell (2009:182) refers to as being "differently-mobile." Because of this, no two protests are the same. Participants must have an ability to engage in multiple activities, such as carrying placards, chanting slogans, looking around, and walking and talking with fellow protesters, all without bumping into other people. This point-of-view image required that I simultaneously walk and look through my camera's viewfinder at the expense of my peripheral vision and of those around me (Figure 12.1, lower left). I do remember setting up other shots when, as I was walking, the rhythm of the participants around me changed, and the pace suddenly became slower. Adjustments to my rhythm occurred frequently as I responded to others' movement around me. Although I came close, I never bumped into another participant. The only contact I experienced was when a neighboring participant, for a reason unknown to me, flailed his right arm, bumping my left shoulder. I was attempting to walk and write field notes, so I did not look up, but he apologized seconds later.

Not all participants conform to an event's rhythmic mobility. Sit-ins became a well-known tactic during the 1960s civil rights movement when African Americans resisted Jim Crow laws through nonviolent acts of disobedience by occupying and refusing to leave private businesses, usually lunch counters (Martin 2004). Several events I attended borrowed similar tactics of immobility where participants occupied and remained in an area juxtaposed to a monumental object. The police then gave several orders for participants to disperse. When some participants refused, officers set up a perimeter using yellow police tape and arrested those within. Often, participants would sit down on the sidewalk, some locking arms, making it more difficult for officers to remove individual violators. Sidewalks and other public spaces became temporary cites of illegal assembly because a group refused to be mobile, while outside the police tape the remaining participants freely assembled. Spontaneous running also rejects an event's rhythmic mobility, which might be considered hypermobility in relation to walking.

During a January 19, 2003, event, several participants approached a stationary line of motorcycle officers who were blocking a side street. The participants wanted to continue walking down the side street, so they began to verbally challenge the officers. The officers sat on their motorcycles, expressionless, as participants taunted them, took their pictures at close range, and wrote down their names and badge numbers. The officers seemed annoyed but remained professional. After a few minutes I walked away. A block from the motorcycle officers, and for unbeknownst reasons, dozens of participants began running down the street. I ran, too. It was my first time in Washington, and I did not know where I was going, or who I was running from; I just followed a pack of several people. Although these seconds are blurry, I do remember motorcycle officers approaching us from behind. One officer accelerated past, just a few feet to my left. The sharp, staccato popping from the motorcycle's tailpipes startled me. I looked over my right shoulder—I didn't want to get run over—and darted toward the sidewalk, where I thought I could find safety. Moments later I wandered over to a group of participants shouting at the police who had just arrested a young man for trespassing on the White House grounds. Perhaps the motorcycle officers were in pursuit of the trespasser or responding to something else, but I was fortunately not of interest.

I never felt the need to run at subsequent events. On occasion, I would walk quickly or jog to catch up to a developing situation. For the most part, protests move at a comfortable pace. Under normal conditions, running down a city street conveys a sense of urgency. Running within Washington's public spaces, especially in the post–September 11 United States, would arouse people's interest and likely be viewed as suspicious, or even elicit concern. Walking is the body's everyday mobility, a movement that takes place at three miles per hour (Solnit 2000). This may be why stagnation in public spaces is met with frustration or often not tolerated, such as with waiting in line or loitering. Running and stagnation have their place, but walking is the normative practice during a public protest. And although protesters may assemble at and remain in a single location to express dissent, one must walk to mobilize.

Walking as an Embodied Protest Tradition

During the height of the 1960s antiwar movement, *Life* columnist Hugh Sidey noted, "It could be that protest is at last being recognized as a part of the American way of democratic life" (1971:2B). Several years later, *Washington Post* columnist Haynes Johnson (1978:A3) stated, "Whatever the politics of the moment, or lack, selfish individualistic introspective '70s as opposed to activist mass movement '60s, one thing remains constant, Washington has become, in season and out, the demonstration capital of the world." Such media accounts affirm that public protests have developed into a time-honored social practice and part of an American cultural tradition. Some, however, feel that public protests in Washington have become too much of a tradition. In response to an event on January 18, 2003—my first protest in Washington—Hank Stuever (2003:C1) of the *Washington Post* wrote: "For all the energy present Saturday, a march on Washington always seems to feel like a rerun." And this is precisely because public protests in Washington have become an established practice. In some ways events are competitive, so a way of distinguishing one event from the others is to attract thousands of participants. The expectation of a large crowd will likely draw more media attention; media frequently report the estimated number of people. For many, the greater number of people will correlate with a greater importance of the cause. On the ground, large events provide a different experience than smaller events do, even if is a similar cause.

For me, large events were when the police rerouted traffic so that participants could walk in the streets, whereas small events describe when participants were relegated to the sidewalk. Regardless of whether an event attracts several hundred or tens of thousands, being in the streets gives participants a temporary sense of collective ownership, and this ownership speaks on behalf of the cause. Furthermore, disrupting the regular uses of the city's streets feels powerful and liberating, for participants during large events do not obey regular traffic laws or have to watch for vehicles. In fact, walking through red lights was necessary to remain mobile. Prior to the January 18, 2003, event, I wandered over to an area on the National Mall, around Seventh Street Southwest, where organizers erected a stage and public address system for activists to inspire the protesters. Perhaps one hundred feet away, a crew had also constructed a media tower where camera operators and reporters could broadcast, which was well above the amassing participants. Someone next to me yelled up to a reporter on the media tower and asked him the size of the crowd. The reporter said the crowd was solid and extended back to the Washington Monument, an approximate distance of one-half mile. After the activists' speeches, organizers told the crowd to begin walking. I remember feeling exuberant, as I and countless people around me spilled onto Independence Avenue (where I later jumped atop a two-foot-high retaining to observe the protest). As an individual, being on the street made me feel small, yet I also felt empowered because I was part of large, unified group.

Large events I attended, such as an antiwar protest on September 24, 2005, drew an estimated three hundred thousand people, according to organizers (Dvorak 2005). This protest was significant because it attracted people from across the United States and received national media coverage. In fact, none of the other protests during my fieldwork in Washington ever quite matched its scale, number of people, and presence of law enforcement. This event was significant for another reason, as well: It revealed that large-scale protests are infrequent occurrences in Washington. Most protests in Washington are underwhelming in that they may draw only a handful of local participants and receive little if any media coverage. As such, a majority of public protests are routine and blend into Washington's everyday activities; so much so many are nearly invisible.

The event on September 14, 2006, represents a small-scale protest that was underwhelming, not because its participants lacked enthusiasm or its cause was unimportant. Rather, this event—and the thousands like it that have contributed to Washington's protest history—fit in with the city's everyday mobile practices of cars, taxis, buses, and pedestrians. Approximately two dozen protesters walked along Washington's downtown sidewalks (Figure 12.1, lower right). Some participants carried signs, several more took turns carrying a large banner, and a few others distributed flyers to passing bystanders. September 14 was a Thursday, and this event occurred in the late afternoon as many people were leaving work. Most bystanders seemed indifferent, although some would glance over at the protesters. In fact, nothing seemed out of the ordinary, even though protesters were chanting slogans noisily and their handheld signs and banners were highly visible. In fact, I wrote in my field notes that it seemed like an "average day" on Washington's streets. Protesting in Washington does not directly change U.S. domestic or foreign policies. Certain events have stood out for their significant impact: For instance, both the 1913 "Woman's Suffrage Procession and Pageant" and 1963 "March on Washington for Jobs and Freedom" galvanized stakeholders, leading in part to voting rights for women and civil rights for people of color, respectively. These legacy events, however, have been the exception. Protests by the thousands have received minimal, if any, mention in the annals of Washington's history, yet—collectively—these smaller and obscure events ensure that protesting remains a national tradition.

Washington's public spaces are where various people can assemble and stake a physical claim, creating a temporary sense of community. Anecdotally, I encountered few participants from Washington. During the event on January 19, 2003, several activists, using a bullhorn to energize the crowd, asked participants to shout what state they were from. About three dozen participants responded, but not one stated Washington, D.C. I left thinking this was interesting but trivial. It was not until I moved to Washington that I began to notice its importance. Toward the end of my fieldwork, I asked a middle-aged participant from Texas about any previous visits to Washington. She told me it was her "first time east of Ohio and riding a subway." Thus, people travel from all over the United States to assemble in Washington; they take time out of their lives and spend their own money to join with other like-minded participants—most of whom are strangers—and engage in political dissent. Even though many of Washington's protests go unreported by the media, their "most effective use," Barber writes, "has arguably become personal affirmation and movement building" (2002:227). When I asked one participant why he traveled to Washington, he told me that the decisions made in the nation's capital impact the future of so many people. Protesting in Washington, he elaborated, allows a place for individuals with similar grievances to connect and express solidarity—to then go back home, in his case to Vermont, feeling energized about politics.

The focus of this chapter has been to recognize public protests in Washington as ephemeral and recurring events, so much so that their physical presence is often seen as ordinary, making them as much a part of Washington's landscape as its visible material culture of monuments and other symbols of state power. In this light, what has made protesting in Washington an established tradition are not the large-scale demonstrations that mobilize thousands of participants and attract the national media but the many small, routine events that draw only a handful of people. Underlying this routine is participants' mobility. Walking in Washington's public spaces takes place every day, whether it is walking on the street to get to work as a resident or across the National Mall to assemble near a monument as a protester—at some point, one must walk to arrive.

Many people have been drawn to Washington because of the cultural significance of its built environment, particularly its iconic monuments. Savage (2009:10) explains: "The memorial landscape of Washington is the one place, above all, where people come to find the nation and to engage with it as citizens." Throughout Washington's protest tradition, organizers have juxtaposed their events with monumental objects in the landscape, a mobile practice that dates back to 1894 when Coxey's Army walked to Washington and petitioned Congress on the grounds of the United States Capitol (Barber 2002). Washington's landscape offers protesters a location for open and collective political action. In turn, protesting in Washington sets a national and international standard for other places to follow. Access to Washington's public spaces means its iconic monuments are not in the distance but ensure that people are part of the landscape. As a mobile participant, whether on the street during large events or relegated to sidewalks for small ones, I had time to reflect while walking and could not help placing my own inscriptions on Washington's monumental objects. No doubt that walking affected other participants, perhaps also in meaningful ways, as Solnit (2000:216) recalls being "deeply moved by walking through the streets en masse." I felt sensations of collective empowerment at every event I attended, regardless of the number of participants or their political objectives. Walking has become a precedent for how protesters engage in Washington's public spaces and, through this embodied experience, maintains a tradition of peaceful assembly and political dissent.

REFERENCES

Adams, Paul C. 2001. "Peripatetic Imagery and Peripatetic Sense of Place." Pp. 186–206 in *Textures of Place: Exploring Humanist Geographies*, edited by Paul C. Adams, Steven Hoelscher, and Karen E. Till. Minneapolis: University of Minnesota Press.

Adey, Peter. 2006. "If Mobility Is Everything Then It Is Nothing: Towards a Relational Politics of (Im)mobilities." *Mobilities* 1(1):75–94.

———. 2010. *Mobility*. New York: Routledge.

Akatiff, Clark. 1974. "The March on the Pentagon." *Annals of the Association of American Geographers* 64(1):26–33.

Barber, Lucy G. 2002. *Marching on Washington: The Forging of an American Political Tradition*. Berkeley: University of California Press.

Beckmann, Jörg. 2005. "Mobility and Safety." Pp. 81–100 in *Automobilities*, edited by Mike Featherstone, Nigel Thrift, and John Urry. Thousand Oaks, CA: Sage.

Bissell, David. 2009. "Conceptualising Differently-Mobile Passengers: Geographies of Everyday Encumbrance in the Railway Station." *Social and Cultural Geography* 10(2):173–195.

Butz, David and Kathryn Besio. 2009. "Autoethnography." *Geography Compass* 3(5):1660–1674.

Cresswell, Tim. 2001. "The Production of Mobilities." *New Formations* 43(1):11–25.

———. 2003. "Landscape and the Obliteration of Practice." Pp. 269–281 in *Handbook of Cultural Geography*, edited by Kay Anderson, Mona Domosh, Steve Pile, and Nigel Thrift. Thousand Oaks, CA: Sage.

———. 2006. *On the Move: Mobility in the Modern Western World*. New York: Routledge.

de Certeau, Michel. 1984. *The Practice of Everyday Life*. Berkeley: University of California Press.

Dragićević-Šešić, Milena. 1997. "Street as a Political Space: The Space of Carnivalization." *Sociologija* 39(1):95–110.

Dvorak, Petula. 2005. "White House Sidewalk Protest Leads to Arrest of about 370." *Washington Post*, 27 September, p. B1.

Edensor, Tim. 2000. "Moving through the City." Pp. 121–140 in *City Visions*, edited by David Bell and Azzedine Haddour. New York: Pearson.

Erdei, Ildiko. 1997. "Alice's Adventures in Studentland: Narrative Multiplicity of the Student Protest." *Sociologija* 39(1):111–133.

Fernandez, Luis A. 2005. "Policing Protest Spaces: Social Control in the Anti-Globalization Movement." Ph.D. dissertation, School of Justice Studies and Social Inquiry, Arizona State University, Tempe.

Goffman, Erving. 1971. *Relations in Public: Microstudies of the Public Order*. New York: Basic Books.

Hannam, Kevin, Mimi Sheller, and John Urry. 2006. "Editorial: Mobilities, Immobilities, and Moorings." *Mobilities* 1(1):1–22.

Ingold, Tim. 2004. "Culture on the Ground: The World Perceived through the Feet." *Journal of Material Culture* 9(3):315–340.

Jansen, Stef. 2001. "The Streets of Beograd: Urban Space and Protest Identities in Serbia." *Political Geography* 20(1):35–55.

Johnson, Haynes. 1978. "Washington Remains Demonstration Capital of the World." *Washington Post*, 19 July, p. A3.

Lorimer, Hayden. 2005. "Cultural Geography: The Business of Being 'More-Than-Representational.'" *Progress in Human Geography* 29(1):83–94.

———. 2008. "Cultural Geography: Non-Representational Conditions and Concerns." *Progress in Human Geography* 32(4):551–559.

Marcuse, Peter. 2006. "Security or Safety in Cities? The Threat of Terrorism after 9/11." *International Journal of Urban and Regional Research* 30(4):919–929.

Martin, Bradford D. 2004. *The Theater Is in the Streets: Politics and Public Performance in Sixties America*. Amherst: University of Massachusetts Press.

McCarthy, John D. and Clark McPhail. 2006. "Places of Protest: The Public Forum in Principle and Practice." *Mobilization: An International Quarterly* 11(2):229–247.

Metropolitan Police Department. 2012. "Application for Parade Permit." Washington, DC: Metropolitan Police Department. Retrieved June 12, 2014. http://mpD.C..D.C. .gov/publication/parade-permit-application.

Mitchell, Don. 2003. *The Right to the City: Social Justice and the Fight for Public Space*. New York: Guilford.

Noakes, John A., Brian V. Klocke, and Patrick F. Gillham. 2005. "Whose Streets? Police and Protester Struggles over Space in Washington, D.C., 29–30 September 2001." *Policing and Society* 15(3):235–254.

Normark, Daniel. 2006. "Tending to Mobility: Intensities of Staying at the Petrol Station." *Environment and Planning A* 38(2):241–252.

Ryave, A. Lincoln and James N. Schenkein. 1974. "Notes on the Art of Walking." Pp. 265–274 in *Ethnomethodology: Selected Readings*, edited by Roy Turner. Baltimore: Penguin.

Savage, Kirk. 2009. *Monument Wars: Washington, D.C., the National Mall, and the Transformation of the Memorial Landscape*. Berkeley: University of California Press.

Schwartz, Dona. 2002. "Pictures at a Demonstration." *Visual Studies* 17(1):27–36.

Sheller, Mimi and John Urry. 2006. "The New Mobilities Paradigm." *Environment and Planning A* 38(2):207–226.

Sidey, Hugh. 1971. "Something Different in Spring." *Life*, 23 April, p. 2B.

Solnit, Rebecca. 2000. *Wanderlust: A History of Walking*. New York: Penguin.

Spasić, Ivana and Đorđe Pavićević. 1997. "Symbolization and Collective Identity in Civic Protest." *Sociologija* 39(1):73–93.

Staeheli, Lynn. A. and Don Mitchell. 2008. *The People's Property? Power, Politics, and the Public.* New York: Routledge.

Stuever, Hank. 2003. "The Art of Peace: Deploying Posters and Body Paint, the Antiwarriors Take a Scattershot Approach." *Washington Post*, 20 January, p. C1.

Urry, John. 2007. *Mobilities.* Cambridge: Polity.

Wylie, John. 2007. *Landscape.* New York: Routledge.

Zajko, Mike and Daniel Béland. 2008. "Space and Protest Policing at International Summits." *Environment and Planning D: Society and Space* 26(4):719–735.

13

Walking, Social Movements, and Arts Activities in the United States, Canada, and France

BRIAN B. KNUDSEN, TERRY NICHOLS CLARK,
AND DANIEL SILVER

T his chapter investigates how walking in different types of neighborhoods relates to the arts and social movement politics in the United States, Canada, and France. Walking is an intimate, direct, embodied means of experiencing the city and its diverse social and built forms. Through these direct engagements with one's social and environmental surroundings, walking heightens awareness and raises consciousness, elicits impressions and sentiments, conjures feelings, encourages imagination, and increases desires for expression. Walking thus enhances people's creative engagement with their cities. The artistic implications of walking are evident, from Charles Baudelaire to Walter Benjamin and beyond. We argue, however, that walking has significance beyond the life of the artist and the aesthete, in particular, for *politics*: Modern political activism has an expressive and imaginative character that makes experiences traditionally conducive to the arts also conducive to political mobilization.

To assess this claim, this chapter examines whether walking independently impacts social movement and arts activity. Specifically, we propose several hypotheses about how social movement organizations (SMOs), arts activity and arts jobs, walking, and several components of walkable urban form relate to one another. Multiple regression analyses allow us to test these propositions across local areas in the United States, Canada, and France. Findings suggest strong and significant effects of walking that hold in all three countries when we replicate the core models: We repeatedly find that artistic and social movement activities are higher in locales with more walking and walkable contexts. These effects are robust to a number of sensitivity analyses. Cities have long been presented as social settings conducive to both artistic production and revolutionary or movement politics; our analyses and results provide substantial empirical support for this view.

Social Qualities of Walking

Walking is rooted in many purposes, mentalities and cultural outlooks.[1] One can walk for exercise, for a utilitarian purpose like rushing to work, to simply enjoy the company of a friend, as a way to enjoy pastoral nature scenes, and possibly as an egalitarian experience as one is confronted in an immediate way with the indigent. While walking has these and other cultural meanings, we focus on those linked to our dependent variables of SMOs and arts.[2] For instance, given the shared expressive and experiential resemblances between contemporary activist politics and artistic production, we extend the perspective of the *flâneur* that portrays walking as an "aesthetic practice" (Careri 2002) at the core of arts and SMOs. Kramer and Short (2011:323) depict the classic *flâneurs* playfully traversing cities on foot to absorb "[their] affective intensities for aesthetic translation." Thus, we focus on specific "social benefits" (Demerath and Levinger 2003) of walking. The *flâneur* is just one kind of intellectualized walker; most walkers are neither *flâneurs* nor actively aesthetic. Nevertheless this form of walking has been depicted so repeatedly by novelists and poets from Honoré de Balzac and Walt Whitman and beyond that it remains a challenge for social science to specifically demonstrate how walking can join the aesthetic and the political. That task has just begun, but we contribute to it below. We develop testable hypotheses positing specific relationships between walking, SMOs, and arts activity and employment, but first we briefly expand on some conceptual links between these constructs.

Arts, Social Movements, and the Walking City

David Graeber (2009:110) notes that artists have often been drawn to revolutionary politics because of a "direct link between the experience of first imagining things and then bringing them into being (individually or collectively) . . . and the ability to imagine social alternatives." In other words, the arts and movement politics are closely related phenomena in that they both involve imagining new ways of living and working to bring them about. Walking is a primary urban act conducive to imaginative, creative, experiential, and expressive

---

[1] Some points in this section build on Knudsen and Clark (2013).

[2] From the 1970s to early 1990s many of the New Social Movements (Offe 1985) took on hierarchical and bureaucratic elements. By contrast, some later groups seek to recover noninstitutional politics by more explicitly emphasizing organizational horizontality, leaderless decentralization, and individual autonomy (Clark and Kallman 2011; Graeber 2003; McDonald 2006). Examples of these *New* New Social Movements include alter-globalization protests at International Monetary Fund and World Bank meetings in the late 1990s as well as the Occupy concerns after 2011. There has been minimal reconceptualization. Our approach recognizes such distinctions but moves in a broader comparative direction by analyzing patterns across types of environmental, human rights, protest and other types of SMOs, using new sources for social movement and social capital research, from the U.S. Census of Business, Canadian Census, and French SIRENE database (register of companies and establishments).

activities like contemporary social movement organizations and the arts (Silver and Clark, forthcoming). Walking links the physical and the social in the city and contributes to SMOs and the arts through social interactions with one's environment and other people. By enhancing contact with the city's diverse environments and by permitting individuals to have frequent casual face-to-face contact, walking builds connections to people and place. This potentially elicits sentiments, helps build shared meanings, and stimulates the imaginative processes, creativity, expressiveness, and innovativeness that are the core of political and artistic activity.

For instance, Francesco Careri (2002:32) describes walking as the "non-utilitarian time *par excellence*," an activity akin to play that gives individuals opportunities for intellectual and creative exploration and speculation, the precursors to both artistic production and activist politics. Similarly, Tim Ingold (2010:15) suggests there is little difference "between walking on the ground, in the landscapes of 'real life,' and walking in the imagination, as in reading, writing, painting, or listening to music." Instead, "the terrains of the imagination and the physical environment, far from existing on distinct ontological levels, run into one another to the extent of being barely distinguishable." By creating opportunities for diverse social interactions, walking may activate both artistic and political expression and creativity by heightening awareness and allowing time for free intellectual and creative exploration and speculation. Therefore, among the many cultural meanings and experiences of walking, one important one is as an artistic-political act that should increase artistic *and* modern social movement activities.

In summary, walking through the modern city to directly and intimately observe, experience and feel urban energies is implicated in creative production. By enabling face-to-face encounters with diverse social influences, walking serves as an authentic source of creative inspiration and thus stimulates and empowers individuals to utilize diverse information for political and artistic ends.[3] These are clearly the impacts noted by walking enthusiasts. We next translate these ideas into several testable hypotheses.

Hypotheses

The first set of hypotheses concentrate on walking, while the second set explores components of walkable urban form. *Walkability* refers to the opportunity to walk, whereas *walking* refers to the act. Substantial research links several specific urban contextual traits to walkability, finding that density, mixed urban use, and connectivity (the ease of moving between origins and destinations) provide the opportunity to walk by promoting proximity and directness of travel (see

[3] Our analysis may apply more to modern Western societies because, comparatively, these cities may have more open civic activities and active citizens. But recent changes globally where social movements of all sorts have played key roles encourages more attention to such new patterns.

Boarnet and Sarmiento 1998; Craig et al. 2002; Frank and Pivo 1994; Greenwald and Boarnet 2002; Saelens, Sallis, and Frank 2003). For example, David Berrigan and Richard P. Troiano (2002:75) find that even after controlling for gender, race, education, income, and health level, walking is significantly more prevalent among U.S. adults who live in older homes and traditional urban neighborhoods with "sidewalks," "denser interconnected networks of streets," and "a mix of business and residential uses." We therefore codify not only walking but also walkability—conceived of as density, connectivity, and mixed uses—as they relate to both the arts and social movement politics.

Walking Hypotheses
> *Hypothesis 1:* Locales with more walking have more social movement organizations.
> *Hypothesis 2:* Locales with more walking have more arts establishments.
> *Hypothesis 3:* Locales with more walking have more arts jobs.

Walkability Hypotheses
> *Hypothesis 4a:* Locales with higher density have more social movement organizations.
> *Hypothesis 4b:* Locales with higher connectivity have more social movement organizations.
> *Hypothesis 4c:* Locales with more mixed uses have more social movement organizations.
> *Hypothesis 5a:* Locales with higher density have more arts establishments.
> *Hypothesis 5b:* Locales with higher connectivity have more arts establishments.
> *Hypothesis 5c:* Locales with more mixed uses have more arts establishments.
> *Hypothesis 6a:* Locales with higher density have more arts jobs.
> *Hypothesis 6b:* Locales with higher connectivity have more arts jobs.
> *Hypothesis 6c:* Locales with more mixed uses have more arts jobs.

Interaction Hypothesis
> *Hypothesis 7:* Walking in locales with more arts activity will have more impact on the incidence of SMOs.

Data and Results

Data

To test these ideas, we use national databases of local area characteristics in the United States, Canada, and France. The ZIP Code Tabulation Area (ZCTA) is the unit analyzed for the United States,[4] the Forward Sortation Area (FSA) is the unit for Canada,[5] and the commune is the unit for France.[6] We use ZCTAs, FSAs, and communes primarily because they are the smallest geography for which the arts and social movement dependent variables are available.[7] These small units allow more fine-grained measurement of urban contextual elements than larger units like entire cities, metro areas, or states used in much past research.[8]

Dependent Variables: Social Movement Organizations

We use data primarily from national economic censuses and electronic yellow pages to construct social movement organization indices for the United States, Canada, and France. Variables and data sources are in Table 13.1.

These data are powerful in providing such large numbers of small units: SMO totals for each of the approximately thirty-three thousand U.S. ZCTAs, sixteen hundred Canadian FSAs, and thirty-six thousand French communes.[9] This broad coverage permits analysis of how the density of such organizations compares across each country, as well as within-country variations to test hypotheses, thus overcoming the multicollinearity and sample selection bias of small N studies. We have only the self-reported categories of organizations in terms of North American Industrial Classification System (NAICS) codes and French APE codes, and thus cannot directly assess how much each may be strongly egalitarian, idealistic, or narrowly NIMBY in style.[10] Clearly, there is variation among movement groups, but this is equally true of many social movement studies, and the NAICS and APE items also include "religious groups," "business groups," and other categories that we compare with SMOs. To the best of our knowledge, this is the first project to analyze these sorts of data, especially for international comparison of arts firms, arts employment, and new social movements.

---

[4] ZCTAs "are generalized area representations of U.S. Postal Service (USPS) ZIP Code service areas." For additional information on ZCTAs, see the ZCTA Technical Documentation at www.census.gov.
[5] An FSA is the first three characters of the Canadian postal code, designating a stable and well-defined postal delivery area within Canada. For additional information, see the Postal Codes Conversion File (PCCP), Reference Guide, Catalogue no. 92-153-G at www.statcan.gc.ca.
[6] Communes are the smallest administrative unit in France. Our data employ communes, except for Paris, Lyon, and Marseille. where municipal arrondissements (ARMs) are used instead.
[7] Whereas ZCTAs are the units for most of the independent variables, ZIP Code Business Patterns uses USPS ZIP Codes. This may be a small source of measurement error in our analyses.
[8] While some data are available at the tract level, they are more often volatile and incomplete because of small Ns. Thus ZCTAs and FSAs are the smallest geographies for which we can obtain and use data for our dependent variables.
[9] Documentation at INSEE, France's Census, recommends using data for areas with populations of more than five hundred. Our regressions therefore use the 16,486 communes with populations of more than five hundred.
[10] APE codes are principal activity codes. See www.insee.fr for more details.

234 Chapter 13

TABLE 13.1   DEPENDENT VARIABLES

Variable	Country	Source	Computation
Social movement organizations			
2011 Social Movement Organizations Index	United States	ZIP Code Business Patterns	Sum of Environment, Conservation, and Wildlife Organizations (NAICS 813312); Human Rights Organizations (NAICS 813311); Other Social Advocacy Organizations (NAICS 813319)
2006 Environmental Organizations	United States	Yellow Pages	Count of environmental organizations
2011 Social Advocacy Organizations	Canada	Canadian Business Patterns	Count of establishments in NAICS 813310 (includes human rights, environmental, other social advocacy)
2009 Gay and Lesbian Organizations	Canada	Yellow Pages	Count of gay and lesbian organizations
2009 Environmental Organizations	Canada	Yellow Pages	Count of environmental organizations
2009 Yellow Pages Index	Canada	Yellow Pages	Sum of gay and lesbian, environmental organizations
2009 Protest, Advocacy, Voluntary, Civic, and Social Establishments	France	SIRENE	Count of Protest, Advocacy, Voluntary, Civic, and Social Establishments (APE 9499Z)
2009 Associations de Defense de l'Environnement	France	Yellow Pages	Count of establishments
Arts organizations			
2011 Arts Index	United States	ZIP Code Business Patterns	Sum of establishments in thirty-six NAICS arts categories
2006 Arts Index	United States	Yellow Pages	Sum of establishments in forty-seven Yellow Pages arts categories
2011 Percentage of Arts Jobs	United States	ZIP Code Business Patterns Industry Detail File	Arts jobs divided by total jobs
2011 Arts Index	Canada	Canadian Business Patterns	Sum of establishments in thirty-four NAICS arts categories

TABLE 13.1   *(continued)*

Variable	Country	Source	Computation
2009 Arts Index	Canada	Yellow Pages	Sum of establishments in thirty Yellow Pages arts categories
2011 Percentage of Arts Jobs	Canada	Canadian Business Patterns	Arts jobs divided by total jobs
2009 Arts Index	France	SIRENE	Sum of establishments in twenty-one SIRENE arts categories
2009 Associations Culturelles, Educatives, de Loisirs	France	Yellow Pages	Count of establishments
2009 Percentage of Arts Jobs	France	SIRENE	Arts jobs divided by total jobs

Note: Business Patterns establishments are classified according to the 2007 NAICS, and defined as "a single physical location at which business is conducted or services or industrial operations are performed. . . . Establishment counts represent the number of locations with paid employees any time during the year." SIRENE is the French national company and establishment register. It is similar to both ZBP and CBP, although the industrial and establishment categories differ. SIRENE is compiled by INSEE, the French Census. Complete information on categories used to compute arts indices is available upon request. Percentage of arts jobs includes employment in the same categories used for the arts indices.

Dependent Variables: Artistic Measures

We again employ economic census and yellow pages data to compute a number of arts variables for the three countries. Specifics are in Table 13.1. We construct two types of arts variables. First, we create indexes that are sums (counts) of arts establishments in ZCTAs, FSAs, and communes. Second we use employment data to compute percentages of arts jobs.

Independent Variables: Walking and Walkability Measures

For each country, we measure walking as the percentage of workers who walk to work. While we would prefer to have walking for additional purposes, walking to work is the only walking measure in these three censuses. Second, we calculate population density for each local unit (for example, ZCTA, FSA, or commune). Third, our connectivity measure is an estimate of city block density, available for the United States and Canada.[11] We divide the number of Census blocks in a ZCTA (for the United States) or dissemination blocks in an FSA (for Canada) by land area. Finally, we use Peter M. Blau's (1977) index of heterogeneity to measure housing age diversity as an indicator of mixed use. It measures the probability that two randomly chosen housing units in a locale were built in different year ranges.

[11] We have no connectivity data for France.

Independent Variables: Demographic and Socioeconomic Control Measures

Besides walking and urban context variables, other demographic and socioeconomic factors potentially predict the dependent variables, and are therefore included. We created similar variables for each country, although there are slight differences (the regression tables show details).

Results

We begin with simple Pearson correlations of the dependent variables—arts and social movements—with walking and walkability. For all three countries, correlations are consistent with the above hypotheses. In the United States and Canada, walking to work and density relate consistently and positively to both SMOs and arts, as does connectivity. In France, density is very strongly correlated to the arts and SMOs, as are walking and housing age diversity, albeit more weakly. These broadly hold in the subsequent regression models, which add variables and explore consistency across countries and specifications.

We estimate several regressions to examine the effects of walking and walkability on (1) the incidence of SMOs, (2) the incidence of arts establishments, and (3) arts jobs, in the United States, Canada, and France. We report standardized slope coefficients, computed after mean centering each independent variable and then dividing by two standard deviations.[12]

Coefficients on percent walked to work test H1, H2, and H3. First, in Tables 13.2 (United States), 13.3 (Canada), and 13.4 (France), we observe for all three countries significant increases in the incidence of SMOs with increases in the percent walking to work. Walking counts: It is significant in each of the SMO regressions, and often one of the largest standardized coefficients. Therefore, the regressions robustly support H1 across countries and different SMO types as dependent variables.

Turning to the arts, in Tables 13.5 (United States), 13.6 (Canada), and 13.7 (France), coefficients on percent walking to work (columns 1 and 2 for each table) test H2. Again, for all three countries we observe significantly more arts establishments in areas with a higher percent walking to work. H2 is supported, again robustly, across countries and arts indicators.

Next for arts jobs, in Tables 13.5, 13.6, and 13.7, coefficients on percent walking to work in column 3 test H3. Table 13.5 shows that in the United States arts jobs increase with walking. But not so in France and Canada. H3 holds only in the United States.

In sum, we find substantial evidence that walking undergirds both contemporary social movement politics *and* artistic activity. For all three countries,

---

[12] Andrew Gelman (2007) argues for using two standard deviations as it places all variables—continuous and binary—on a common scale. Tables 13.2–13.7 report Gelman standardized coefficients for regressions relating the dependent variables to the independent variables described above.

TABLE 13.2 U.S. ZCTA-LEVEL REGRESSIONS: SOCIAL MOVEMENT
ORGANIZATIONS AS DEPENDENT VARIABLE

Variable	1	2	3	4
Social and economic				
Population (1,000s)	0.469**	0.508**	0.263**	0.242**
Median Age	−0.405**	−0.290**	−0.067**	−0.048*
Percent B.A. Degree and Above	0.956**	0.839**	0.338**	0.305**
Percent Nonwhite	−0.195**	−0.111**	−0.138**	−0.107**
Median Gross Rent (100s)	−0.066	−0.121**	0.086**	0.071**
Median Household Income (1,000s)	−0.278**	−0.256**	−0.085**	−0.096**
Mean Travel Time to Work	0.067*	0.078**	0.028*	0.034**
Percent in Same House, Five Years	−0.172**	−0.142**	−0.022	−0.013
Percent Married	−0.217**	−0.202**	−0.127**	−0.114**
Percent with Children	−0.664**	−0.491**	−0.204**	−0.165**
Foreign-Born Diversity	0.037	0.044	−0.018	−0.015
Percent Renters	0.162**	0.215**	0.166**	0.153**
Density				
Population Density (1,000s)	0.183**	−0.307**	−0.212**	−0.300**
Connectivity				
Census Blocks per Square Mile	0.653**	0.653**	0.221**	0.228**
Land-use mix				
Housing Age Diversity	0.274**	0.207**	0.113**	0.104**
Walking				
Percent Walked to Work	0.630**	0.485**	0.162**	0.158**
Interactions				
Art Index			0.338**	0.187**
Art Index × Walking			0.551**	0.052**
n	26,705	26,705	27,107	26,705
R^2 (adjusted)	0.200	0.263	0.127	0.144

Note: Gelman standardized regression coefficients. The dependent variable in columns 1 and 2 is the 2011 U.S.
Social Movement Organization Index, which is the sum of U.S. ZIP Code Business Patterns Environmental
Organizations (NAICS 813311), Human Rights Organizations (NAICS 813312), and Other Social Advocacy
Organizations (NAICS 813319). The dependent variable in columns 3 and 4 is 2006 Yellow Pages Environmental
Organizations.
**$p < 0.01$, *$p < 0.05$ (two-tailed)

percent walking to work positively and significantly covaries with social movement organizations and arts activity. These relationships also hold across different SMO and arts measures. For the SMO regressions, the large standardized
coefficients on walking suggest its relative importance compared to the other
variables included in the regressions.

Density, connectivity, and housing age diversity are our indicators of walkability, and their coefficients test H4, H5, and H6. Tables 13.2, 13.3, and 13.4
provide substantial support for H4, especially for the United States and France.
In the two countries with connectivity variables (United States and Canada),

TABLE 13.3 CANADIAN FSA-LEVEL REGRESSIONS: SOCIAL MOVEMENT ORGANIZATIONS AS DEPENDENT VARIABLE

Variable	1	2	3	4	5	6	7	8
Social and economic								
Population (1,000s)	1.730**	1.518**	0.398**	0.412**	0.002	0.012	0.400**	0.424**
Percent Fifty-Five Years and Older	-0.035	0.163	-0.318**	-0.138*	-0.009	-0.002	-0.327**	-0.140*
Percent B.A. Degree and Above	0.704**	0.452**	0.123	0.045	-0.013	-0.009	0.110	0.036
Percent Visible Minority	0.461	0.695*	-0.022	-0.021	-0.013	-0.023	-0.035	-0.044
Average Gross Rent (100s)	-0.134	-0.212	-0.112	-0.116	-0.004	-0.000	-0.116	-0.117
Median Household Income (1,000s)	-0.146	-0.038	-0.048	-0.026	0.005	0.003	-0.043	-0.023
Percent Moved in Last Five Years	0.236	0.266	0.038	0.028	0.020	0.017	0.058	0.045
Percent Married	0.008	0.161	0.087	0.146*	0.001	0.000	0.088	0.146*
Percent with Children	-0.285	-0.034	-0.446**	-0.194*	-0.025*	-0.014	-0.471**	-0.208**
Percent Immigrants	0.555**	0.695**	0.009	0.034	-0.001	-0.005	0.009	0.029
Percent Renters	1.132**	1.338**	-0.074	0.151	-0.046**	-0.035**	-0.120	0.116
Density								
Population Density (1,000s)	-0.710**	-1.052**	-0.052	-0.342**	0.076**	0.066**	0.025	-0.275**
Connectivity								
Dissemination Blocks per Square Kilometer	14.241**	14.117**	2.518**	1.636*	-0.128	-0.195*	2.390**	1.441*
Land-use mix								
Housing Age Diversity	0.072	0.107	0.049	0.025	0.017*	0.013	0.065	0.038
Walking								
Percent Walked to Work	1.350**	1.228**	0.442**	0.245**	0.033**	0.022*	0.475**	0.267**
Interaction								
Art Index		0.913**		0.153*		-0.026**		0.127
Art Index × Walking		0.149		0.741**		0.058**		0.798**
n	1,539	1,539	1,547	1,539	1,547	1,539	1,547	1,539
R^2 (adjusted)	0.408	0.431	0.187	0.336	0.069	0.091	0.195	0.349

Note: Gelman standardized regression coefficients. The dependent variable in columns 1 and 2 is 2011 Canadian Business Patterns Social Advocacy Organizations (NAICS 813310, includes human rights, environmental, etc.). The dependent variable in columns 3 and 4 is 2009 Canadian Yellow Pages Environmental Organizations. The dependent variable in columns 5 and 6 is 2009 Canadian Yellow Pages Gay and Lesbian Organizations. The dependent variable in columns 7 and 8 is 2009 Canadian Yellow Pages Social Movement Index, the sum of gay and lesbian organizations and environmental organizations.

$**p < 0.01$, $*p < 0.05$ (two-tailed)

TABLE 13.4 FRENCH COMMUNE-LEVEL REGRESSIONS: SOCIAL MOVEMENT
ORGANIZATIONS AS DEPENDENT VARIABLE

Variable	1	2	3	4
Social and economic				
Population (1,000s)	27.054**	20.756**	0.783**	0.632**
Percent Fifty-Five Years and Older	−2.139**	−1.187**	−0.061**	−0.046**
Percent with University Degree	0.358*	0.693**	0.029**	0.037**
Percent Foreigners	−1.487**	−0.680**	−0.049**	−0.029**
Average Net Income of Tax Households (1,000s)	1.132**	−0.167	0.001	−0.025**
Percent in Same House as of Five Years Ago	−1.137**	−0.533**	−0.031**	−0.014
Percent of Families, Married	−0.649**	−0.198	−0.026*	−0.016
Percent of Families, Zero Children under Twenty-Five	3.680**	1.848**	0.106**	0.072**
Percent Principal Residences, Renter Occupied	−2.154**	−0.743**	−0.087**	−0.053**
Density				
Population Density (1,000s)	0.963**	−2.439**	−0.027**	−0.104**
Land-use mix				
Housing Age Diversity	−2.427**	−0.828**	−0.048**	−0.018
Walking				
Percent Walked to Work	2.407**	1.066**	0.044**	0.019*
Interactions				
Art Index		3.159**		0.115**
Art Index × Walking		10.252**		0.120**
n	16,482	16,482	16,286	16,286
R^2 (adjusted)	0.779	0.891	0.439	0.474

Note: Gelman standardized regression coefficients. The dependent variable in columns 1 and 2 is 2009 France SIRENE Protest, Advocacy, Voluntary, Civic, and Social Establishments (APE 9499Z). The dependent variable in columns 3 and 4 is 2009 France Yellow Pages Associations de Défense de l'Environnement.
$**p < 0.01$, $*p < 0.05$ (two-tailed)

SMOs rise with connectivity. Housing age diversity also increases with SMOs for the United States. Finally, density in the United States and France is significant (column 1 of Tables 13.2 and 13.4). Therefore, across countries and variables, we find support for the hypothesis that increasing the opportunity to walk increases SMOs.

For the arts, Tables 13.5, 13.6, and 13.7 report density, connectivity, and housing age diversity in columns (1) and (2) to test H5. Again, we find the most support in the United States and France. Observe especially that when connectivity and housing age diversity increase in the United States, so do arts establishments. Also, results from the three countries support our conjecture that arts establishments rise with density. This is moderate support for hypothesis (H5)

TABLE 13.5   U.S. ZCTA-LEVEL REGRESSIONS: ARTISTIC DEPENDENT
VARIABLES

Variable	1	2	3
Social and economic			
Population (1,000s)	7.325**	9.339**	−0.153**
Median Age	−2.197**	−1.134**	0.165**
Percent with B.A. Degree and Above	7.584**	5.115**	0.849**
Percent Nonwhite	−2.881**	−2.759**	0.083
Median Gross Rent (100s)	2.133**	0.488*	0.208**
Median Household Income (1,000s)	0.078	0.567*	−0.064
Mean Travel Time to Work	−0.682**	−0.491**	0.128**
Percent in Same House, Five Years	−0.017	−0.564**	−0.009
Percent Married	−1.456**	−1.496**	−0.207**
Percent with Children	−5.410**	−4.100**	−0.124*
Foreign-Born Diversity	−0.924**	−0.499**	−0.008
Percent Renters	2.729**	2.907**	0.307**
Density			
Population Density (1,000s)	7.815**	2.150**	0.108*
Connectivity			
Census Blocks per Square Mile	0.004	2.375**	0.064
Land-use mix			
Housing Age Diversity	1.727**	1.695**	0.023
Walking			
Percent Walked to Work	1.006**	1.450**	0.137**
n	26,705	27,107	26,705
R^2 (adjusted)	0.238	0.401	0.044

Note: Gelman standardized regression coefficients. The dependent variable in column 1 is the 2011 U.S. ZIP Code
Business Patterns Arts Index. The dependent variable in column 2 is the 2006 U.S. Yellow Pages Arts Index. The
dependent variable in column 3 is 2011 U.S. Percentage Arts Jobs.
**$p < 0.01$, *$p < 0.05$ (two-tailed)

positing that opportunities to walk increase arts organizations, although less
strong than H4.

Does walkability increase arts jobs? Tables 13.5, 13.6, and 13.7 test H6 with
these same three measures in column 3. We find limited support for the H6
hypothesis. In the United States, Canada, and France, density covaries with
the percentage of arts jobs, supporting H6a. Neither H6b nor H6c is anywhere
supported.

This is relatively clear and powerful evidence that these three urban contextual factors—of walkability—encourage both social movement activity and
the arts in the United States, Canada, and France. The strongest support is for
social movements. We note also that, especially in the United States, walkability
rises with arts organizations. Yet we find little evidence linking walkability to
arts *jobs*, at least paid jobs reported to the census.

TABLE 13.6   CANADIAN FSA-LEVEL REGRESSIONS: ARTISTIC DEPENDENT VARIABLES

Variable	1	2	3
Social and economic			
Population (1,000s)	27.413**	8.524**	−0.078
Percent Fifty-Five Years and Older	−20.589**	−1.295	−0.178
Percent B.A. Degree and Above	30.616**	3.485**	0.875**
Percent Visible Minority	−30.525**	−5.319**	−0.814**
Average Gross Rent (100s)	9.988**	0.951	0.169
Median Household Income (1,000s)	−13.980**	−1.431	−0.528**
Percent Moved in Last Five Years	−3.754	2.839**	−0.016
Percent Married	−17.899**	−0.310	−0.689**
Percent with Children	−25.029**	−3.210**	−0.328
Percent Immigrants	−17.383**	−1.736**	−0.303*
Percent Renters	−20.545**	1.800	−0.729**
Density			
Population Density (1,000s)	36.380**	0.594	1.721**
Connectivity			
Dissemination Blocks per Square Kilometer	−8.374	0.532	−3.430*
Land-use mix			
Housing Age Diversity	−4.928	0.640	−0.134
Walking			
Percent Walked to Work	10.412**	4.350**	0.002
n	1,539	1,547	1,539
R^2 (adjusted)	0.436	0.385	0.218

Note: Gelman standardized regression coefficients. The dependent variable in column 1 is the 2011 Canadian Business Patterns Arts Index. The dependent variable in column 2 is the 2011 Canadian Yellow Pages Arts Index. The dependent variable in column 3 is 2011 Canadian Percentage Arts Jobs.
**$p < 0.01$, *$p < 0.05$ (two-tailed)

What if we combine the effects of walking and the arts? This is H7, which is substantially supported (in even-numbered columns of Tables 13.2, 13.3, and 13.4). For each country, we multiply walking by the arts index (ZBP arts index in the United States, CBP arts index in Canada, and SIRENE arts index in France) to create an arts-walking multiplicative interaction term. The interaction terms discriminate between walking in arts sparse scenes versus arts rich scenes. We then include this interaction term and its two individual components, walking and the arts index, in our regressions. The dramatic results are that the interaction term shows stronger impact on SMOs than just walking, in all three countries (in the United States, Table 13.2, column 2; in Canada, Table 13.3, columns 4, 6, and 8; and for France, Table 13.4, columns 2 and 4). These results are especially interesting and important. Walking amid the arts—as measured by the interaction of art and walking—is distinctively conducive to SMOs, as

TABLE 13.7   FRENCH COMMUNE-LEVEL REGRESSIONS: ARTISTIC DEPENDENT
VARIABLES

Variable	1	2	3
Social and economic			
Population (1,000s)	58.735**	12.844**	0.035
Percent Fifty-Five Years and Older	−2.226*	−0.737**	0.032
Percent with University Degree	−2.891**	−0.019	0.330**
Percent Foreigners	−5.751**	−0.668**	0.099**
Average Net Income of Tax Households (1,000s)	7.238**	0.404**	0.062
Percent in Same House as of Five Years Ago	−5.386**	−0.471**	−0.111*
Percent of Families, Married	−3.832**	−0.291**	−0.048
Percent of Families, Zero Children under Twenty-Five	9.886**	1.252**	0.062
Percent Principal Residences, Renter Occupied	−12.399**	−1.344**	0.035
Density			
Population Density (1,000s)	28.231**	0.495**	0.075**
Land-use mix			
Housing Age Diversity	−7.730**	−1.015**	−0.113*
Walking			
Percent Walked to Work	6.504**	0.552**	−0.058
n	16,482	16,286	16,479
R^2 (adjusted)	0.657	0.694	0.014

Note: Gelman standardized regression coefficients. The dependent variable in column 1 is the 2009 France SIRENE Arts Index. The dependent variable in column 2 is 2009 France Yellow Pages Associations Culturelles, Educatives, de Loisirs. The dependent variable in column 3 is 2009 France Percentage Arts Jobs.
**$p < 0.01$, *$p < 0.05$ (two-tailed)

shown by the larger coefficients for the walking X arts interaction than for the walking variable alone. These strong coefficients show that effects of walking on SMOs are heightened when joined with more artistic surroundings. The capacity to imagine alternative political worlds seems encouraged when walking and the arts combine. The spontaneous, self-selective meandering and pondering we do more when surrounded by examples of aesthetic creativity can spark creative ideas in other domains, like those pursued by SMOs. While walking can be the atomistic activity of the solitary *flâneur* or outsider, it can also feed into the surrounding buzz that energizes political movement organizations.

These walking and walkability regression coefficients are robust to tests for multicollinearity. They are also robust to the inclusion of a dummy variable of 1 if a ZCTA or FSA is in a city or metro area with at least a 250,000 population, and when regressions are reestimated with the subset of ZCTAs and FSAs from cities with populations of at least 250,000.[13] We also tested if the main walking

[13] Communes are different from ZCTAs and FSAs in that they are less often nested within larger cities. Therefore, these size-based regressions are not carried out for France.

regression coefficients were driven primarily by some influential data points, using DFBETAs. Specifically, DFBETAs indicate the amount of change in a regression coefficient for walking and walkability resulting from deletion of the ith case. We observe some interesting patterns. The most potentially influential ZCTAs, FSAs, or communes are from large cities: Washington, D.C., New York City, and Los Angeles in the United States; Toronto, Montreal, Ottawa, Vancouver, and Quebec City in Canada; the Parisian municipal arrondissements in France. These local areas are influential in potentially driving the national results. However, filtering the observations with the largest walking or walkability DFBETAs out of the SMO and arts regressions does not substantially impact the coefficients of interest for the United States, Canada, or France. We also reestimate regressions for different types of organizations, like religious groups instead of social movements, and compare effects. We conclude that especially in the United States and France the SMO variable—compared with the other dependent variables—is most consistently and significantly related as predicted by the hypotheses.[14]

Conclusions

Social movement activism and the arts resemble one another; both are creative acts. Yet they are not randomly distributed in geographic or social space; they are concentrated in distinct local environments. Walking and walkability, we find, are consistently key elements of environments conducive to cultural and political creativity. Walking thus undergirds both contemporary social movement organizations and artistic activity. This is a rather simple idea, but we have never previously seen it coherently articulated or tested.

To evaluate this general idea, we formulated a series of specific testable hypotheses linking walking, walkability, the arts, and SMOs. Results support many of these hypotheses. Most notably, we find that walking raises the incidence of SMOs and arts establishments in U.S. ZCTAs, Canadian FSAs, and French communes. Walking also leads to more arts jobs in the United States (but not in Canada or France). These findings are robust across different SMO and arts indicators. We often find, moreover, not only that connections exist between *walking*, the arts, and SMOs but that these connections are sometimes

---

[14] For all our analyses the standard caveats apply: We cannot crisply distinguish causality from association. Our regression models include the main factors that experts have used in this field, but not every factor is included owing to time and data availability. There are many types of walking and art and social movements; each has partially distinct dynamics. Some processes are stronger in some locations than others, in ways that we do not detail here. We have probed each of these and other such dynamics in multiple ways, such as adding other variables, left and right political parties and other components (areas with left parties also have more social movements), contrasting more and less participatory types of art as (more participation encourages social movements). See Silver and Clark (forthcoming); da Silva, Clark, and Cabaço (2014); Clark (2014); and draft memos from Knudsen (available upon request).

stronger than standard urban variables such as density and housing age diversity. In our results walking appears as one of most powerful drivers of creativity. We also find some evidence that places with *walkable* urban form—dense neighborhoods with interconnected streets and mixed uses—exhibit higher SMO and arts activity. Walkability is higher in areas with more SMOs in all three countries, and with arts establishments in the United States. Finally, walking, the arts, and social movement activism are not only separate processes. They enhance one another. Walking amid the arts appears to heighten imaginative openness to new social and political possibilities, energizing SMO activity more powerfully than walking on its own. Walking is important, but not all walking is the same, and when it occurs in locales with more arts activity, its impact on SMOs is greater. These interaction processes illustrate the dynamics elaborated in our related work (for example, Silver and Clark, forthcoming), which combines variables that synergistically create distinctive local "scenes" that foster values such as self-expression and egalitarianism. The arts add power to distinct scenes by enhancing emotion, elaborating symbols via colorful images and text, and linking acts like singing and parades to deeper values. These can in some cases combine to generate buzz—a signal that "something is happening here"—in popular magazines, electronic media, posters, and interpersonal conversations, enhanced via large crowds in public squares. Such buzz is a major new political resource that social movement activists from Cairo to Kiev to Paris have mobilized, even if social scientists have not fully appreciated their power (but see Clark 2014; Silver and Clark 2013; Silver and Grodach 2013; Storper and Venables 2004). This sort of attention to the political energy generated by local scenes also represents a conceptual break with much past political and social movement theorizing (Leach and Haunss 2009), which stresses occupation, class, social backgrounds, and hierarchy as main cleavages (Gelman 2009; Verba, Schlozman, and Brady 1995). By contrast, scenes point toward local differences in spatial confluences of cultural practices and venues—such as walking, bars, cafés, churches, hunting lodges, music, yoga studios, auto racing, poetry readings, and the like—that define political cleavages in ways not reducible to traditional variables such as education, income, or race (Silver and Clark, forthcoming).

This chapter illustrates new social dynamics featuring the political and artistic potential inhering in direct, active experiences generated by walking. Past work on walking typically considers these themes theoretically or through ethnographic case studies of one or a few cities. By contrast, our comprehensive quantitative data on walking, social movements, and the arts in three countries permit systematic empirical analyses with generalizable results while identifying contrasts across countries. Controls for education, income, marriage, children, and other factors adjust for the biases inherent in selecting any one or two locations. This approach provides a broadened perspective on walking not otherwise possible. Our empirical results also point to interesting future directions. Research should explore not only cross-national similarities but also where and why walking in different countries has different impacts. Likewise it is important to extend the analysis beyond the arts and walking to a broader set of amenities and activities that may also support self-expression and creativity. Future work could better distinguish between different types of art, different types of walking, and different types of walkability using all sorts of data and methods. This chapter has taken crucial steps forward, however, conceptually articulating and empirically demonstrating in three countries how walking affects both political and artistic activity separately, and how walking in artistic surroundings substantially raises walking's impact on social movement activity.

REFERENCES

Berrigan, David and Richard P. Troiano. 2002. "The Association between Urban Form and Physical Activity in U.S. Adults." *American Journal of Preventive Medicine* 23(Supplement 1):74–79.

Blau, Peter M. 1977. *Inequality and Heterogeneity*. New York: Free Press.

Boarnet, Marlon G. and Sharon Sarmiento. 1998. "Can Land-Use Policy Really Affect Travel Behaviour? A Study of the Link between Non-Work Travel and Land-Use Characteristics." *Urban Studies* 35:1155–1169.

Careri, Francesco. 2002. *Walkscapes: Walking as an Aesthetic Practice*. Barcelona: Gustavo Gili.

Clark, Terry N. 2014. *Can Tocqueville Karaoke? Global Contrasts of Citizen Participation, the Arts, and Development. Research in Urban Policy.* Bingley, UK: Emerald.

Clark, Terry N. and Meghan Kallman. 2011. *The Global Transformation of Organized Groups: New Roles for Community Service Organizations, Non-Profits, and the New Political Culture.* Beijing, China: Ministry of Civil Affairs.

Craig, Cora L., Ross C. Brownson, Sue N. Cragg, and Andrea L. Dunn. 2002. "Exploring the Effect of the Environment on Physical Activity: A Study Examining Walking to Work." *American Journal of Preventive Medicine* 23:36–43.

da Silva, Filipe Carreira, Terry Nichols Clark, and Susana Cabaço. 2014. "Culture on the Rise: How and Why Cultural Membership Promotes Democratic Politics." *International Journal of Politics, Culture, and Society* 27:343–366.

Demerath, Loren and David Levinger. 2003. "The Social Qualities of Being on Foot: A Theoretical Analysis of Pedestrian Activity, Community, and Culture." *City and Community* 2:217–237.

Frank, Lawrence D. and Gary Pivo. 1994. "Impacts of Mixed Use and Density on Utilization of Three Modes of Travel: Single-Occupant Vehicle, Transit, and Walking." *Transportation Research Record* 1466:44–52.

Gelman, Andrew. 2007. "Scaling Regression Inputs by Two Standard Deviations." *Statistics in Medicine* 27:2865–2873.

———. 2009. *Red State, Blue State, Rich State, Poor State: Why Americans Vote the Way They Do.* Princeton, NJ: Princeton University Press.

Graeber, David. 2003. "The Globalization Movement and the New New Left." Pp. 325–338 in *Implicating Empire: Globalization and Resistance in the 21st-Century World Order*, edited by Stanley Aronowitz and Heather Gautney. New York: Basic Books.

———. 2009. "Anarchism, Academia, and the Avant-Garde." Pp. 103–112 in *Contemporary Anarchist Studies: An Introductory Anthology of Anarchy in the Academy*, edited by

Randall Amster, Abraham DeLeon, Luis A. Fernandez, Anthony J. Nocella II, and Deric Shannon. New York: Routledge.

Greenwald, Michael, and Marlon Boarnet. 2002. "The Built Environment as a Determinant of Walking Behavior: Analyzing Non-Work Pedestrian Travel in Portland, Oregon." *Transportation Research Record* 1780:33–42.

Ingold, Tim. 2010. "Ways of Mind-Walking: Reading, Writing, Painting." *Visual Studies* 25:15–23.

Knudsen, Brian B. and Terry N. Clark. 2013. "Walk and Be Moved: How Walking Builds Social Movements." *Urban Affairs Review* 49:627–651.

Kramer, Kathryn and John Rennie Short. 2011. "Flânerie and the Globalizing City." *CITY: Analysis of Urban Trends, Culture, Theory, Policy, Action* 15:323–342.

Leach, Darcy K. and Sebastian Haunss. 2009. "Scenes and Social Movements." Pp. 255–276 in *Culture, Social Movements, and Protest*, edited by Hank Johnston. Burlington VT: Ashgate.

McDonald, Kevin. 2006. *Global Movements: Action and Culture*. Oxford: Blackwell.

Offe, Claus. 1985. "New Social Movements: Challenging the Boundaries of Institutional Politics." *Social Research* 52:817–868.

Saelens, Brian E., James F. Sallis, and Lawrence D. Frank. 2003. "Environmental Correlates of Walking and Cycling: Findings from the Transportation, Urban Design, and Planning Literatures." *Annals of Behavioral Medicine* 25:80–91.

Silver, Daniel and Terry Nichols Clark. 2013. "Buzz as an Urban Resource." *Canadian Journal of Sociology* 38:1–32.

———. Forthcoming. *Scenes*. Chicago: University of Chicago Press.

Silver, Daniel and Carl Grodach. 2013. *The Politics of Urban Cultural Policy: Global Perspectives*. New York: Routledge.

Storper, Michael and Anthony J. Venables. 2004. "Buzz: Face-to-Face Contact and the Urban Economy." *Journal of Economic Geography* 4:351–370.

Verba, Sydney, Kay Lehman Schlozman, and Henry Brady. 1995. *Voice and Equality: Civic Voluntarism in American Politics*. Cambridge, MA: Harvard University Press.

Contributors

Nazgol Bagheri is an assistant professor of political science and geography at the University of Texas at San Antonio. She received her Ph.D. in geography and sociology from the University of Missouri–Kansas City. She received a B.A. in architecture, a B.S. in computer science with a minor in geographic information science, and a M.A. in urban design and planning from the National University of Iran (Shahid Beheshti), all with honors. In Iran, she has worked as a licensed architect and a project manager for urban design projects at an international design firm. Her dissertation on "Modernizing the Public Spheres in Tehran" examined the interplay of gendered places, multiple modernities, and space politics in Tehran's public spaces. Her dissertation was funded by the Association of American Geographers and the American Association of University Women. Her ultimate goal is to advance the understanding of Iranian women's social life in public spaces by not simply importing Western theories but instead by hearing their voices and stories.

Kevin Beck is a doctoral student in the Department of Sociology at the University of California, San Diego. He holds an M.A. in sociology from UCSD and an M.A. in Latin American regional studies from Columbia University. His current research focuses on housing and support networks in U.S. cities.

Evrick Brown is an assistant professor in the Department of Behavioral Sciences and Human Services at Kingsborough Community College, City University of New York. His current research focus is on the vast social dynamics of an urban ethnic community that includes Afro-Caribbean and African American interethnic relations. He previously coedited *Walking in the European City* (Ashgate, 2014) with Timothy Shortell and contributed a chapter entitled "An Ethnography of Local Politics in a Brooklyn Caribbean Community" to *The World in Brooklyn: Gentrification, Immigration, and Ethnic Politics in a Global City* (Lexington Books, 2012). His areas of interest include race and ethnicity, urban sociology, political sociology, and social movements.

Ernesto Castañeda received a Ph.D. in sociology from Columbia University. He has taught at Columbia University, Baruch College–City University of New York, and the University of Texas at El Paso. He has been a visiting scholar at the Sorbonne, the Institut d'Études Politiques de Paris, the Zolberg Institute on Migration and Mobility at the New School for Social Research, and the Centre on Migration, Policy, and Society (COMPAS) at the University of Oxford. He is affiliated with the Center on Health, Risk, and Society and the Center for Latin American and Latino Studies at American University in Washington, D.C., where he is an assistant professor of sociology.

Terry Nichols Clark is a professor of sociology at the University of Chicago. He holds M.A. and Ph.D. degrees from Columbia University and has taught at Columbia, Harvard, Yale, the Sorbonne, University of Florence, and UCLA. He has published some thirty books. He has worked on how cities use culture to transform themselves, especially in the books *The City as an Entertainment Machine* (JAI/Elsevier, 2004) and *Building Post-Industrial Chicago* (University of Chicago, 2012). He has worked at the Brookings Institution, the Urban Institute, Department of Housing and Urban Development, and U.S. Conference of Mayors. He coordinates the Fiscal Austerity and Urban Innovation Project, surveying twelve hundred cities in the United States and thirty-eight other countries. Since 2004, he has focused on Scenes, comparing neighborhood cultures in forty-two thousand U.S. zip codes and in monographs on Chicago, Paris, Seoul, and other key cities.

Judith N. DeSena is a professor of sociology at St. John's University. Her work centers on community, neighborhoods, and gender studies. Her latest research agenda articulates how gentrification affects community relationships in Brooklyn, New York. She has authored *Protecting One's Turf: Social Strategies for Maintaining Urban Neighborhoods* (University Press of America, 1990 and 2005) and *People Power: Grass Roots Politics and Race Relations* (University Press of America, 1999). She has edited readings in sociology and ethnic studies, is editor of *Gender in an Urban World* (2008), and coeditor, along with Timothy Shortell, of *The World in Brooklyn: Gentrification, Immigration, and Ethnic Politics in a Global City* (Lexington Books, 2012). She has also published various research articles in the area of residential segregation, women's community activism, and gendered space. Her latest book, *Gentrification and Inequality in Brooklyn: The New Kids on the Block* (Lexington Books, 2009), is a social class analysis of gentrification and the neighborhood dynamics it creates. At St. John's, she is currently the faculty coordinator of Discover New York, a component of the Core Curriculum, and director of the Interdisciplinary Minor Program in New York Studies.

Marlese Durr is a professor of sociology at Wright State University in Dayton, Ohio, where she has taught for fourteen years. Her research focuses on organizations, work and occupations, and race and gender. She is the author of *The New Politics of Race: From Du Bois to the 21st Century* (Praeger, 2002) and *Race, Work, and Family in the Lives of African Americans*, with Shirley A. Hill (Rowman & Littlefield, 2006). Her most recent publications include, "Inner-City African-American Women's Adolescence as Stressful Life Events: Understanding Substance Abusing Behavior," *Journal of African American Studies*, with La Fleur Small and Eloise Dunlap; "Small Town Life: A Study in Race Relations," *Ethnography*; and *Keep Your "N" in Check: African American Women and the Interactive Effects of Etiquette and Emotional Labor.*

Michelle Hall is a QUT doctoral candidate who is researching the ways that consumption experiences can support community in inner-city environments. In particular, she is interested in the ways that interactions within public and quasi-public spaces, such as cafés, bars, retail stores, and shopping centers, can be understood as experiences of community. Also of interest to this research are the ways that these consumption experiences can shape an individual's understanding of neighborhood identity. Her current research extends her earlier work in this area, with the aim of developing its potential to inform business practices, urban development policy, and place-making activities. She has presented her research at Australian and international sociology, urban studies, and consumer research conferences, and published book chapters and journal articles.

Brian B. Knudsen is a research associate at Urban Innovation Analysis. He received his Ph.D. from the Heinz College at Carnegie Mellon University. His research focuses on walking, experience of cities, and new social movements.

Josué Lachica is a furniture designer and maker who studied at the North Bennet Street School in Boston. He holds a bachelor's degree and a master's degree in sociology, both from the University of Texas at El Paso. He has published on the transnational aspects of homelessness along the U.S.-Mexico border and on health disparities among Latinos. He has conducted ethnographic research in Oaxaca, London, and Denver, as well as having worked with homeless populations in nonprofit organizations for fourteen years. He currently runs a woodworking business based in El Paso.

Shanshan Lan is a research assistant professor in the David Lam Institute for East-West Studies at Hong Kong Baptist University. She is the author of *Diaspora and Class Consciousness: Chinese Immigrant workers in Multiracial Chicago* (Routledge, 2012). Her research interests include urban anthropology, race and immigration, class and social service, multiculturalism, and interethnic relations. She has conducted ethnographic fieldwork among Chinese, Latino, and Korean immigrants in the larger Chicago area. Her articles have appeared in *Asian American Law Journal, City and Society, Amerasia Journal*, and others. She is currently carrying out an ethnographic project on African migrants in Guangzhou, China.

Timothy Shortell is a professor of sociology at Brooklyn College, City University of New York. He currently serves as the editor of *Visual Studies*, the journal of the International Visual Sociology Association. He has published numerous book chapters and journal articles on social semiotics and the public sphere. Since 1997, he has collaborated with Jerome Krase on an online photographic archive of urban neighborhoods in global cities (www.BrooklynSoc.org). He coedited *The World in Brooklyn* (Lexington Books, 2012) with Judy DeSena and *Walking in the European City* (Ashgate, 2014) with Evrick Brown.

Daniel Silver is an assistant professor of sociology at the University of Toronto. His research focuses on social theory, culture, and urban sociology. He received his M.A. and Ph.D. from the Committee on Social Thought at the University of Chicago.

Paul R. Watts is an assistant professor of geography in the Department of History and Geography at Nicholls State University. Academic interests include performance-based aspects of public protests, notions of place, and various forms mobility and immobility. His published work includes mapping narratives of individual experiences from the 1992 Los Angeles riots to more broadly understand complex social and inherently spatial phenomena. He is currently researching the use of family photographs as a visual archive to elicit meanings and memories of place.

Amber N. Wiley is an architectural and urban historian whose research interests are centered on the social aspects of design and how it affects urban communities. She is an assistant professor of American studies at Skidmore College. Her areas of focus combine architectural theory and history with cultural issues of race, class, collective memory, city planning, and urban policy. She received her doctorate in American studies from George Washington University, where she specialized in architectural history, urban history, and African American cultural studies. She also holds a B.A. in architecture from Yale University and a master's in architectural history and certificate in historic preservation from the University of Virginia School of Architecture. She sits on the board of the Latrobe Chapter of the Society of Architectural Historians.

Kristen A. Williams earned a Ph.D. from the University of Maryland, College Park, in 2010. She joined Miami University of Ohio in the fall of 2010 as a visiting assistant professor in American studies. Her scholarship focuses on the co-constitution of place, labor, and flows of migration. Her doctoral dissertation, "Waterfronts for Work and Play: Mythscapes of Heritage and Citizenship in Contemporary Rhode Island," examines the relationship between heritage sites, urban culture, and civic life in present-day Rhode Island. She is currently researching a new project entitled *Of Communes and Compounds: The Origins and Cultural Politics of Contemporary Self-Sufficiency Movements*, about the resurgent interest in home-based craft and food production within self-sufficiency movements both across the United States and around the globe.

Rebecca Williamson is a Ph.D. candidate at the University of Sydney in the Department of Sociology. Her research will involve an urban ethnography of new migrants in a multicultural suburb of Sydney, Australia, focusing in particular on women's settlement experiences as mediated through access to housing and use of suburban public spaces. Rebecca is also a postgraduate researcher for the Social Transformation and International Migration ARC-funded research project, led by Professor Stephen Castles. She has previously worked as research assistant and administrator at the Institute for the Study of Muslim Civilisations, London, and prior to that, as a social researcher for the Ministry of Social Development in New Zealand. She received a master of arts in social anthropology and B.A. (hons) from Victoria University of Wellington, New Zealand.

Index